101 WONDERS OF America

101 WONDERS
OF
America

By the Editors of Country Beautiful

Published by Country Beautiful Corporation

Waukesha, Wisconsin

Country Beautiful: Publisher and Editorial Director: Michael P. Dineen; Executive Editor: Robert L. Polley; Senior Editors: Kenneth L. Schmitz, James H. Robb, Stewart L. Udall; Art Director: Buford Nixon; Associate Editors: D'Arlyn M. Marks, John M. Nuhn; House Editor: Kay Kundinger; Art Assistant: Tom McCann; Production Manager: Donna Griesemer; Administration: Brett E. Gries; Editorial Secretary: Jane Boyd; Staff: Bruce L. Schneider.

Country Beautiful Corporation is a wholly owned subsidiary of Flick-Reedy Corporation: President: Frank Flick; Vice President and General Manager: Michael P. Dineen; Treasurer and Secretary: August Caamano.

PHOTO CREDITS

Frontispiece: A harvest moon over Priest Lake, Kaniksu National Forest, Idaho, highlights fall color.

CONTENTS

VII. *Wilderness Of Rock:* WONDERS IN COLORADO AND UTAH

VIII. *Sculptures Of Wind And Water:* THE GREAT DESERT I

IX. *Views Along The Mesas:* THE GREAT DESERT II

X. *Cascade Cathedrals:* THE PACIFIC NORTHWEST

XI. *Granite Domes And Pacific Shores:* THE SIERRAS TO THE SEA

XII. *The Outer Limits:* ALASKA, HAWAII AND THE VIRGIN ISLANDS

POCKETS OF PEACE
AND REACHES OF ROCK
The Atlantic Coast

Allagash River, Maine

In the morning sunlight touching the Atlantic Coast, the wild surf crashes against the rock, the great spruce forests carpet in emerald the inland stretches, and another day begins for the variety of wild creatures harbored along the beaches, inlets and outcroppings of mute and seemingly immutable rock. Between the high tides of twenty-eight feet at Calais, Maine, and the clash of ocean currents at Diamond Shoals off Cape Hatteras, North Carolina, lies the fascinating Eastern seaboard.

ACADIA NATIONAL PARK

There is an air of aristocracy about Acadia National Park, but nothing of the lukewarm, weak-tea flavor that sometimes surrounds that word. It is an "aristocrat" in the same sense that the noble Americans who first tried to preserve this place were called by that name—because they could appreciate the many moods of dashing splendor in man and nature.

Maine's Acadia National Park holds itself sometimes aloof in fog-shrouded mystery and sometimes spreads its inner resources of sea and sunshine with a lavish freedom born of ancient riches. Sometimes it flaunts its elegance unconcerned and unquestioning, and sometimes, with an overplus of hospitality, it opens its arms to any who come to its door.

It was here, after the Civil War, that the first families of America's inherited wealth came and invited the leisure classes of the world to join them for their summer pleasures. Like called to like, and those of princely tastes came to these islands of royal beauty.

Here is the pink granite of Cadillac Mountain (highest point on the Eastern seaboard); here is the wild crashing sea surging into Thunder Hole; here

are the wide, still waters of Somes Sound; here is the variety and grandeur of nature that brought the wealthy socialites of a by-gone age to vacation at Bar Harbor at the turn of this century.

This society has passed away. The Bar Harbor "cottager" whose "cottage" required a dozen household servants to maintain is no longer the chief visitor to Acadia, now, since 1919, a national park (called Lafayette National Park until 1929). The new aristocrat, the American vacationer appreciative of nature's wonders, comes bringing his family to this graceful leisure land where the smell of the great spruce forests and the briny tang of the sea, and the tangle of blueberries there for the picking, and the fish-filled streams for his rod and reel, and the lobster traps that are emptied at morning for his purchasing, these all let a man live like a king.

In 1820 Maine became a state and what is now Acadia National Park supported a thinly settled fishing economy. But in the nineteenth century artists rediscovered the beauty of the area, and summer boats from Boston brought it out of the wilderness and

Acadia's miles of cliffs and rocky shorelines (left) are easily accessible by scenic roads. The tip of Schoodic Peninsula (above) is the only part of the park located on the mainland.

9

Whitecaps rush upon the rocky coast, slowly wearing down the formidable shore line where the struggle between land and the ocean continues.

within the reach of the affluent, who responded to its loveliness.

In 1901 some of those vacationers, fearful that the beauty of their island would be ravaged by commercial exploitation, formed a corporation "to acquire and hold for public use lands in Hancock County, Maine, (because of their) beauty (and) historical interest . . . ." They donated a square rod of land "for public use" (that is about sixteen feet square: room enough perhaps for a bench and a drinking fountain), and in a dozen years had acquired about six thousand additional acres. The corporation donated this land to the Federal Government, which, in 1916, created out of this gift the fifty square miles that make up Acadia National Park.

East of Mount Desert Island, across Frenchman Bay, there is another portion of the park on Schoodic Peninsula, and southwest of Mount Desert is the park's truly isolated wilderness of Isle au Haut ("High Island") which can be reached only by boat.

But to most of the visitors, who arrive in great numbers only to be swallowed by the winding trails and sheltered glens and surf-tossed beaches, Acadia National Park lies along the loop of Ocean Drive—a major park road curving along the Atlantic, gliding in and out of spruce and fir forests, dipping beside quiet inland ponds, suddenly surprising a feeding band of deer that with unfrightened speed gracefully vault into the deeper forest on one side of the road, with the elegance of the yachts, large and small, seen in the distance on the road's other side.

Most visitors come to Acadia in the summer, but spring and fall are pleasant too and the park is more one's own. Cool nights and rain are known to all three seasons. It is only winter—from December through April when snow and ice close the park road system—that is inhospitable.

MOOSEHORN NATIONAL WILDLIFE REFUGE

Moosehorn National Wildlife Refuge is the essence of Maine. Rocky shores take the shapes of little inlets, bays and secret coves, with evergreens marching right to the sea's edge. The offshore islands are covered with pine, and the ocean waters are crowded with buoys marking the locations of lobster pots. Inland the air is sweet with the smell of balsam fir, hemlock and pine growing on the rolling landscape, and among stands of trees are meadows, lakes, marshes, bogs and streams called flowages.

Almost all of the East Coast refuges were established for birdlife, and thus were built around marshes, but Moosehorn is mostly uplands.

Located on the extreme eastern tip of Maine, Moosehorn is divided into two units: the Baring Unit on the north near the town of Calais (locally pronounced "callous"), and the Edmunds Unit twenty miles south near Whiting. Part of the boundary of the Baring Unit touches the St. Croix River separating Maine from the Canadian province of New Brunswick. The Edmunds Unit borders on Cobscook Bay. Cobscook is an Indian word meaning "boiling tides," and although the tides at Cobscook are large, the biggest tides in the United States (outside of Cook Inlet, Alaska) are at Calais, with a difference of twenty-eight feet between rise and fall.

In spite of its name, Moosehorn was established primarily for the protection of the woodcock, a small, brown nocturnal bird. With a short tail and rounded wings, it flies rapidly and erratically when flushed from cover. Feeding on worms which it finds by probing the damp earth with its long, pointed beak, it is extremely hard to see because of its camouflage and is thus a rather secretive creature.

Two hundred other species of birds have been identified on the refuge, many of them nesting here. Ring-necked ducks are abundant, along with a great variety of teals, grebes, mergansers, loons, hawks, ospreys, warblers, sparrows and the handsome snowy owl, rare in the East and seen only in winter.

Of course, the refuge does have moose, for Maine is one of the few states where one still sees "moose crossing" signs on main highways. Largest of the deer family and tallest mammal of the Americas, it stands six or seven feet at the withers and weighs up to 1,200 pounds. Moose are extremely strong and of uncertain temper. If surprised by man, they will blindly crash through the forest, though normally they are very stealthy. They are strict vegetarians, dining on twigs, bark, leaves and roots of plants.

Another interesting animal in the refuge is the fisher, a large, dark weasel with a bushy tail and rounded ears. It is about the only animal that makes a habit of assaulting porcupines. If a fisher eats a porcupine, the quills pass harmlessly through his digestive system, but many fishers carry quills around in their bodies for many weeks as their reward for tangling with this pugnacious rodent.

But the sighting of an adult moose in the wilds of these Maine forests, with its horns sparkling white after ridding itself of their moss, is a memorable experience for any outdoorsman.

The snowy owl, rare in the East and even there seen only in winter, exists in Moosehorn in comparatively large numbers.

BAXTER STATE PARK

According to Indian legend, Mount Katahdin was created by the Council of Gods to serve as their meeting place. One of the lesser dieties, Pamola, became angry when refused a position on the council and retreated less than a mile east to Pamola Peak. From there he supposedly destroys anyone who ventures up Katahdin. Reminders of his wrath seem evident when storm clouds collect on the summit and the wind cuts across the rocks.

In the three hundred million years since a mass of granite rock was thrust up, the mountain's countenance has been carved and rearranged by erosion and glacial action, particularly by the great continental ice sheet of the Pleistocene which passed over the peak and planed off a section. As the ice sheet moved and melted, it dropped boulders from its collections of other mountains. One of the peak's most famous visitors, Henry David Thoreau, wrote that "the mountain seemed a vast aggregation of loose rocks, as if it had some time rained rocks."

Highest point in the state of Maine and main attraction in Baxter State Park is Mount Katahdin, the northern terminus of the well-known Appalachian Trail. The park's 200,000 acres are honeycombed

Rarely found away from water, a bull moose (below) forages for aquatic plants while a cow rests. Highest peak in Maine, Mount Katahdin (right) is reflected in Daicey Pond.

Rushing over a rocky bed through a corridor of hardwoods and conifers, Big Niagara Falls is a highlight of Nesowadnehunk Stream to the southwest.

with more than 130 miles of trails that wind through the rocks and forests of one of the largest state parks in the country. Less than thirty miles north of the town of Millinocket, the hearty camper or climber can enjoy accommodations that range from quite well developed to the more challenging and invigorating primitive areas. Although visitors have passed through the area for more than one hundred years, and loggers once enthusiastically began transforming virgin timber into ships' masts, the charm of Katahdin prevails.

A prime ingredient in the mysterious attraction of Baxter State Park is its variety and abundance of wildlife. The lordly moose is free to crash through the bushes and then hunt with his broad muzzle for succulent aquatic plants in the park's clear waters. White-tailed deer often visit the campsites of quiet and patient campers. Although the black bear accepts handouts, he is normally timid and grows cantakerous when his food supply is not as easily available. Smaller mammals include mink, weasels, the snowshoe hare and two species of marten.

In Baxter two distinct vegetation zones are found. The forest zone features hardwoods—beech, birch and maple—and conifers—black spruce and balsam.

Dotting the almost endless array of mosses, lichens, clubmosses and liverworts are painted trillium, starflower yellow clintonia, goldthread, bunchberry and rose twisted-stalk specimens. The low matted forest known as *Krummholz*, found in the alpine zone along the steep upper slopes and tableland of Mount Katahdin, features short spruce and fir trees that have grown stunted and gnarled in retaliation from the strong winds. Among the Arctic plants that flourish are the alpine bearberry, bog laurel, mountain cranberry and Lapland rosebay. Matlike growths of vegetation consist of Arctic shrubs such as the black crowberry, dwarf birch and herblike willow.

The park is the gift of philanthropist and former governor Percival P. Baxter, who tried during his legislative and gubernatorial terms to persuade the state to purchase the Katahdin region and set up a park. After leaving office, his determination to preserve the area led him to buy up the land piece by piece and donate it to the state. At Thoreau Spring on the mountain reads a plaque from that visionary: "Man is born to die. His works are short lived. Buildings crumble. Monuments decay, wealth vanishes, but Katahdin in all its glory forever shall remain the mountain of the people of Maine."

CAPE COD NATIONAL SEASHORE

Cape Cod is a slender rampart jutting more than seventy miles from the Massachusetts coast into the wind and waves of the turbulent Atlantic Ocean. A large section of it became part of the National Park System as a result of the interest and leadership of President John F. Kennedy. The storm-lashed seas surge over the shoals and dash against marine scarps and, miles away, these same seas gently lap the slopes of barrier beaches. The Cape, one of the nation's most dramatic headlands, is the northernmost of our national seashores. Its high, shifting dunes, great ponds and historic places make a fascinating outdoor playground in summer or winter.

Cape Cod is shaped much like a man flexing his arm muscles. It was named by explorer Bartholomew Gosnold in 1601 for the "grate stoare" of codfish in the vicinity. The Cape, aided by the lengthening of a sandspit called Monomoy Island which extends south from the "elbow" of the Cape, is responsible for the relatively quieter waters of Cape Cod Bay and Nantucket Sound. Sandbars and shoals surrounding the Cape have been a burying ground for ships from the time of the Pilgrims, who first touched New World soil at what is now Provincetown on the extreme northern tip of the Cape.

The exhilarating aspects of winter storms on Cape Cod moved naturalist Henry David Thoreau to write that these periods were the best time to visit the area. Thoreau is credited with giving the name Great Beach to the seaside sands of the Cape. "A man can stand there and put all America behind him," he wrote. The elemental forces that shape life cycles are evident here in the biting sting of salt water spray borne in the teeth of a northeaster or in the offshore breeze of a quiet July afternoon.

Rooted strongly in sand dunes and silts, the cattails, marsh grass, bearberry, heath and pitch-pine woods stand against the rasping waters, collecting new sand from each windstorm. Glacial movement in the area resulted in an overlapping of northern and southern plant life growing on the Cape. Extensive geological evidence found in the accumulation of glacial drift makes the Cape a lodestone for geo-oceanographers.

Some of the most spectacular sand dune formations are found at Province Lands and Truro at the northern tip. The dunes were formed after glacial action thrust clay and boulders into the coastal plains area while the ocean was still shallow. Erosion of the scarps by wave action caused sandbars, then sandspits and later the dunes. As the dunes were formed, they buried whole forests, and when they moved on, remnants of these forests reappeared. Even today, these forces of nature are clearly visible at Province Lands and Truro.

The wild turkey, once native to this region and traditionally part of the Pilgrims' Thanksgiving, became extirpated in 1850. But the sea gulls on Nauset Light

Dead pitch-pine trees are being covered with sand as an active dune moves across the land in the Province Lands area. Advancing dunes may cover entire forests.

Beach find no shortage of "wild game." They hover fifteen or twenty feet above a rock, drop clams or mussels onto it, and then swoop down to pick the meat from the broken shells. Gone with the wild turkey are the forests the Pilgrims described. However, most of the tree species, possibly in smaller sizes, still are native to the Cape. A remnant of this past, not far from National Park Service headquarters at Wellfleet, is an Atlantic white-cedar swamp considered unusual because it is located so near salt water. This swamp can be reached by one of the many trails recently established by the park service.

Extensive forests cause an entire change of scene between the highlands and beaches on the west side of the Cape. Here are many deep, freshwater ponds, and nearby, the "Cliffs" area arises to a height of 175 feet above Great Beach. In lower altitudes to the south are some of the only natural cranberry bogs in the Western Hemisphere.

Ornithologists describe Monomoy Island as an unparalleled area in which to observe shorebirds. Since its establishment as a wildlife refuge in 1944, more than three hundred bird species have been identified here. During seasonal migrations millions of shore, sea and marsh birds stop over at the island regularly. The island is abundant in rich sea life for the birds who visit this 3,300-acre barrier beach.

Such unusual birds as the Hudsonian godwit, the American oystercatcher and the golden plover have been spotted on Monomoy along with thousands of commonly seen Canada geese and black ducks. Monomoy is roadless and entirely undeveloped, and this guarantees a glimpse of wild nature at its best.

The one who seeks a rare experience of life, whether it be solitude, which is indeed becoming rare, or the thrill of seeing a slice of unsullied shoreland, will find both at Cape Cod seashore or Monomoy refuge.

Cape Cod National Seashore, established in 1961, consists of almost 27,000 acres along the outermost one-third of the Cape, primarily facing east and north directly onto the Atlantic. Three large areas have been developed thus far: Province Lands Area on the Cape's tip has a visitor center and provides a splendid panoramic view of the sea from Ocean View Lookout; in the Pilgrim Heights Area a few miles to the east is the spring where the Pilgrims found their first fresh drinking water; and Marconi Station Area contains Thoreau's Great Beach and the site where the first wireless station in the United States was set up in 1903. Smaller areas include Coast Guard Beach Area where, on Nauset Light Beach, there is some of the finest protected saltwater swimming anywhere. A mile and a half inland from this beach is another visitor center and an amphitheater near the main highway, and just across Salt Pond Bay is Hemenway Landing.

The two visitor centers provide information about exhibits, special programs, guided walks and self-guided nature trails. Six privately operated campgrounds are on the Cape near the national seashore. A number of bicycle trails have also been constructed and one, in the Province Lands Area, is nine miles long.

Because Monomoy Refuge is maintained by the Bureau of Sport Fisheries and Wildlife to preserve its wild qualities, there are no facilities. Nearby towns provide accommodations as well as boat rentals.

Walt Whitman wrote, perhaps of this scene, "... the long bar of maroon-tint, ... the fragrance of salt marsh and shore mud ..."

ASSATEAGUE ISLAND NATIONAL SEASHORE

A vast expanse of sand and sea makes up Assateague Island National Seashore. Thirty-seven miles long and generally a mile to a mile and a half wide, this barrier island has many moods—from a quiet summer evening with the soothing wash of waves and the crying of terns the only sounds, to a winter storm raging over the sand, the surf thundering onto the shore.

The island was born of the sea and will die of the sea, as it is rapidly pushed toward the Delmarva Peninsula where three states (Delaware, Maryland and Virginia) share the Atlantic coastline.

The change in topography is phenomenal. Before 1933 Assateague was actually a peninsula, but a storm that year cut an inlet separating it from the barrier island to the north, which has nearly completed its cycle of being pushed into the mainland. At the south end of the island is a small cove called Tom's Cove which did not exist in 1850. The Assateague Beach Coast Guard Station, now abandoned, was built on the very tip of the island in 1922, and since then two more miles of beach have been formed below it, curving around into a "hook." A pier recently ex-posed on the ocean shore near the north end was actually built on the bay side about thirty years ago.

The sand dunes, built up of grains carried and deposited by ocean currents and surf and then blown above the tide marks by winds, protect the inland portions of the island. The dunes are fragile and unstable, anchored only by grasses that are tolerant of salt spray but vulnerable to feet.

Beyond the dunes, loblolly pines and thickets of wax myrtle, bayberry, sumac, rose and greenbrier have a hold in the packed sand; and deer, foxes, raccoons, and forest birds dwell here. Marshes and many small islands make up the bay shoreline, and in Chincoteague Bay itself, named for a vanished tribe of Indians who lived in this region, are found oysters, clams and crabs which are the source of a substantial fishing industry.

But it is the Assateague beach that draws the most attention. Thirty-seven miles long, it has a gently sloping bottom, fine surf and lack of strong undertow, making it attractive to bathers.

19

As purple and blue clouds fly overhead, wild ponies graze among grasses and bayberry.

About two-thirds of the national seashore is in Maryland; the Virginia third (the southern third), is comprised of the Chincoteague National Wildlife Refuge. There is a marked difference between the upper and lower portions of Assateague Island—the lower is greater in vegetation and its marshes are larger, providing excellent cover for more than 225 species of birds. Each season has its own species. In March wintering flocks of ducks, geese, and swans leave the refuge to go north. Other flocks, coming from the south, linger shortly and then continue on. By late April all the waterfowl are gone except for black ducks, blue-winged teals, mallards and gadwalls that nest here.

During April and May enormous numbers of shorebirds, such as sandpipers, plovers, oystercatchers, willets and yellowlegs, gather on mudflats and freshwater ponds. In summer, egrets, herons, ibises, avocets, terns, gulls and black skimmers reside on the ponds and small islands. Shorebirds return in July and August, and autumn is marked by the arrival of hawks and flickers.

On an early, chilly October morning, pintails, widgeons, shovellers, Canada and snow geese and greenwinged teals can be seen by the noisy thousands. Scoters in offshore waters parallel the beach for miles, and buffleheads, goldeneyes, mergansers, brants, loons and grebes congregate in Tom's Cove. Many of these birds terminate their flights at Chincoteague

In winter the winds pile dry snow into drifts, or "snow dunes," along the beaches.

and stay for the winter. Dikes have been constructed around the freshwater pools and marshes at Chincoteague to protect their habitat from storms. These areas provide growths of smartweeds, spikerushes, bulrushes, sago pondweeds and widgeon grass.

One of the most interesting aspects of Assateauge Island is its herd of wild ponies. Legend says they are the descendants of ponies that swam ashore from a shipwrecked Spanish galleon, but no one really knows their origin. Most of them are in the refuge, but separate groups are maintained on lands administered by the National Park Service. Their diet consists of marsh grasses and bayberry leaves, and each July a roundup is held by the Chincoteague Volunteer Fire Department, which owns the ponies roaming the refuge portion of the island, to sell some of them and keep the population in balance. Seeing these ponies trotting along the wet sands of the beach is a memorable sight for the visitor.

Sika deer, native to Japan, were introduced onto Assateague in 1923 by some Boy Scouts. Smaller than white-tailed deer, they have flourished under the adverse conditions of the island and can often be seen in marshy meadows.

Assateague Island National Seashore almost failed to become a reality. Although the National Park Service had recommended the island for seashore status in the 1930's, this seemed to be foreclosed when a private developer bought a large section of the island

and chopped it into over eight thousand beach homesites and sold them to gullible buyers. But in March 1962, a powerful northeaster storm struck Assateague, destroying most of the man-made structures. This gave conservationists a second chance, and in 1965 President Lyndon B. Johnson signed a bill to make Assateague the largest public seashore on the mid-Atlantic Coast.

Some facilities are located at the south end in Chincoteague refuge, and the "hook" will be developed as a recreational area. Assateague State Park on the north, within the seashore boundaries but administered by the State of Maryland, contains a campground, picnic areas, a protected beach and other facilities. The extreme northern portion of the island will be left in its natural state.

In her book, *Gift from the Sea,* Anne Morrow Lindbergh might refer to Assateague when she writes:

> *Rollers on the beach, wind in the pines, the slow flapping of herons across sand dunes, drown out the hectic rhythms of city and suburb, time tables and schedules. One falls under their spell, relaxes, stretches out prone. One becomes, in fact, like the element on which one lies, flattened by the sea; bare, open, empty as the beach, erased by today's tides of all yesterday's scribblings.*

The most common of the "sea gulls" (left) are the herring gulls and the ring-billed gulls. Bodie Island lighthouse (right),on the northern end of the Hatteras seashore, stands sentinel against the treacherous sea of North Carolina's Outer Banks.

CAPE HATTERAS NATIONAL SEASHORE

A northeaster storm on Cape Hatteras has to be experienced to be believed. Raging wind blows sand with such force that it can be heard hitting a building, and the brushy plants bend away from the gusts, as if bowing to this master of violent nature. The seas crash their breakers into the shore, spray is hurled into the wind, and skies are ominously dark, the air filled with a cold, misty rain. A walk along the beach at this time is a walk in total loneliness, an experience unique to a place facing the sea such as this.

Hours later, after the storm has passed, the beach takes on a different character. A warm breeze ruffles the drying sea oats and the setting sun plays with the clouds. A ghost crab scurries into the wet sand at your approach; scavenging shorebirds look for culinary delights at the edge of each dying breaker. Small sand dunes now exist where earlier there had been none, and others have disappeared.

The storms of the Cape are so feared that seamen call North Carolina's Outer Banks the Graveyard of the Atlantic. Since 1585, when the British ship *Tiger* was sunk in Ocracoke Inlet to the south of the Cape, and possibly before that, mariners have dreaded passing near Diamond Shoals at the tip of Cape Hatteras. The clash of warm Gulf Stream and cold

Arctic waters, over twelve offshore miles of underwater shifting sandbars, plus enemy submarines in wartime, have combined to send more than seven hundred ships to the bottom from Cape Henry at the entrance of Chesapeake Bay to Cape Fear in southern North Carolina.

Among these relics are the skeletal remains of a World War II LST and U-85, a German submarine sunk in 1942 while preying on Allied shipping. And perhaps someday shifting sands will expose the rusty hulk of the *Monitor,* the first Federal ironclad of the Civil War, which went down with sixteen men somewhere off the Cape in 1862.

The raging storms wreck not only ships but the sands themselves. An especially violent storm on March 7, 1962 (called the Ash Wednesday storm), cut an opening into Hatteras Island at the town of Buxton, creating an inlet which was finally closed a year later with the combined efforts of the Army Corps of Engineers, Federal funds, hundreds of volunteers, two dredges, tens of thousands of sandbags and dozens of junked automobiles. Nature occasionally does this filling-in job herself: Nine miles south of Oregon Inlet at the northern part of the Cape, the road passes over land that just over a

decade ago was "New Inlet." The remains of the ill-conceived bridge that once spanned this inlet are visible several hundred yards off the highway.

The history of the Outer Banks, which extend some thirty miles from the mainland at their farthest point at the tip of Cape Hatteras, is nearly a history of the United States. In 1585, and two years later, Sir Walter Raleigh started unsuccessful settlements on Roanoke Island at the northern point of Pamlico Sound which separates the Cape from the mainland. The second English attempt at colonization in the New World was marked by the birth of the first child of English parentage born in America, Virginia Dare, but the settlement mysteriously disappeared. Raleigh had left for England and when he returned in 1590 he found only the word "Croatoan" carved on a stockade post. Fort Raleigh National Historical Site marks the probable spot of the "Lost Colony."

During the eighteenth century, colonials from Virginia and Maryland moved onto the Cape, becoming fishermen, navigators and sailors. They were called "bankers" and they founded the various towns along the Cape.

In 1874 these people started the U.S. Life-Saving Service, and their acts of heroism were commonplace, as in 1899 when a banker on patrol singlehandedly saved ten of the fourteen people on a small cruise ship grounded during a hurricane. The maxim of these volunteer sailors was "The rules say you gotta go, not that you gotta come back," and family cemeteries and scattered lonely graves bear lasting testimony to this conviction.

The Life-Saving Service was merged with the Revenue Cutter Service in 1915 to form the U. S. Coast Guard, and the new organization continued the valiant traditions of the old. In 1918 a dramatic sea rescue took place as the men of the Chicamacomico Coast Guard Station saved most of the men of the burning tanker *Mirlo*. During World War II the men had the important job of coastal defense and saving the lives of victims of German submarines.

On December 17, 1903, on a sandy plain called Kitty Hawk near the town of Kill Devil Hill, about ten miles north of the national seashore, Wilbur and Orville Wright flew the world's first successful power-driven airplane.

At the southern tip of the seashore on Ocracoke Island is a spot called Teach's Hole, believed to have been the lair of Edward Teach, better known as the pirate, Blackbeard, feared by merchantmen all along the Atlantic seaboard.

Cape Hatteras National Seashore was established in 1953. It covers forty-five square miles stretched along seventy miles of shores of three barrier islands, each separated by an inlet. The eight villages are excluded from the seashore. Visitor centers are located at the Hatteras and Bodie Island lighthouses

and at Ocracoke village. Seven campgrounds are within the seashore's boundaries. The entire beach length is open for swimming. No vehicles of any kind are allowed on the dunes.

At the tip of Cape Hatteras is the tallest lighthouse in the United States, 192 feet above low-tide level. Built in 1870, it is one of three on the Cape and easily recognized by its "barberpole" striping.

Ocracoke, Hatteras and Bodie islands are barrier islands believed to have been formed by ocean currents and wave action on what were originally shoals to the east of the present shoreline. The islands are not more than three miles in width and are covered with sand dunes which have not been stabilized and are still moving. The largest dunes on the Atlantic seaboard are near the town of Nags Head, just north of the seashore. Salt marshes line the western shores of the islands.

Wildflowers grow profusely in this humid climate, even in December when the flats behind the barrier dunes are bright with flowering gaillardia. Growing individually on sand ridges are live oaks and thickets of evergreen yaupon, a species of holly. Sea oats and beach grass thrive on the dunes. Near the Hatteras

The salt marshes of Bodie Island and those in the Pea Island Wildlife Refuge are one of the winter homes for the greater snow geese, which are protected from hunting and encouraged to browse here among the brushes and weeds, planted to attract a great variety of waterfowl and shorebirds.

Lighthouse is Buxton Woods, with stands of loblolly pine, American holly and live oak growing on the ridges and slopes. Marshy valleys lie between the ridges and support dense banks of ferns, shrubs and clinging vines.

The head of the Cape, about three miles south of the Hatteras Lighthouse, provides a close-up view of the dangerous Diamond Shoals. The sudden shallow water a couple of hundred feet out from the beach combined with the mixing of the two large ocean currents cause the waves to tumble over each other at angles, making a thunderous roar and much foam.

Surf fishermen consider the Cape a great spot to catch channel bass, ocean perch, sea mullet (whiting), sea trout, Spanish and king mackerel, flounder and assorted sharks. During the summer, however, fishing is best offshore where marlin, dolphin, bluefish, false albacore and tuna may be caught. Gray trout and flounder swim in Pamlico Sound, and there is some freshwater fishing in ponds which hold largemouth bass and bluegill.

Although animal life is limited to a few deer and some marsh rabbits, birdlife is abundant. Over three hundred species can be found here. Pea Island Na-tional Wildlife Refuge—named after the upper island which existed when New Inlet split Hatteras Island—is renowned for being the wintering grounds of great numbers of Canada and snow geese. This 6,700-acre reserve, established in 1938, has the only large concentration of gadwall nesting on the Atlantic seaboard. Other birds found here are royal terns, black skimmers, laughing gulls, black ducks, loons, red-breasted mergansers, glossy ibises, snowy and common egrets, whistling swans, pheasants, grebes, hawks, warblers and many kinds of herons.

From the top of Hatteras Lighthouse, the Cape curves into the horizon on the north and south; to the west lie the fairly calm waters of Pamlico Sound. But your gaze keeps returning to the east—the wide expanse of the Atlantic and, closer to shore, the herringbone designs of white-capped breakers at Diamond Shoals, spreading scalloped sheets of surf obliquely on the beaches on either side. A dramatic "water confrontation" occurs at Hatteras, and those who know and love this area return again and again because these great sand banks tell important chapters of our history and offer a singular seashore experience.

CAPE LOOKOUT
NATIONAL SEASHORE

In the first grays of morning the lighthouse throws its beam many miles into the Atlantic, repeating over and over its set pattern. The eastern sky, rosy pink, reflects onto the foam of the breakers as they hit the beach and spread over the sands. Sandpipers prance on this wet sand, and gradually the light increases until the sun, already above the horizon, finally lifts itself free of the distant clouds.

Dawn on Cape Lookout may be much the same as dawn on other Atlantic barrier beaches with one exception—here man is no longer an intruder. Unlike Cape Hatteras National Seashore to the north, Cape Lookout National Seashore has no roads, no campgrounds and no thriving towns. Only the lighthouse, the extremely small town of Portsmouth on the north end (with a few summer residents only), and a number of shacks scattered along the shores give evidence of civilization.

It was not always this way. The same colonials from Virginia and Maryland who traveled down Cape Hatteras and established homes and towns came to the lower banks, but there were not as many.

Spanish privateers were a problem for citizens in the 1740's, but after they were gone, the North Carolina Assembly established a "maritime town" named Portsmouth on the island of the same name at Ocracoke Inlet. The town grew to over five hundred residents because Ocracoke Inlet was the only navigable inlet in the central and lower banks, and heavy draught ships had to stop here to transfer their cargos to boats able to navigate Core and Pamlico sounds. In 1846, however, Hatteras and Oregon inlets opened up farther north, and the town's prosperity died until today there are far more homes than people.

The first Cape Lookout Lighthouse was constructed in 1812 and the present one completed in 1859. The lighthouse, 150 feet in height, has a distinctive black and white diamond pattern.

The U. S. Life-Saving Service, and subsequently the U. S. Coast Guard, maintained patrols along the shores of Core Banks and Portsmouth Island, saving the lives of many victims of the sea whose ships had floundered on the sandbars offshore. With automation and ship safety improvements the patrols no longer proved necessary, and many of the Cape's residents left.

Geographically, Cape Lookout differs from Cape Hatteras in that there are many small islands, mostly tidal marshes, off the west side of the Cape in Core Sound. These marshes support a variety of birdlife, such as sea gulls, terns, boat-tailed grackles, sandpipers and black skimmers. Bottle-nosed dolphins can often be seen playing in the breakwater close offshore, and channel bass, mackerel, bluefish and sea trout are abundant.

Most of the lands of Cape Lookout National Seashore were bought and preserved by the State of North Carolina until Congress enacted a law in 1966 making the entire area a national seashore. Under current development plans, Shackleford and Core banks and Portsmouth Island will remain completely roadless, reached only by ferries or private boats. The fifty-eight mile seashore contains about 15,800 acres, although actual acreage fluctuates with each large storm.

Once while visiting Cape Lookout, former National Park Service Director George B. Hartzog reportedly kicked off his shoes and scampered over the dunes, calling the seashore "simply terrific." Terrific for everyone, for the lower banks of North Carolina are now protected against all enemies but nature herself. And if nature decides to change the land a little, that is as it should be. After all, it was hers to begin with!

A setting, hazy sun silhouettes a number of sanderlings as they play touch and go with the foamy white breakers.

ANCIENT GREEN MOUNTAINS
The Appalachian Chain

Shenandoah Valley, Virginia

To the quiet forests come the seekers of peace, to the aged mountains come the searchers after tranquility. The chain of mountains ranging south exude the charm and dignity of revered tribal elders. The rocky ancients, worn smooth through eons of sunrises and snowfalls and crowned by wisps of fog, remain a sanctuary to visitors. Walking is the best way of enjoying the pleasures of the Appalachian Trail that stretches from Mount Katahdin in Maine to Springer Mountain in Georgia. Particularly enchanting are the Smokies, the Blue Ridge Mountains and the Shenandoah Valley at any season of the year.

Along the trail, a picturesque covered bridge spans Madison River at Warren, Vermont, in Green Mountain forest.

APPALACHIAN TRAIL

"Give me," says William Hazlitt, "the clear blue sky over my head, and the green turf beneath my feet, a winding road before me, and a three hours' march to dinner—then to thinking. It is hard if I cannot start some game on these lone heaths. I laugh, I run, I leap, I sing for joy."

There are many fine walks over the "lone heaths" and the high hills of the national forests. They are for hikers, climbers, slow strollers and even for invalids; they are for everyone in the country.

The trails in the national forests are well used, for walking is one of those simple pleasures within economic reach of all citizens. Figures show that walking ranks among the most popular forms of outdoor recreation. Conditions of the times demand that it be so: A people whose everyday lives are circumscribed by mechanization and urbanization clamor for respite, a return to native ways. In order to survive and prosper as a race of thinking beings, we need to exercise our bodies in natural surroundings, for man is no synthetic creature, but a living offspring of the earth.

President Lyndon B. Johnson gave recognition to the New Age of Walking Americans in 1966 when he called for the establishment of many more trails for walking, hiking, horseback riding and cycling, both in rural areas and the back country. "Old and young alike can participate," he said. "Our doctors recommend and encourage such activity for fitness and fun."

Recreational trails have been the subject of proposed Federal legislation for many years, but as a result of the President's statement, a new concept was placed before Congress, providing for the establishment of a National System of Scenic Trails. The prime component of this system is a number of choice trails with high natural, scenic or historic qualities, each one over several hundred miles in length, with overnight shelters at appropriate intervals, linked with other trails branching out to nearby points of special attraction. Such values would be safeguarded and enhanced for the benefit of generations to come.

The major arteries of three of the proposed National Scenic Trails run through the National Forest System, along the ridgelines, mountaintops, streams and lakeshores, harmonizing with the natural areas they cross, affording the visitor communion with the natural world and a feeling of true inspiration.

The genius of the trails that now exist derives from the devotion of people who love the land. The U. S. Forest Service has been aided—and spurred—by the ideas, energy and unselfish activity of local outdoor clubs and individuals. Such groups have laid out, marked and maintained trails, cleaned the litter left by others, and encouraged wise use.

The Appalachian Trail has been envisioned as the foundation unit of the new national system. It is the longest marked path in the world, covering 2,021 miles along the crest of Appalachia from northern New England into the Deep South. It traverses fourteen states. Virginia has the longest section, 500 miles; West Virginia, the shortest, 10 miles. The trail embraces 507 miles in eight national forests (White Mountain, New Hampshire; Green Mountain, Vermont; George Washington and Jefferson, Virginia; Pisgah and Cherokee, North Carolina and Tennessee; Nantahala, North Carolina; and Chattahoochee, Georgia, where it reaches its southern terminus at Springer Mountain), as well as 172 miles through two national parks, 452 miles through state lands and the remainder of the trail through private lands.

The "AT" is more than a footway; it is a concept of recreation brought to reality almost entirely through the voluntary efforts of patriotic people who felt the need to stir the pioneer spirit and to provide new generations of Americans with the lure of exploration. "This is to be a connected trail," declared the Constitution of the Appalachian Trail Conference, after its organizational meeting in 1925, "running as far as practicable over the summits of the mountains and through the wild lands of the Atlantic seaboard and adjoining states, from Maine to Georgia, to be supplemented by a system of primitive camps at proper intervals, so as to render accessible for tramping, camping, and other forms of primitive travel and living, the said mountains and wild lands, as a means of conserving and developing within this region, the primeval environment."

The idea of the Appalachian Trail was proposed in 1921 by the eminent Benton MacKay, forester and regional planner. He formulated the project for the mountain footpath from his wanderings in his native New England forests. In 1922 the first part of the trail was constructed by hiking clubs of New York and New Jersey. New England had much to add with the trail systems of the Appalachian Mountain Club, Green Mountain Club and the Dartmouth Outing Club. In time other clubs were formed farther south. Now these non-professional enthusiasts cooperate in maintaining the route with Federal and state agencies.

The walker who sets out to cover the entire Appalachian Trail and averages seventeen miles a day will complete his journey in 123 days and nights. He will be within 150 miles of half a dozen of the country's largest cities—Boston, New York, Philadelphia, Baltimore, Washington, Atlanta—and cross an occasional motorway, but essentially he would be far removed from the works of man. His lodgings would be campsites, shelters and cabins. He would know that what makes a mountain trail a supreme adventure is the combination of natural diversity, the touch of intimacy at hand, and the fullness of distant vistas. The AT has all of these elements.

New Englanders have a long and vigorous tradition on the trails, dating from explorers like Henry David Thoreau and some of the oldest hiking clubs in the country. The Appalachian Mountain Club began cutting its first trails in 1876; its goals then, as now, were to "explore the mountains of New England and adjacent regions, and in general to cultivate an interest in geographical studies."

The AMC huts constitute the only system of its kind for the tramping vacationer who desires a degree of comfort, well cooked food and a bunk for the night at modest prices. The Madison Huts are near the highest hiking trail in the Northeast, within reach of the Great Gulf. Pinkham Notch, the largest hut (accommodating one hundred in two buildings), lies just off a main road, but within minutes the hiker is enveloped in deep woods, then up the headwall of Tuckerman Ravine, a great glacial cirque enroute to the summit of Mount Washington, New Hampshire.

The forest service and AMC have lived in close understanding for many years. When Gifford Pinchot developed the concept of modern conservation, and Theodore Roosevelt popularized it, the AMC was prepared to join in their campaign. It sponsored lectures by Pinchot, advocated the Weeks Bill to establish national forests in the East and collaborated with other organizations of like convictions. Its efforts have benefited many people, through maintenance of hundreds of miles of hiking trails, construction of free trailside shelters, a wide program of education in canoeing, mountaineering and natural history, and in publication of guidebooks, maps and pamphlets.

A hiker's reward is a view of White Water Falls in North Carolina's Pisgah National Forest.

WATKINS GLEN STATE PARK

On the edge of the northern plateau of New York's Catskills lies a huge area haphazardly sprinkled with lakes, as if a daydreaming god had let his giant fingers trace symbols of his thoughts in the rocks and valleys and then walked off, leaving his indecipherable etchings to be filled up with clear water by the rain gods. The Finger Lakes region in the center of the state was in fact formed by mile-high glacier ice thousands of years ago. Later the abrasiveness of water on the Devonian shale shaped the glens and waterfalls.

The gem of all the lakes is Seneca, and crowning its southern tip is the Watkins Glen Gorge, a deep winding canyon worn through the shale that originated as the mud deposit of spring-fed streams flowing into an ancient inland sea. Along two miles of its most breathtaking part, the stream drops seven hundred feet from waterfall to waterfall, until a total of nineteen can be counted.

Trails wind along the defile that plunged to an almost sunless three hundred feet past, behind and above Sentry Bridge, Minnehaha Falls and Frowning Cliff. The triple cascades of Rainbow Falls are the most celebrated. The spray from these falls captures rainbows which can be seen from many different angles. The falls were named by a New England newspaperman, Morvalden Ells, who began making paths and staircases in the Glen for others to see the loveliness he spent hours studying.

The forests around the gorge are northern deciduous — aged beech, maple and oak with red pine scattered throughout. Among the many ferns and lichens, spring wildflowers brighten the greenery—wake robin, jack-in-the-pulpit, moccasin flower and Dutchman's breeches. Fall is a breathtaking season, when the scarlets and golds add touches of majesty to the woodland.

If one is quiet and patient enough, one can catch sight of wildlife in the park—white-tailed deer, raccoons, red foxes. Chipmunks and squirrels demand less attentive searching and seem to chirp for attention along the miles of trails available for hikers.

The trails have a particularly natural look, since practically all of the unnatural concrete steps, trails and iron railings were washed out during heavy flooding in 1935. The walkways were then reconstructed of native stone to harmonize with the setting. One of the trails follows a path worn first by the Indians. Another brings hikers 165 feet up the wall above the creek bed.

Before white settlers moved in, Iroquois Indians cleared and cultivated the land. The Iroquois Nation confederacy of six tribes—Mohawk, Oneida, Onondaga, Cayuga, Seneca and Tuscarora—was headquartered there, too, until forced out by the Federal government in the late eighteenth century. Although their communal longhouses and storage pits filled with corn, dried venison, nuts, roots and berries can no longer be seen, their influence is apparent in many place names.

The glen entrance site was used by various mills, and when they closed, Watkins Glen became a privately owned business attraction noted, of course, for its visual qualities, but also appealing because of its mineral waters, said to equal those of Europe. Two men from Connecticut named Watkins and Flint purchased the area and called it Salubria for promotional purposes. The region again became Watkins Glen in the late 1800's. By the time the State of New York purchased the area in 1906, the region had gained a considerable measure of fame and popularity.

Watkins Glen has a quality of quietness that invites introspection. Charles Lindbergh has aptly expressed it:

> *In wildness I sense the miracle of life, and beside it our scientific accomplishments fade to trivia. The construction of an analogue computer or a supersonic airplane is simple when compared to the mixture of space and evolutionary eons represented by a cell. In primitive rather than in civilized surroundings I grow aware of man's evolving status, as though I were suddenly released from a hypnotic state. Life itself becomes the standard of all judgment. How could I have overlooked even momentarily, such an obvious fact?*

The stream in the spectacular gorge at Watkins Glen drops seven hundred feet in two miles, falling over nineteen waterfalls. The almost vertical walls are from 100 to 300 feet high.

NIAGARA FRONTIER STATE PARKS

The Niagara River, actually a strait, flows in a northerly direction for only thirty-four miles connecting Lake Erie to Lake Ontario. Erie, however, is 572 feet above sea level, and Ontario, 246 feet. Niagara Falls is the result of this great drop of 326 feet along the river's course, most of it occurring in a collected series of falls and rapids that has the high falls as the central attraction. Here, at the "Thundering Waters," as the Indians named the spot, fifteen million cubic feet of water a minute plunge down the escarpment. Nearly a mile wide at this point, the falls are divided into two main areas, the American and the Canadian or Horseshoe Falls.

The Canadian Falls carries ninety-four percent of the water and has a crest line of 3,010 feet and a drop of 158 feet. The American Falls has a crest line of 1,060 feet, but a drop of 167 feet. While the foot of the American Falls is shallow and rocky, the pool below the Canadian Falls reaches a depth of 160 feet.

Between them is Bridal Veil Falls, well known as the sight favored by honeymooners. Dramatic views can be seen from Luna Island that is connected by a foot bridge to Goat Island, which in turn is connected to the bank by the American Rapids Bridge.

The area around the falls was strategically important in colonial times, since it is the only break in an all-water route between the upper St. Lawrence River and the upper Great Lakes. In 1805 an entrepreneur, Augustus Porter, bought the area around the falls, established a grist mill and named it Manchester, after the great English industrial center he envisioned the small town would become. Niagara has become a world-renowned hydroelectric center and the nucleus of a well-known manufacturing community.

While the ancient Indians worshipped the falls as a most powerful diety, and visitors today stand in awe at the thunderous rush of water, a handful of daring people found the spot a challenge. Going over the falls in a barrel, walking a tightrope stretched over the gorge, jumping into the water from a platform on Goat Island, riding the rapids in a rubber suit— all were tried with more or less success since the 1850's. Such stunts are now illegal.

The State Reservation at Niagara was established in 1885 and is called the first state park in New York. A dozen state parks have since been established in the area, sufficient to accommodate and offer recreational opportunities for the many visitors who come to see the falls, this legend of living water.

The tremendous falls along the Niagara River include the American at the left, Bridal Veil in the center, and the Canadian or Horseshoe on the right.

MONONGAHELA NATIONAL FOREST

Man cannot cast his shadow on the rising of the sun, or halt the flow of the winds, or alter the rhythm of the waves. But he can enrich his humanity with appreciation of the greater world that lies above and beyond his own.

Wilderness is the tangible essence of the greater world placed within our grasp to touch and feel, and to test our sensitivity.

In Monongahela National Forest, almost a million acres in eastern West Virginia, man can come close and touch the wilderness. The many recreation areas, hiking trails and highlights of Monongahela leave an indelible image of vigor and spontaneity.

Spruce Knob, the highest point in West Virginia (4,860 feet), is bordered by many species of plant life found far south of their normal range. Roadside overlooks are numerous at high elevations, with beautiful vistas into valleys of both Virginia and West Virginia. A trail leads to the cool summit.

A unique natural area where orchids and cranberries grow in mountain bogs—similar to vegetation in the low areas of Maine—is the subject of the Cranberry Mountain Visitor Center near Richwood. Two miles west of the center a self-guiding boardwalk trail leads across a small portion of the famous Cranberry Glades and introduces the visitor to plants, birds and mammals of the northern tundra. The soil is mainly sphagnum and sedge peat up to eleven feet deep underlain with algal ooze and clay.

Carnivorous sundew and horned bladderwort, rare in the southern Alleghenies, are highly esteemed.

In Spruce Knob-Seneca Rocks National Recreation Area, whitewater canoeing is popular with experts on swiftflowing streams that form the headwaters of the Potomac River. An especially favorite course starts at Mouth of Seneca and winds downstream through canyons for fifteen miles. In addition, Seneca Rocks at Mouth of Seneca is one of the highest, most impressive rock formations in the East. Rock climbers come from hundreds of miles away to test their skills. According to legend, Snow Bird, the daughter of a Seneca chieftain, held a contest here to choose the brave she would wed. The first warrior to scale the cliff (which she had been able to climb since childhood) won her hand, so the story goes.

One hundred million people live within five hundred miles of the parallel mountain ridges contained within the National Recreation Area. But its purpose is not only to provide recreation for today but to "preserve important resources for future generations." Accordingly, the quiet green character in the heart of the hills is protected through cooperative regional planning to "promote a harmonious and unified development of the National Recreation Area and the surrounding region." This beautiful but economically depressed region may yet come into its own through the wise use of its rich recreational resources.

Serene Spruce Knob Lake in the Monongahela forest is set amid the misty, ancient Allegheny Mountains and some of the East's most breathtaking country.

The unforgettable sound of the elk rises to a bugle tone heard for miles, then flattens out to a grunt and bay.

HOCKING HILLS STATE PARK

Hollowed by the constant force of water for the last million years, the Rock House in Ohio's Hocking Hills State Park stands massive, with huge openings separated by large columns of stone letting sunlight into the only true cavern in the area. Situated halfway up a hundred-foot vertical cliff, Rock House is a straight natural tunnel with five "windows" overlooking Laurel Run. One of several principal scenic attractions in the southeastern Ohio park, Rock House displays attractive coloring: bright buff at freshly exposed spots, deep red and brown on weathered surfaces and pale green where covered with lichens and moss. With a reputation for sometimes having housed robbers, horse-thieves and their ilk, the cavern is occasionally called "Robbers' Roost."

North of the Rock House is Cantwell Cliffs, a gigantic horseshoe precipice slowly changing in appearance because of the headward erosion of Buck Run. Weathering along joints also causes changes, for instance, when large blocks separate from the rock mass and move downhill away from the face of the cliff in a process called slumping. The magnitude of slumping ranges from a few inches to tens of feet.

South of Cantwell Cliffs is a rocky gorge considered to be the deepest in Ohio, Conkle's Hollow, named for an explorer who carved his name on the west wall of the gorge in 1797. The most active erosion of valley walls in the area is taking place in the half-mile-long ravine. Almost everywhere else in the park, the rock face has been casehardened, that is, a cement effect from mineral-saturated water that has evaporated on the surface of porous rock causes erosion to be retarded. Where casehardened rock has been broken, rapid erosion of the sandstone beneath is evident.

The gorge is sometimes as narrow as three hundred feet across at the top. In the spring or after a heavy rainfall, spectacular waterfalls cascade from the numerous small side valleys entering the gorge. The valley has such a thick growth of hemlocks, birches, ferns and scrubs that parts of the forest floor never see sunlight.

Two miles from the hollow is Old Man's Cave, the most popular site for Hocking's campers, hikers and climbers. Surrounded by tumbling waterfalls, evergreens clinging to rock walls and mirrorlike pools, an old fugitive made the cave his hermitage for many years after the Civil War and now reportedly lies buried beneath the rocks he loved.

Nearby, Ash Cave, the largest overhanging ledge in the area, received its name from huge piles of ashes, the remnants of countless Indian campfires, found by settlers in the early eighteenth century. The ancient peoples of the Adena culture enjoyed the rugged cliffs and caves at the time of Christ. Later, Wyandot Indians moved to the spot to escape their more savage neighbors. The squaws baked corn bread in crude natural ovens in the larger caves called "hominy holes," while the smaller recesses became weapon-making workshops for the braves. The Indians often hunted in the wild country, using the rock shelters for temporary homes. Layers of relics of their escapades have been unearthed and date back to 6000 B.C. Artifacts, such as pottery, arrow and spear points, and bones of successfully-downed prey—deer, bison, elk and wild turkey—have accumulated on the cave floor.

Like other recesses in the park, Ash Cave was weathered by heavy rainfall and the sapping action of the plunge pool, in addition to the other erosive forces. Horseshoe-shaped, the cave measures ninety feet from the rim to the plunge pool of the falls and one hundred feet from the rim to the back wall. Because of the remarkable acoustical qualities and a natural "pulpit rock", the overhang has been used for many camp meetings.

Early visitors came to hunt the elk, the bison and the deer. People come to Hocking Hills today when looking for a quiet haven of beauty, for a place to commune with the land.

Sights as charming as Cedar Falls characterize Hocking, where miles of trails also follow gorges that are wild, lonely and austere, such as the one leading from here to Old Man's Cave.

SHENANDOAH NATIONAL PARK
AND BLUE RIDGE PARKWAY

This is a humble place where beauty is quiet and does not shout, where there is a tranquility, a charm of blushing shyness that only gradually captures the visitor's awareness. But once its cup of gentle refreshment is drunk, one will find his pleasure.

This is Shenandoah, cradled against the breast of gentle mountains grown mellow with the age of the eastern half of our continent, spread in a generous north-south sweep down northwestern Virginia, encompassing great but not unconquerable mountains and brooks running in a grandfatherly way through the coolness of stately trees.

Yet, compared with other national parks, Shenandoah seems a lesser light until first the geological history is realized; finally its subtlety shines and one realizes there are few places left that can match its serenity. "Oh, Shenandoah, I Love Your Daughter," pleads the American folk song, and one wonders if its composer refers to the daughter of an Indian chief or the land named for the sachem. It is moot, for Shenandoah whispers of love, love of the land and its creatures.

This scene of green coolness and a long mountain range like a vein of blue is a great gift, for within a day's drive, over half of the nation's population can escape the tedium and anxieties of urban existence and sink into its quiet pleasure.

The Blue Ridge Mountains were first seen by Captain John Smith, and later by Alexander Spotswood, the colonial governor of Virginia who crossed near what is now Swift Run Gap. George Freeman Pollock visited the Blue Ridge in 1886, and inspired by its beauty, spent a lifetime building a resort on Stony Man Mountain to let others succumb to the region's charm.

Pollock and friends proposed Shenandoah to a national committee, formed in 1925 to seek suitable park sites in the East. It was not an easy time for them; they struggled most of a night answering the committee's questionnaire, finishing it only a scant few hours ahead of the deadline.

Harry Flood Byrd, Sr., then governor of Virginia, supported their proposal and appointed his commissioner of conservation and development to oversee the purchase of lands for Shenandoah. The state legislature appropriated a million dollars, a vast sum in the time of hard cash, to help the park along. Added to it was $1.25 million in the pennies, nickels and dimes of Virginians and others.

It was not until the eve of the Fourth of July, 1936, that Shenandoah National Park was a reality. President Franklin Delano Roosevelt dedicated it in ceremonies at Big Meadows, for the "recreation and re-creation which we shall find here."

Re-creation. It is two things spelled one way; only the pronunciation is different. For many who see Shenandoah, the accent is on the first syllable, for they are *re*-created here. They usually come by the Skyline Drive, a winding, 105-mile road threading across the crest of the Blue Ridge, offering seventy-five parking overlooks of the valleys and mountain slopes. Often they stop to leave the pavement and walk some of the two hundred miles of foot trails. The hardy few who traverse the entire Appalachian Trail walk through Shenandoah, more than ninety miles of it.

Walking is the best way to enjoy the subtle pleasures of the park, such as seeing water shift its course to the other side of a rock, or feeling beneath one's feet the crunch of the brown, needle-strewn floor of the forest. A few yards beyond may be a handful of gnarled apple trees, unpruned for generations, surrounding a small clearing being rapidly overgrown with trees. Look closely, for here was the cabin of an early settler, one of the fur-capped frontiersmen who crossed these mountains on their way west. Some continued on, some remained. These old mountains were not really much of a natural barrier, but one so attractive many stayed, making it their home.

Hikers often climb Old Rag Mountain, starting near Nethers, Virginia, to complete the ascent and descent of eight miles in a day. There are shelters nearby. Others clop slowly along on horseback on the miles of bridle paths lacing the park.

The Shenandoah Valley was recognized as the Confederacy's "breadbasket" and the back door to the nation's capital during the Civil War. General Stonewall Jackson brought troops within the park's boundaries during the struggle, and in Browns Gap there are earthworks believed to have been built by Confederate forces when they occupied the pass.

This is an old part of our land, more than a billion years in creation. Craggy peaks were smoothed by time into the gentle slopes of today, often wearing a mantle of the blue haze which gave the famous Blue Ridge its name.

The four seasons are each brilliant, painting new colors on the landscape from a palette of pastels with a handful of vivid shades. The dogwood and redbud come early in the spring as leaves from the eighty-odd species of trees begin to unfold in the new-found warmth. Nearly seven-eighths of the park is forested, and in deep shaded glades the winter snows disappear slowly. Finally the sun brushes away the last patches of white, the water seeping into the ground to give life to plant and animal alike, often appearing as a cool spring a mile away or cascading down a hill.

(continued on page 43)

The frequent bluish haze seen about the rolling hills of the Virginia Piedmont, for which Blue Ridge Parkway was named, is evident at Craggy Gardens near Asheville, North Carolina.

As the Blue Ridge Parkway extends 469 miles through the southern Appalachian Mountains, it tells the story of the original settlers, an independent people, through their homesteads and settlements.

Then the azaleas and locust come into bloom, followed by the pink and white mountain laurel. In patches of deep shade live the Dutchman's breeches, a delicate, odd-appearing wildflower sharing the rich, moist soil with beard tongue and red blossoms of the cardinal-flower. Pushing its way through the carpet of black leaves here and there is the snowy trillium, a cousin of the turk's-cap lily.

In fall, as summer gives way to a new season so that living things might sleep and regain their strength for a new spring, so that the mountain laurel will bloom again, come the colors—the wild reds, oranges, yellows and browns.

The Blue Ridge Parkway, separately administered but actually an extension of Shenandoah and Great Smoky National Parks, winds slowly from its lowest elevation crossing the James River in Virginia upward to its highest point of more than six thousand feet in elevation in the Balsams south of Asheville, North Carolina. From it one can see the rolling hills of the Virginia Piedmont, across the fertile fields of the Great Valley, to the Alleghenies and then onward to the Black Mountains and the Great Smokies. Adjacent to the parkway are three national forests—the George Washington, the Jefferson and the Pisgah, which contains the first large tract of managed forest in this country.

The parkway area is also rich in the folk history of the late 1700's: Log cabins and gristmills are preserved; Daniel Boone's Wilderness Road crosses the parkway in North Carolina.

Pleasures on a human scale are abundant in Shenandoah or along the Blue Ridge Parkway.

GREAT SMOKY MOUNTAINS NATIONAL PARK

Rising high between the states of North Carolina and Tennessee are the Great Smoky Mountains, the highest range of the Appalachian Chain which extends from Gaspé, Canada, to northern Georgia. The lofty range of the Smokies is the climax of the Appalachians and is the backbone of Great Smoky Mountains National Park.

Known as the cradle of eastern American vegetation, this area supplied plants and animals to the land exposed for the first time in thousands of years as the glacial ice sheet retreated northward. Primeval and timeworn as they are, vegetation densely covers the Smokies with a sea of green from base to summits, some rising more than six thousand feet.

At first, the Great Smokies may appear to have a certain sameness, then suddenly the delight unfolds: The presence of junglelike plant life together with the prevalent haze charms many who visit the park. Wisps of fog rise from the valley as low-hanging clouds roll through the gaps following the summer rainstorms when most of the precipitation falls. Blue, cold water falls into rushing streams, tipping over the edges of stone after stone. A half-light hovers at the doorway to a mysterious, beckoning cave.

The mountains are steep, but not nearly unconquerable, faced with high rock, but not having the sheer face of the Tetons. Nature has mellowed the Great Smokies with time, gently filling deep valleys and rounding sharp peaks so that they have a graceful, undulating rhythm. The harshness has been worn away and replaced with placidity.

All this took time, 880 million years of it, before the Ice Age's glacial sheet covered the central United States down to the Ohio River, destroying all that lay before it. The Great Smoky Mountains escaped the earth-gnawing glaciers since they were beyond their reach and their climate an anathema to the masses of ice.

Gravel, sand and mud deposits first covered the region, the layers compressing the ones beneath until time and weight solidified them more than three miles thick. Then the land began to rise and side pressures caused the once-solid formations to break or buckle, forming faults in the surface. This disturbance affected much of North America.

Then the ice sheet destroyed and restricted much of the vegetation and animals around the Great

Flowers bloom amid the trees that round the Great Smokies. A blue-green mist, for which the mountains were named, rises from the dense plant growth.

*The Little Pigeon River (left) adds
to gentle scenic beauty at Smoky.
A sunset at Mount Le Conte (right)
colors the skies with a prism of hues.*

Smoky Mountains. The region was at first refuge, then provider, when the ice retreated to the north, furnishing plant and animal life to the land which was raped.

As life began to spread outward from what is now part of the park, the rivers came and cut channels through the land mass, creating valleys in a haphazard pattern. The ages have done the rest, wearing away mountain peaks, brushing away harsh corners and filling too-deep valleys with rock and silt so that vegetation might live and bring still more beauty to this ancient geological structure.

Most of the trees survived the rigorous climate to become the nucleus of deciduous trees which eventually spread and reforested the land with Eastern hardwood trees.

There is no timberline; wide expanses of trees cover the hills with a mantle of green, shedding a fraction of their used vegetation each fall to build the humus for the enormous variety of flora for which the Smokies are noted.

Here are the broadleaved trees—yellow poplar, white ash, American beech, black cherry and northern red oak, growing below the mountain ash and red spruce in the cooler regions at higher altitudes. Surprisingly, the forests overlap because of environmental factors, but the spruce and fir stands are generally found in the Canadian zone above five thousand feet.

The trees are a part of an ecological cycle existing because of the protection given the region by its national park status. Their life is interrelated with smaller plants, the rhododendron, ferns and a gamut of wildflowers. They, in turn, are links in the chain of survival for fifty species of mammals, two hundred types of birds, and fish hovering silently in deep stream-pools.

This country attracted settlers who were hardy, self-sufficient people mostly from Scotland and England. They vied for hunting and fishing lands with the Cherokee Indians whose reservation is now adjacent to the park on the south. The customs, speech and names of those pioneers cling to the region today.

Some of their descendants lived in Cades Cove, Tennessee, which was an isolated community until World War I and some of its citizens joined the armed services. It was seven years after the armistice before a good road linked this tiny town with the world around it. Today Cades Cove visitors can see the cabins and churches and the mill grinding cornmeal which was left when these mountain people sold their properties to the Government at the time the area became a national park.

Today, there are nearly eight hundred square miles for the people's pleasure in this region where all that is gentle and soft is supreme; a mass of green winter and summer, a climate kind to man, an abundant supply of water to nourish the natural treasures preserved in these venerable mountains.

MAMMOTH CAVE NATIONAL PARK

The darkness grips the visitor, then the depths slowly come into focus as the eyes adjust themselves to the underworld of Kentucky's Mammoth Cave, which has been a lure to awestruck men since it was first trod by primitives.

It is still a place of mystery, this partially unexplored hollow land beneath the surface. The ancients braved superstition and penetrated more than three miles of its vaulted passages, seeking gypsum. The dry, even temperatured air has preserved for centuries their worn-out sandals and burnt torch ends, scattered here and there among footprints before sheer walls hacked with rude stone tools. Why they sought the soft mineral is not known. The remains of one of them is still there, his body mummified after he was crushed by a six-ton boulder while gathering the stone 2,400 years ago.

The yawning cavern was rediscovered by an unknown white man in 1798, and a few years later by another seeking saltpeter, or potassium nitrate, a prime ingredient of black gunpowder. The bored-out tree trunks used to carry the chemical solution to vats are still here, along with other well-preserved artifacts of the operation.

The saltpeter industry died after the War of 1812; then began Mammoth Cave's career as a tourist attraction, although much of it remained unexplored. Jenny Lind sang here, her voice echoing and reechoing through the rooms of stone. Edwin Booth, the great Shakespearian actor, intoned the philosophy of Hamlet in this apt surrounding and Grand Duke Alexis of Russia paid the cave a visit along with thousands of others who linked it with Niagara Falls as a great attraction.

In 1837 a fifteen-year-old boy named Stephen Bishop, among the cave's first guides, crossed the Bottomless Pit on a slender pole, opening the way to extensive uncharted corridors and passages. Bishop guided the many eminent scientists who visited the cave thereafter, and achieved world renown before he died in 1859. He is buried in what is now the park. Later the cave became an underground tuberculosis sanitarium. It was proposed as a national park in 1911; that was accomplished thirty years later.

The cave is a maze of corridors connecting huge, domed chambers and deep pits. They were formed 340 million years ago when the limestone was the bed of an ancient sea. The land rose, and water inched

Blindfish (below), which inhabit the subterranean Echo River, have developed acute senses of touch and smell. They are small, colorless and translucent. Iron oxide in the calcium carbonate gives the Golden Fleece (right) its golden color.

into the rock, eroding the giant passages seen today. The formations have quaint, picturesque names— Fat Man's Misery, a narrow channel out into the floor of a large room; Frozen Niagara; the Snowball Room. Echo River is the world's best-known underground stream. Nearly a million persons a year visit this great natural wonder.

Above ground, two lovely rivers flow through the park, winding past deep green forests and a blaze of colorful wildflowers, a strange paradox to the weird, wonderful world spread out down below.

The Rotunda, one of Mammoth Cave's largest rooms, was used to mine saltpeter, a prime ingredient of black gunpowder, during the War of 1812.

Juniper Springs, Ocala National Forest, Florida

SWAMPS, BOGS AND ALLIGATORS
Florida and The Gulf Coast

A "river of grass," the mystifying Everglades of Florida is a haunting lushness of subtropical wilderness. Mangroves with their roots clustered above the water add a note of fantasy to the landscape, as do the dark coastal forests tangled with abundant vegetation. To the north lies another incomparable swampland, Okefenokee, the "Land of the Trembling Earth," festooned in brown and gray draperies of Spanish moss. Stretching for miles and miles to the west, breaker islands, reefs and sugar sand beaches border the Gulf of Mexico. The desolate, wind-swept beauty of Padre Island offers a curious contrast to the beaches of the Gulf Islands.

51

EVERGLADES NATIONAL PARK

Quiet, calm, flat, mysterious—the Everglades are a unique part of the American landscape, the largest subtropical wilderness in North America.

Lake Okeechobee, massively spilling over to the north, created this river of grass, broad, short and shallow, with multifarious water creatures—wading birds, alligators, turtles, otter and fish—thriving in and about its swampy lushness in Florida.

All this lush, growing green can be seen best from the jungle spots on elevated islands called hammocks. Towering trees, dangling vines, carpets of ferns, West Indian in character, flourish here, where thrive the Liguus trees snails, so beautiful in aspect and so rarely seen elsewhere.

Here, where dark, tangled coastal forests drove Spanish horsemen to more maneuverable coasts, are ghostly clusters of mangrove trees, cypress heads, bayheads and stands of Caribbean pine. Many trees grow above tangles of crooked, interlocking roots which sustain their trunks above the water. The pines are slender-tufted, fire-resistant and fire-perpetuated and they have been used extensively in the building of termite and rot-resistant structures.

(continued on page 55)

The osprey (above), the only hawk that dives into water, sails toward his nest on a small island of mangroves. Palm trees (right) rise high over the abundant variety of plants flourishing in the renowned swamp.

Dead and rotting logs lay across a vast swamp (left) which is interlaced with placid waterways. At Everglades many tropical plants and animals are interspersed with species found in the temperate zone. Seen frequently is the cormorant (above), an expert fisherman that often swims with just its neck and head showing and then dives sharply to pursue and capture a fish in its strongly hooked beak.

The Everglades thermometers do not fluctuate sharply during the two characteristic seasons, the wet summer and dry winter. During the rainy season, great cloud formations are sculptured battlements over the terrain, colored and dominated by dark thunderheads. Sometimes a hurricane will move in from the tropical seas, wreaking havoc: Sea beasts are washed ashore, vegetation stands bare and wind-stripped, water everywhere, salt and fresh alike, inundates the land.

Midway to Flamingo from park headquarters, the salt area begins. This enormous brackish zone is

One of the Everglades' famous wading birds, the American egret spends the dry season (winter) in its rookery.

nature's inaccessible nursery for numerous game fish and the coveted pink shrimp. Spawn and prawn, a swampy matrix of infant, edible fish life, is permitted to grow and eventually fills the demands of commercial and sport fish operations amid the Keys and along the Gulf Coast.

Here, too, are the mangrove trees, grotesque on the aforesaid prop roots. The citizen of Copenhagen would wonder at the rookeries of storks in this region, increasing and multiplying, a continent removed from the storied stork-nest roofs of Denmark.

The dark memory of the ruthless plume hunters can be vividly recalled in this expanse, where exploiters once threatened to bring exquisite species of waterfowl to the point of extinction.

Once a rustic fishing village, Flamingo is now a gateway to the water wilderness of the park, the bays and rivers. Along the rich and intriguing Florida Bay shore there is no perceptible dividing line between land and sea. Beyond is Cape Sable, a pristine retreat whose immaculately white sands shelter the eggs of huge, lumbering loggerhead turtles, which may grow to weigh nearly half a ton.

The park by night is a jungle of sound and movement. The cries of night birds, the watery thrashings of alligators seeking garfish in the sloughs, the crackling predatory movements of raccoons and panthers, the choruses of insects, toads and frogs arise in sporadic crescendo, and all are weirdly, momentarily illuminated by streaks of lightning in the ebony sky.

The experienced explorer knows the threat and rudeness of the terrain—a few poisonous snakes (including the diamondback rattlesnake), trees which shake off blister-yielding rain drippings, the pits and pinnacles of the trails. Add to this the steamy humidity of summer, the severe winds and drenching rains. But the prize is worth the worry and strain. It now is attainable in areas of minimal discomfort for the bird-watcher, the naturalist, the boater. The strange beauty of the Everglades is ours.

Hardy coconut palms line rough coral-rock shores in Biscayne monument.

BISCAYNE NATIONAL MONUMENT

Wild bird calls and the splash of marine life are the only interruptions to the peaceful silence of the narrow, low-lying islands and barrier reefs of the upper Florida Keys. The higher ground of these keys, nine or ten feet above the tidal marshes, has rare Sargent palms, mahoganies and dense mangrove thickets.

Here in the northern limits of living coral reefs along United States coasts—protected at last by national park conservation practices—small numbers of the endangered North American crocodiles may still maintain haunts in the quiet waters. The rare manatee (sea cow) and bottle-nosed dolphin share the waters surrounding the keys with the many colorful and varied fish. This locale is also the northernmost breeding area for several species of rare West Indian land birds.

Located a few miles south of Miami, Biscayne National Monument contains about 4,200 acres of uplands and more than 92,000 acres of submerged reefs.

Elliott Key, Adams Key, Old Rhodes Key and Sands Key form an almost continuous island barrier bisecting the submerged areas of the monument. The submerged lands form two broad, divided habitats. On the Biscayne Bay side, the bottom is a deposit of marl mud and marine grasses.

Underwater terrain on the Atlantic Ocean side of the islands is more variable with the bottom gradually deepening to the edge of the rubble reefs. The rocky limestone outcroppings, bottom shoals, coral, coralline algae and marine grasses support an extremely rich and varied tropical marine biota. The ecosystems here are so fragile that any distinct major disturbance by man would damage them irreparably.

Although this area has been near a well-traveled sector of the Atlantic Coast since the beginning of European occupation, and in earlier times by Indians, it remains relatively undisturbed. Relics of the boisterous era of Spanish galleons loaded with gold bullion and English sea rovers searching the seas for the loot lie rotting in these reefs.

To the south is John Pennekamp Coral Reef State Park. Homestead Bayfront Park on the mainland side of the bay complements the monument, and a short distance inland is the entrance to Everglades National Park. Within the monument itself is ninety-acre Elliott Key Park with boat docks and a marina.

Yet the peace and solitude of these isles can be shared with birds, fish and wildlife visible in sudden flashes of bright color. The brilliant green subtropical forests lend a feeling of tranquility, making this a remarkable reef preserved as a national treasure.

LOXAHATCHEE NATIONAL WILDLIFE REFUGE

The Everglades once covered most of southern Florida. Wildlife was extremely plentiful because of a perfectly balanced ecosystem. The Colusa and Seminole Indians living there took care not to upset this balance, but then the Europeans came with their desire to conquer the wilderness. Ponce de Leon trekked over the Everglades looking for his evasive Fountain of Youth and was killed near here by the Colusas in 1521. Then came other Spanish explorers and finally settlers. Conflicts mounted in the early 1800's, and when the Indians were subdued, the glades were open to human despoilment. Today all too few acres of this swamp remain undisturbed.

One of the largest remaining areas of glades is Loxahatchee National Wildlife Refuge, containing 220 square miles and located between Lake Okeechobee and Fort Lauderdale. Established in 1951, the refuge preserves the habitat of a fantastic number of birds and animals.

Loxahatchee is roughly pear-shaped, bounded by levees on all sides. Just inside are the canals which expedite the movement of water in or out of the region as called for by the rainfall, which averages sixty-two inches annually. It was originally the bottom of a great sea, but dying vegetation has built up a large body of organic soil rising up to fifteen feet above sea level.

Although crisscrossed with questionable drainage ditches, much of the unique beauty of this section of the Everglades remains. Dense stands of Tracey's beakrush flourish in shallow water flats, and sawgrass continues to cover large areas. Smartweeds, white water lilies and other wet-soil aquatic plants grow here, while the tree islands support mixed stands of redbay, wax-myrtle and holly.

Both wading birds and waterfowl come here by the thousands all year round. The rarest bird found on the refuge is the Everglade kite, of which there are

Portions of Loxahatchee are jungle glades of ferns, semitropical flowers and trees (opposite) while others are swamps and shallow water flats. The Florida sandhill crane (above) is found in this state and in Cuba. In Loxahatchee, its numbers are protected.

only about one hundred in existence. Medium-sized birds with a black body, white tail bands and, during the breeding season, a red patch between the eyes and the sharply hooked beak, the kites are very sensitive in their eating habits, feeding only on a particular species of freshwater snail. Thus they can survive only in areas where the snails are fairly plentiful. Perching on snags in the marshes after capturing their prey, they deftly pull it from its shell with their specialized beaks.

Two birds that are uncommon outside of the glades are the limpkin and the Florida sandhill crane. The limpkin, a long-legged, long-beaked bird with a brown body and distinctive white arrowhead-shaped spots, feeds on the same species of snail as does the kite, and also other mollusks and insects. The sandhill crane, largest bird found on the refuge, can be easily recognized by its large size and tufted tail. In flight the long neck is outstretched, and its call, once heard, cannot soon be forgotten. During winter a number of cranes may roost in the flooded fields near the refuge headquarters on the eastern boundary near Delray Beach. They build their nests less than a foot above the water, which may be six to eighteen inches deep.

The bald eagle visits Loxahatchee occasionally, but does not normally nest here, preferring instead to travel sixty miles south to Everglades National Park. The American osprey can be found in the region in small numbers most of the year.

The great white heron's breeding range lies south of Loxahatchee, and the number of these graceful long-legged wading birds visiting at any one time is usually small. But the great blue heron is common here, and can be seen along the trails as it stalks through the waters looking for animals to feed upon.

A large white bird with yellow beak and black legs seen in the refuge is the common egret, brought to near extinction by plume hunters around the turn of the century. Its smaller cousin, the snowy egret, can be recognized by its black bill and black legs with yellow feet. Egrets feed primarily on small fish, frogs and other water creatures.

During winter one of the most plentiful birds is the coot, a duck-like bird with a white bill. Also abundant at this time of year, and residing here all year round, is the white ibis with its red face and decurved bill. A close relative, the glossy ibis, is identified by its dark bronze plumage.

The roseate spoonbill, a large white and pinkish wader with a bill which flattens out at the tip, is an occasional visitor. Still other birds found in Loxahatchee are common and purple gallinules, anhingas, Louisiana herons, turkey and black vultures, killdeer, mourning doves, smooth-billed anis (normally a bird of the tropics), screech and great horned owls, grackles and mockingbirds.

Loxahatchee is the southern terminus of the Atlantic Flyway, and twenty or more species of ducks

A great blue heron, distinguished by two black plumes on its white head, nests in the refuge.

migrate here annually. The Florida duck, mottled duck and wood duck nest here, and ring-necked ducks, pintails, blue-winged and green-winged teals, American widgeons, shovellers and baldpates winter in the marshes.

Alligators, though an endangered species nationally, seem to thrive in this refuge. These reptiles can be seen floating partially submerged or sunning on the edge of a canal. Armadillos were introduced into the area about 1920 and forage for insects early or late during the day and at night. This odd mammal, with its suit of armor protecting it from all enemies, was named by Spaniards who found it in Mexico and called it the "little fellow in armor."

Rabbits, bobwhite quail, raccoons, river otters, Florida water rats (small, round-tailed versions of the muskrat), bobcats and white-tailed deer also inhabit the glades. An occasional cougar, locally called the Florida panther, may wander into the refuge at times.

Fishing in Loxahatchee is good with largemouth bass, bream and crappies in the ditches and shallows.

Only part of Loxahatchee is open to the public. A concession at the south end carries supplies, and rental boats and guides are available. Boat launching facilities and picnic shelters are located at the extreme northern boundary, and a boat launching ramp is also located near the headquarters building. Accommodations are numerous along Florida's Gold Coast, twelve miles to the east.

This section of the once vast Everglades may yet survive as a natural area if the Florida development "fever" does not encroach upon it further.

OKEFENOKEE NATIONAL WILDLIFE REFUGE

Those who want to study an unimpaired swampland environment should come to Okefenokee. One of the largest, oldest and most primitive protected swamps in the United States, it covers 412,000 acres in extreme southeastern Georgia. Vegetation includes many huge cypress trees mixed with blackgum and redbay. The uplands around the swamp and the islands within it are covered principally with pine and occasional hardwood patches, called hammocks. From May to October the evergreen foliage of the gordonia, one of the swamp's most distinctive trees, is spotted with large white flowers.

About sixty thousand acres of Okefenokee is prairie, or open marsh. During spring these areas are carpeted with white and yellow water lilies, yellow-spiked "neverwet," white floating hearts, purple bladderwort and pickerelweed.

Sometimes a large piece of peat will break away from the swamp bottom and float on the surface. Smaller plants take root until trees and large brush grow on these floating islands. Locally called "houses" because of the many animals and birds that live and nest on them, the islets frequently become anchored by the trees extending their roots down through the water to the bed of peat below, which may be as thick

as twenty feet. The stamping of feet on one of these peat islands will cause the nearby trees to shake, thus the Choctaw name *owaquaphenogau* ("Land of the Trembling Earth"). Okefenokee is simply an anglicized version of this Indian word.

A major characteristic of Okefenokee is the Spanish moss, which is actually an air-breathing plant. Found throughout the Southern states, it festoons all the swamp vegetation with long, flowing draperies of brown and gray.

A few small inlets at the north end of the swamp furnish the only source of water streaming into Okefenokee. The water, coffee-colored due to tannic acids from partially submerged trees, moves slowly through the swamp to the two outlets at the south—the Suwanee River (immortalized in song by Stephen Foster) which drains into the Gulf of Mexico, and St. Mary's River which flows past Jacksonville into the Atlantic.

The most readily recognizable animal in the swamp is the American alligator, rare in almost every other part of the country, but abundant here. This holdover from prehistoric times is known throughout the United States, even by small school children ("A is for Alligator"), as a vicious villain; while actually,

Okefenokee Swamp is characterized by dark, murky waters and long strings of Spanish moss festooning the trees. One of the largest swamps in the nation, most of it is protected as a national wildlife refuge.

*A common egret rests in a slash-pine tree.
This yellow-billed bird has up to fifty long plumes,
or aigrettes, on its back during breeding season.*

at birth, and growing a foot every year until maturity at six feet, they become easy prey for herons, fish, mammals and even other alligators. With these odds, only about one in seven baby gators grows to maturity. The young alligators will eat almost anything that moves if it is smaller than they are, such as tadpoles, snails or insects.

Other animals in the swamp include opossums, otters, raccoons, white-tailed deer, black bears and wild turkeys. The Eastern spadefoot toad, with smooth instead of warty skin, rings out its call on spring nights, and the cottonmouth water moccasin, shy but with a deadly poisonous bite, slithers through the waters in search of frogs.

Practically all of the Atlantic Flyway's species of ducks are here in season, and many stay all year. The anhinga, or snakebird, a large black bird that feeds solely on fish, rests frequently on branches with outstretched wings drying in the sun. Its name comes from its ability to swim completely submerged except for its long snakelike neck. Sandhill cranes majestically fly up from the water, long necks extended, and egrets and herons stalk through the swamp waters in search of food. During the day a red-shouldered hawk may scream overhead, and at night barred owls hoot in the darkness, sending echoes among the cypresses.

Four-fifths of the swamp is under the protection of the Bureau of Sport Fisheries and Wildlife as the Okefenokee National Wildlife Refuge. The establishment of this refuge in 1937 marked the culmination of a long fight to save the swamp from "developers." Beginning in the sixteenth century, when Hernando de Soto may have explored the swamp, Okefenokee was threatened with drainage and timber cutting.

Trips into the interior of Okefenokee can be accomplished only by boat, and a guide is required in the closed areas. The Suwannee Canal, heading into the swamp from Lake Cornelia on the eastern boundary, is open for visitors with private boats, and a campground is maintained at Camp Cornelia. Planned for this area are nature trails and boardwalks, an observation tower and service facilities.

Stephen Foster State Park, in the interior of the refuge, can be reached via a paved road through the southwestern portion, and a number of facilities, including cottages and a picnic area, are available here.

Early-day naturalist William Bartram wrote in 1791 of a belief held by the Creek Indians that an island existed in the middle of the great swamp which was the most blissful place on earth. It was inhabited by a tribe whose women were "incomparably beautiful" while the men were fierce and cruel. After gliding silently along on dark waters beneath eerily draped cypresses and seeing alligators peer up from the water surface with inquisitive eyes, a visitor may wonder about this old legend. Certainly there are many unexpected and fascinating pleasures to be seen in this incomparable swampland environment.

unlike its cousin the crocodile, it will normally avoid man unless provoked. Until recent laws made their illegal trade unprofitable, poachers sold their hides to handbag and shoe manufacturers, and reduced their numbers until they were becoming an endangered species.

Growing to a length of up to fifteen feet, the alligator feeds primarily on aquatic life. During winter it is inactive, denning under banks or in water holes it has made, which benefits all the swamp wildlife during seasons of drought. In the April-May breeding season males call for the female with a loud bellow heard for miles. The female builds a nest mound of grass and muck about two feet high and inserts forty to sixty eggs.

Three months later when they hatch, the young gators grunt and the female makes an opening in the nest to let them out. Being only six to ten inches long

Shady stretches of beach provide encompassing views of the sometimes calm Gulf of Mexico.

GULF ISLANDS NATIONAL SEASHORE

Wide, gently sloping beaches of unusually fine, white "sugar" sand, clear blue waters reminiscent of Caribbean bays, unique flora and fauna, and several historically important forts are the characteristics of Gulf Islands National Seashore. Consisting of about 13,600 acres of barrier and offshore islands stretching 150 miles from Florida to Mississippi, the seashore is a prime example of what dedicated citizens can do for the preservation of our natural resources.

Citizen interest in these islands was developed in the 1960's when it was learned that sea erosion was undermining Fort Massachusetts on Mississippi's Ship Island, now included within the seashore. They appealed to their Congressmen and Senators for Federal help in preserving the fort, which was further damaged in September 1965 by Hurricane Betsy. Erosion would not wait for legislation, however, and local residents formed an organization called Save the Fort, Inc., which gained widespread publicity and enough contributions to erect a protective wall around the old structure. A bill authorizing the proposed seashore passed Congress and was signed by President Richard M. Nixon in January 1971.

Saved from further commercial development are some of Mississippi's offshore islands, namely Horn, Petit Bois (meaning "little woods" and locally pronounced "petty boy") and Ship Islands, and in Florida, parts of Santa Rosa Island (formerly the Santa Rosa

National Monument which was deactivated by the Secretary of the Interior in 1946), the eastern half of Perdido Key across the channel from Santa Rosa, and sections of Naval Live Oaks Reservation and the Pensacola Naval Air Station, both on the mainland. The two state areas are separated by Alabama's Gulf Coast.

Santa Rosa, a long, thin barrier island, is significant because of its sandy beaches and clear waters. On the western tip of the island lies Fort Pickens, an old brick fort built in 1834 to protect the important deepwater harbor at Pensacola. Before that, the site had been occupied by the Spanish, French and British. The fort's major role was during the Civil War, when it was one of only three forts in the South successfully held by Union forces, the others being Fort Taylor at Key West and Fort Jefferson on Dry Tortugas. In fact its builder, Captain William Chase, a U. S. Army engineer, planned its defenses and strongholds so carefully that, later as a Confederate general, he himself was unable to seize it.

On Perdido Key, across the narrow ship channel from Fort Pickens, are the foundations of Fort McRee, visible only at low tide. Built shortly after Fort Pickens, it was destroyed by tides and pounding surf. The center of the parade grounds, where the flagpole stood in 1852, is now covered by thirty feet of water in the channel.

Across Pensacola Bay on the mainland's Naval Air Station are two other important forts, San Carlos and Barrancas. Fort San Carlos was built by the Spanish between 1781 and 1790 on the approximate site of an earlier wooden Spanish fort, completed in 1698. Connected to it by a brick tunnel is Fort Barrancas, built between 1839 and 1844 by the United States and held by the Confederates for a short time during the Civil War. Still a third fort, Redoubt, can be seen a short distance away.

The other fort within the seashore is Fort Massachusetts. Completed just as the Civil War broke out and seized by the Confederacy, the fort was soon recaptured by Federal troops and was used as an important part of the naval blockade for the duration of the conflict.

Ship Island itself has an intriguing history. The French first settled the island in 1699, and it re-

Beach grasses try to stabilize the sand on Horn Island, Mississippi (left), but severe storms cause much ecological damage to the offshore islands. In other parts of Horn, beach morning glories spread their creamy white-yellow flowers.

mained an important stopping point for supplies from France, which were then distributed to all of French Louisiana. After the capital moved from Biloxi to New Orleans, the island's importance declined.

Flora in the seashore is extremely varied. For example, Horn Island contains over 204 species of plants. Slim slash-pine trees fight to survive the salt and sand driven by stormy winds. Some of the sand dunes have been stabilized by species of magnolia, palmetto and live oak, while the unstabilized dunes are mostly covered with beach grass and sea oats. The 1,300-acre Naval Live Oaks Reservation is a beautiful stand of large live oaks and represents the nation's first attempt at conservation: President John Quincy Adams set aside the area in 1828 to save these rare oaks from being used for shipbuilding.

Fur-bearing animals find little on which to survive, and rabbits and opossums are the only two mammals still fairly common on the islands. The monument provides many places for the Gulf's increasingly rare sea turtles to lay their eggs, and it is the only habitat for a species of beach mouse which has developed a very light coloration to blend into the white sand.

A great number of birds nest within the seashore, especially on Horn and Petit Bois islands. Here the interior ponds, lagoons and marshes serve as wintering grounds for blue and snow geese and several species of ducks. The beaches support laughing gulls and Sandwich and royal terns; redhead ducks are abundant on the shallow Gulf waters. Other birds include common and snowy egrets; green, great blue and Louisiana herons; willets; snowy and Wilson's plovers; sanderlings; American oystercatchers; killdeer; and occasional ospreys and frigate birds.

The sections of Santa Rosa Island closest to the bridge linking it to the mainland are commercially developed and are not included within the seashore's boundaries, although they contain a number of attractions and facilities for visitors. Other facilities, such as cottages, picnic areas and a campground are located at Fort Pickens State Park at the west end of the island.

The efforts of citizens of the Florida and Mississippi Gulf Coasts should be deeply appreciated by anyone walking on the "sugar" sands of Santa Rosa, photographing a tern robbing a sea turtle's nest on the beach, or simply imagining how an old fort must have looked in earlier days.

At Aransas refuge, Attwater's prairie chicken can be seen performing its prenuptial dance.

ARANSAS NATIONAL WILDLIFE REFUGE

It is truly a magnificent creature, this tallest of North American birds. Five feet in height, with a seven-foot wingspan, the whooping crane gives a piping cry that can be heard over a mile away. It is noble and stately in appearance, with its gleaming white plumage, red patch of bare skin on the crown, black wing tips and graceful flight. But it is not just its appearance that makes the whooper so unusual. It mates for life and lives in a fiercely guarded privacy with a decorum rarely found in birds. The male, who can sense potential danger a mile away, is always ready to challenge an enemy with bugle calls and a head-on charge.

Every autumn, the world awaits word of the arrival of the whoopers on the Texas Gulf Coast after a 2,500-mile flight from their summer nesting sites in Canada, for these birds have been on the verge of extinction for many years. It is believed that they have not been really numerous for centuries and there may have been only 1,400 dwelling on the continent at the time the Pilgrims landed. By 1938 only fourteen remained and today there are about fifty.

One reason for the modest increase was the establishment in 1937 of the Aransas National Wildlife Refuge at the whoopers' winter grounds on Blackjack Peninsula on the Texas Gulf Coast. While there, each pair of birds, including a rusty-colored chick or two if there are offspring, establishes for themselves a territory of about four hundred acres. Because whoopers are so sensitive to intruders, espe-

cially human, the public is not allowed to enter the birds' wintering grounds in Aransas, but the birds can be usually viewed with binoculars from an observation tower which overlooks a portion of this coastal area.

Late in the winter, when mates renew their nuptial bonds, one approaches the other with many stiff bows interspersed with cavorting, trumpeting and flapping as he constantly moves in semicircles. Then he leaps into the air stiff-legged, spreading his great wings; this is repeated as he circles more frantically and jumps increasingly higher until his dance is over.

Another endangered species, Attwater's prairie chicken, once nested in goodly numbers on the tallgrass prairies of the Texas coast, but as this fertile country was settled, drained and cultivated, they were forced to survive in isolated patches or on the fringes of their former habitats.

The marshes, grasslands, brush thickets and woods of Aransas nurture many other species of birds under the supervision of the Bureau of Sport Fisheries and Wildlife. Among the mammals are an abundance of white-tailed deer and an increasing number of javelinas (collared peccaries). The latter is the only wild native piglike animal in the United States. These sturdy beasts favor a terrain in Aransas—the dense thickets—quite different from that of the elegant whoopers, but the important fact is that, like the great rare birds, they have found needed sanctuary on this isolated Gulf Coast peninsula appropriately named for the blackjack oak that grows here.

PADRE ISLAND NATIONAL SEASHORE

Along the Texas Gulf Coast is the longest uninterrupted stretch of primitive, warm-weather beach land in the continental United States. For those who are fascinated by vast expanses of unspoiled shoreline, by a feeling that places where the oceans and land meet have a special message for man—Padre Island will always be memorable.

Over a hundred miles long, Padre is a splendid example of a barrier island formed by lateral currents and waves depositing billions of shellfish, the remains of other animals and eroded sediment from mainland Texas. Finally, about five thousand years ago, the island edged above the surface, the winds began building dunes, and vegetation began to establish a tenuous foothold with plants that are resistant to the scouring effect of wind-blown sand. They must grow faster than the sand can pile up around them or survive periods of inundation beneath this shifting surface, and they must resist the periodic washing by saltwater. The resultant vegetation—including the picturesque, nodding sea oats and the purple-flowered railroad vine (beach morning glory) that stretches its runner for more than twenty-five feet over the sands—are what binds these dunes and

protects them against the strong winds and heavy seas of the Gulf, permitting the dunes to grow.

Padre, like all such barrier islands, is a living and dying piece of the earth. In the natural sequence of events, this island will be pushed, during tens of thousands of years, by wind and waves toward the mainland, gradually becoming part of it—just as another new barrier island may begin to form slowly somewhere offshore. For inevitably the time comes for every dune to become mobile when hurricane winds and tides break through and start moving it toward the mainland again. But the life cycle of Padre has been accelerated because of man. Regrettably, cattle grazing, dune buggies and motorcycles, by destroying vegetation, have contributed to the island's westward movement so that today in some locations Laguna Madre, the shallow body of water between the island and the mainland, is filling in at the rate of fifty feet per year.

Padre Island was discovered in 1519 by a Spanish fleet under Alfonso Alvarez de Piñeda when it was inhabited by the cannibalistic Karankawa Indians. First named *Las Islas Blancas* ("The White Islands"), because of its immense stretches of white rolling

A stretch of diamondlike sand sparkles in the morning sun on Padre Island, a barrier island off the tip of Texas in the Gulf of Mexico. The national seashore section of the island is an 80.5 mile expanse of unspoiled beaches.

The railroad vine, a kind of beach morning glory, has large purple flowers and runners that may extend twenty five-feet.

sands, like other barrier islands, it became known as a graveyard for ships. Probably the worst of naval disasters occurred here in 1553 when thirteen ships of a Spanish fleet were forced by a violent hurricane onto the sand bar known as Devil's Elbow. About three hundred persons survived the storms but only two of these escaped the animosity of the Indians.

The island acquired its present name shortly after 1800 when Padre Nicholas Balli and his nephew received a Spanish land grant that included the island. Their operations continued for about thirty years. John Singer, brother to sewing machine inventor Isaac Singer, was shipwrecked on the island and ranched on it for fourteen years. Patrick Dunn began ranching here in 1879 and his operation lasted until 1971 when most of the cattle were removed because grasslands had become depleted by overgrazing. Ruins of some of the buildings of the Dunn Ranch line camps can still be seen within the boundaries of the national seashore which was authorized in 1962 and dedicated by Mrs. Lyndon B. Johnson six years later.

The seashore includes 80.5 miles in the central portion of the island, with the northern and southern ends occupied by private land and county parks. Motels and restaurants nearest to the seashore are located in these areas. Camping is permitted along the Gulf beach but there are no conveniences. Causeways at both ends provide vehicular access to the narrow island, which ranges in width from a few hundred yards to about three miles. Along the Gulf is a gently sloping beach of sand and, in places, broken shell that is ideal for swimming, surf fishing and other kinds of recreation. Next, paralleling the shore, is an alignment of dunes in various stages of stabilization that sometimes reach a height of forty feet.

Sport fishermen may go after a range of highly prized species—weakfish, channel bass, croaker, red-fish, red snapper, drum, pompano, sheepshead and shark. Occasionally porpoises can be seen leaping near the shore. Birds are plentiful, with 250 species having been recorded on small islands along the Intercoastal Waterway near Padre, including a dozen kinds of gulls and terns. The only white pelican rookery along the Gulf Coast or East Coast is located on a small island in Laguna Madre, but brown pelicans have become quite scarce during the past decade due to the effects of DDT. Other nesting birds include the great horned owl, burrowing owl, American avocet, marsh hawk, horned lark, Eastern and Western meadowlarks, bobwhite, black skimmer and several kinds of herons and egrets, including the reddish egret, an endangered species found only in Texas and Florida. Its name derives from its rusty-brown head and neck. Another distinguishing physical characteristic is its flesh-colored, black-tipped bill, but the most intriguing aspect of the reddish egret is the way it feeds in shallows by rapidly dashing about and making sudden turns and lurches, giving the appearance of a creature somewhat out of its head. An abundant variety of ducks, geese and sandhill cranes winter on Padre.

Sizable terrestrial animals are not as plentiful as on the mainland but the black-tailed jackrabbit and coyote are commonly seen and occasionally white-tailed deer and javelina (collared peccary) swim over to the island from the mainland. However, most of Padre's animal population consists of small rodents, such as spotted ground squirrels, kangaroo rats and pocket gophers, and larger mammals such as raccoons, opossums and badgers.

Among the reptiles are turtles, lizards and a dozen different kinds of snakes, including the secretive and seldom-seen Western diamondback rattler and the curious hognose snake that is quite harmless though it hisses loudly, spreads a cobralike hood and sometimes plays dead. At night scavenger ghost crabs dart back and forth in such numbers that they are almost impossible to avoid.

Padre Island's desolate, windswept beauty and its abundant marine and shore wildlife make it one of the most unusual and inviting national seashores. It has a spaciousness and wildness that will always distinguish it as an unforgettable pleasuring ground in America.

The Upper Mississippi-Great Lakes

Glen Lake, Ottawa National Forest, Michigan

Alone with a fragrance of pine carried on hearty breezes, the traveler in the north woods can refresh himself in the acres of birch, hemlock, quaking aspen, pine and spruce. Cool havens for shore and water birds and mammals, the Chippewa and Superior national forests also form a backdrop for the myriads of sparkling lakes that seem to be smaller versions of Superior's color and charm. Studding the surface of the most western of the Great Lakes are the varied islands of Isle Royale and Apostle Islands. Guarding the shore are Pictured Rocks, the multicolored sandstone cliffs, and the ever-changing Indiana and Sleeping Bear dunes.

Isle Royale has many moods. In one of the most charming, a tranquil beauty descends with night upon the numerous lakes and islands of the archipelago, where man can find the isolated splendor that comes with being in the north woods.

ISLE ROYALE
NATIONAL PARK

Isle Royale, now north woods wilderness held in a lake's solitude, is visibly haunted by the grace and majesty of its geologic past. This handsomely endowed protectorate of vast Lake Superior, in Michigan, and twenty-two miles from the Minnesota shore, is enveloped by the greatest of the Great Lakes, the lake which marks the site of the southern end of an ancient and possibly one of the highest mountain ranges that ever existed on our continent.

The formation of Lake Superior and perhaps Isle Royale itself is explained eloquently by Rutherford Platt in *The Great American Forest:* "Through timeless eras . . . in many places the uplift of mountains so weakened the edge of the Canadian Shield (a shield is a broad, massive, symmetrical rock upheaval) that it gave way, . . . creating depressions for future lakes and river valleys."

The pure copper deposits of Isle Royale and even the mineral riches of its geologic cousin the Mesabi Range are explained by Platt: "The Canadian Shield became the pedestal of the North Woods." He describes the intrusions of plutonic minerals and the ravaging of the area's surface by glaciers, the outcroppings of rock in which, on Isle Royale itself, the Indians found copper "so pure it can be used without smelting. This was the source of copper for Indian artifacts found scattered far and wide through the American wilderness."

Isle Royale, forty-five miles in length, is redolent with the ancient history of Indian copper miners, who reportedly worked there four thousand years ago. Its fjord-like harbors, sheltered bays and interior, parallel ridges attaining a height of seven hundred feet, were first looked upon by white men in 1699. These were heroic French explorers who named the island for Louis XIV.

Yet white men did not recognize that although the copper of Isle Royale was satisfactory for the primitive artisan, it wasn't in sufficient concentration for modern industrial needs. Miners ventured across the lake in the 1840's and 1870's, but by 1900 their mines were abandoned.

The canoe yielded to the motor launch, the small boat to the excursion vessel. Hotels and summer homes were beginning to multiply. A cry was raised and the administration of the second great conservationist Roosevelt responded to their reasoned pleas. In 1936, Franklin Delano Roosevelt signed the Isle Royale National Park Act resulting in its establishment four years later.

Two hundred tiny islands and countless rocks, inviting water explorers, surround the main island; thus the entire park area can be called an archipelago. A coniferous sweep of trees covers the northeast and

71

perimeter of the island, and maple-birch hardwoods dominate the higher interior. Bald ridges, bogs, spruce and cedar swamps dot the landscape, offering additional havens for the water birds.

"The muzzles of moose cut sliding V's on the mirrors of the ponds," as Rutherford Platt suggests of the north woods area. On Isle Royale approximately six hundred of the long-legged, antlered beasts form the relatively large population.

Beavers, red foxes, snowshoe hares and red squirrels find refuge and sustenance here. The lonely cry of the loon, the din of the herring gull, the scream of the bald eagle are heard on the island reaches.

There are no roads on the island. The hiker and canoeist, however, can maneuver here with more than 120 miles of trails to be negotiated amid the wild splendor, although they should remember that the nights are cool and even day temperatures seldom rise above eighty degrees. Many small boats are handy to the seeker of water worlds at Rock Harbor and Windigo. Fishermen call the island "the pike capital of the nation" because of the abundance of pike in the two hundred lakes and ponds. Isle Royale is the north woods in autonomous compactness, with fascination for all.

Away from the mainland's daily routine of hurry and heaviness, a visitor (above) can relish the sharp contrast of color and form. Moose (below) did not come until 1912 when Lake Superior froze across to Canada, fifteen miles away.

PICTURED ROCKS NATIONAL LAKESHORE

From the waters of Lake Superior, the largest fresh-water lake in the world, the afternoon sun brings out the deep colors of the rocky cliffs—the reds, greens, browns and purples—and the various shapes of the rocks are accentuated by long shadows. Inland the sun sparkles on the lakes and cascading streams, and the maples and birches ruffle in the breeze. The scent of pine drifts down the hillsides and, far away, a coyote howls. It is not hard to imagine a young Indian brave named Hiawatha paddling his birch-bark canoe on these lake waters. For this is the land of the Gitche-Gumee, the shining Big-Sea-Water, and near-by is the wigwam of Nokomis, who raised Hiawatha. It was at his wedding feast that Pau-Puk-Keemis danced on the beach and kicked up the sands that are called the Grand Sable Dunes.

Although Longfellow's epic poem is fiction, much of his setting was based upon the Pictured Rocks area of Michigan's Upper Peninsula. The Chippewa Indians resided here for many years, and French explorers and missionaries, including Pierre Radisson and Father Marquette, knew the area well.

The main single attraction are the Pictured Rocks themselves, fifteen miles of multicolored sandstone cliffs rising abruptly from the lake as much as two hundred feet. In the never-ending struggle against erosion, these rocks are fighting a losing battle, for the waves, rain and frost have carved arches, columns, promontories and thunder caves out of the cliffs. Groundwater, seeping to various sandstone levels and collecting minerals and chemicals on the way, drips down the sides of the eroded sculptures, depositing the staining chemicals. The names describe the formations: Miners Castle, Chapel Rock, Lovers Leap, Rainbow Cave and the Battleships. In the early 1900's Grand Portal, a magnificent series of several honeycombed arches jutting six hundred feet into the lake, collapsed, leaving lesser arches, amphitheaters and debris.

Just east of the Pictured Rocks along the shoreline are twelve miles of bluffs neither as steep nor as high and interspersed with many sand and pebble beaches.

Further east are the Grand Sable Banks and Dunes rising 350 feet above the lake. They were formed during the last stages of the Pleistocene Ice Age as sand and glacial silt were dropped to the bottom of an ancient lake made by the receding glaciers. A slight upthrust of the sandstone base pushed the sand several hundred feet up, and winds shaped it into dunes which are still active and moving inland toward the forests and streams.

Inland are many lakes, the most picturesque of which are Chapel and Beaver lakes. Streams connect them with Lake Superior, and along the Pictured

A wave crashes into Chapel Rock, clearly demonstrating how Lake Superior's waters were able to carve these magnificent Pictured Rocks.

Autumnal colors grace the white bark of a birch stand along the lakeshore, which is the fictional home of Longfellow's Hiawatha and a prime example of the north woods.

Rocks shoreline, the water cascades over the palisades in spectacular fashion. Waterfalls are also numerous in the interior—Munising Falls south of the Pictured Rocks drops fifty feet into a large natural amphitheater, and visitors can walk into a cavity behind the falls without getting wet.

A huge lumbering industry in the latter nineteenth century nearly exterminated the pine trees, but today the Pictured Rocks region has extensive second-growth forests, mostly mixed northern hardwoods of sugar and red maple, beech, birch and hemlock. There is one almost pure stand of beautiful white birch in the center beach area. A feeling of the "north woods" is perpetuated with the addition of some quaking aspen, pine and mountain ash. In the bog areas are found white spruce, balsam fir, tamarack and arborvitae. In spring yellow violets, trillium, Dutchman's breeches and orchids cover the forest floor and bogs, and in autumn the blueberry joins the trees in a spectacular array of color.

White-tailed deer are a common sight along the dirt roads, and black bear may occasionally be seen. Other mammals found here are the coyote, otter, fox, bobcat, muskrat, mink, porcupine, beaver and snowshoe hare, and the moose, lynx and wolf are sometimes present in small numbers. Game birds, such as grouse and woodcock, are plentiful, and a great variety of water and shorebirds—bald eagles,

ravens, herring gulls, and migratory Canada geese and loons—may be observed.

In winter this area receives over one hundred inches of snow, an amount exceeded in the Upper Peninsula only in the Huron Mountains one hundred miles west. Yet in comparison to the surrounding regions it remains fairly warm because of Lake Superior.

Pictured Rocks National Lakeshore, approved by Congress in 1966, protects thirty-five miles of Lake Superior shoreline from Grand Marais to Munising. It also includes many thousands of acres of forested slopes and inland waters. Some of the lakeshore is still privately owned, but there are dirt roads and trails to some of the scenic spots, and three primitive campgrounds. Developed campgrounds are located in nearby Hiawatha National Forest and Grand Sable State Forest. The best way to see the Pictured Rocks is from the lake, and tours are available in Munising during the summer. Future developments will include a scenic drive atop the lake cliffs and dunes, camp and picnic grounds and a beach, although Lake Superior waters are too chilly for any but the most hardy.

The fabled days of Hiawatha live on only in folklore, but the wilderness that he might have known remains essentially the same, preserved for all who want to enjoy the untamed beauty of the northern Great Lakes.

SLEEPING BEAR DUNES NATIONAL LAKESHORE

According to ancient Chippewa and Ottawa Indian legends, a black bear and her two cubs attempted to swim across Lake Michigan from the Wisconsin side. Nearing the Michigan shore the cubs became tired and lagged behind their mother, who climbed atop a bluff to watch and wait for her offspring. She is still there, the Sleeping Bear, a solitary sand dune covered with dark vegetation. The cubs still lag a few miles offshore, the forested North and South Manitou islands.

In fact, these massive sand dunes, glistening beaches, green forests, blue lakes and gently flowing streams are the result of glacial action. When the last stage of the Pleistocene Ice Age ended, the land was left in a jumble of glacial features. The basis of the Sleeping Bear region is the three-hundred-foot-high Manistee Moraine, which snakes along a few miles inland. Other moraines, called interlobate moraines, extend out from Manistee and are responsible for the various points jutting out into the lake.

However, at Sleeping Bear Point the erosion carved steep bluffs some four hundred feet high. Continual battering of the eroded material by wind and waves formed sand particles which were blown up over the tops of the cliffs. At this point a decrease in wind caused them to drop and gradually cover the bluffs. Thus the Sleeping Bear Dunes differ from the Indiana Dunes three hundred miles south because they are not pure dunes, but covered cliffs.

Blowouts, breaks in the sand ridges where the sand has been blown away, are also present here. Many of the older dunes have been stabilized with vegetation, but the younger dunes, particularly the Sleeping Bear Dune which towers some 450 feet over Lake Michigan, are continuing to move inland, encroaching on the forests and glacial lakes.

Indians lived in the dunes area and on the Manitou Islands for many years, and Father Marquette visited the region during his explorations, preparing the way for trappers and traders. But most of the land was sparsely settled by whites because it was not especially fertile. South Manitou Island has a fine harbor, however, providing protection against storms, and it became a regular stopping point for Great Lakes steamships. A large lumbering industry developed on the mainland, founding the communities of Empire, Glen Arbor and Glen Haven, outside of the lakeshore. Later, summer vacationers from Chicago, Milwaukee and Detroit began building cottages. Heavy industry however, never took notice of Sleeping Bear, and most of the region remains in a relatively unspoiled state.

Many clear blue lakes, notably Crystal, Platt and Glen lakes, are surrounded by forests of beech and sugar maple. The more sandy areas support pine, oak and aspen. Excellent stands of white cedar exist on the Manitou Islands, and beach grass and cottonwoods grow on the younger dunes of the mainland.

Otter, badger, deer, beaver, bobcat and over two hundred species of birds thrive here, and the two islands support large gull rookeries.

Sleeping Bear Dunes National Lakeshore was authorized in 1970 and contains about 71,000 acres, including sixty-four miles of mainland shoreline and the two offshore islands. Planned developments include a thirty-mile scenic drive with overlooks, hiking trails, campgrounds, picnic areas, visitor centers and beach activity areas. The Manitou Islands will be kept as a wilderness with only primitive facilities.

From the top of Sleeping Bear Dune, Glen Lake sparkles in the middle of the maples, oaks and pines. The miles of curving white beach disappear in the distance, and to the west, Lake Michigan's horizon is indistinct in the bluish haze. Offshore the islands look like two small humps on the white, choppy waters. The mother bear and her cubs can now sleep on forever.

Sparse grasses manage to live on the Sleeping Bear bluffs.

INDIANA DUNES NATIONAL LAKESHORE

Through the pines and hardwoods at the tops of the dunes you can see the setting sun silhouetting the impressive skyline of Chicago, thirty-five miles away across Lake Michigan. However, in the same gaze, you can also see the "dark, satanic" steel mills in East Chicago and Gary with smoke billowing from their tall stacks. This is Indiana Dunes—a natural area squeezed between urbanization and steel mills. In 1919, just after World War I, Stephen T. Mather, the first director of the National Park Service, proposed that forty miles of the Indiana Dunes be preserved as a national park. Mather was ignored and by 1960 those dunes were largely leveled by industry. But a new wave of conservationists took up the cause and the last remnant of these shorelines was saved, less than one third of the original dunes.

These dunes, which reach astonishing heights of up to two hundred feet, were once the sandy shores of a monstrous lake formed by the retreating glaciers. As the lake receded, winds whipped the exposed sand into dunes which "moved" over the area. Through the centuries vegetation gradually covered and immobilized them. New dunes are constantly being formed, however, and sometimes they have gradually covered forests which had established themselves on the older dunes. Occasionally stiff winds blow a niche in a sand ridge, which gradually enlarges to form a "blowout." Five large "blowouts" can be seen in Indiana Dunes State Park, within the lakeshore's boundaries, and the largest one has exposed remnants of a dead forest, killed by the once-advancing sands.

Of equal interest are the bogs and marshes in the area. Large chunks of ice broke off the glaciers as they retreated, and the melting chunks formed kettle-holes which were gradually filled with humus, resulting in the marshes. The lakeshore's bogs are significant because of their lush and varied vegetation: over one thousand species of flowering plants and ferns, making Indiana Dunes one of the most interesting botanical areas in the country.

Plants forced to move south because of the glaciers have somehow managed to survive here, mixing with plants from the south which migrated north during the post-glacier warming period. Thus the prickly-pear cactus of the desert mingles with Arctic barberry.

Jack and white pine grow on the dunes and tamarack and birch in the bogs, separated from their normal range to the north by about a hundred miles, while the tulip tree, black gum and sassafras are at their northwestern limits. Dune grass, dwarf willow, sand cherry and cottonwood begin to stabilize the fore dunes near the shoreline. Black oak, pine, hickory, chestnut and some sugar maple and beech grow on the older dunes and in the sand valleys. Wildflowers include the violet, hepatica, buttercup, jack-in-the-pulpit, dune lily and wild rose. Some typical bog and marsh plants are the cattail, blueberry, mayapple, dogwood, raspberry, blackberry and grapevine. White and showy lady's slippers, rare for the region, are found in Cowles Bog, named for Dr. Henry Cowles who developed the concepts of the science of ecology and who used the dune plant life for much of his studies.

Wildlife was once abundant here, but the over-bearing presence of all-conquering man has exterminated the bear, wolf, lynx, bison, elk and the passenger pigeon. The racoon, opossum, rabbit, fox, mink, squirrel and woodchuck have survived, and deer and beaver have been reintroduced. The six-lined lizard probably migrated here with the cactus and now thrives on the dunes. Many migratory birds stop in the marshes during season, and shorebirds can be seen scavenging on the beach.

Indiana Dunes National Lakeshore contains about 8,200 acres in a number of isolated areas spread along the shore and inland. Eventually, the Ogden Dunes area in the western portion of the lakeshore will be developed for extensive beach recreation, and trails will crisscross the remainder of the lakeshore. The Indiana Dunes State Park has many facilities, including picnic areas, campground, developed beach, bath house and many trails through dunes and marshes. One of them goes to the top of Mount Tom, at 192 feet the highest of the dunes.

A moving dune is slowly covering large trees in the east end of the lakeshore. The sand will soon kill the trees and then move further inland, perhaps to cover whole forests which grow on older dunes.

Wisconsin's Eagle Bay contains a sandy beach strewn with boulders, driftwood and gnarled roots of trees.

APOSTLE ISLANDS NATIONAL LAKESHORE

Lake Superior, the largest of the Great Lakes and the one least polluted by man, has many miles of wilderness shoreline, but nowhere else on Superior is there the scenic variety and wealth of historic association that there is in the Apostle Islands region near the western tip of the lake. Throughout the twenty-three islands and nearby Bayfield Peninsula are heavily forested islands, high lakeside cliffs and wave-sculpted rocky arches, long sandy beaches, marshes, caverns and bays. And yet, despite its primitive, pristine appearance, Wisconsin's Apostle Islands region is rich in history.

The Chippewa Indians entered the region about five hundred years ago, and because of harassment from other tribes, they took refuge on the largest of the Apostle Islands, which they named "The Island of the Golden-Breasted Woodpecker." Today it is called Madeline Island. Here they constructed a great village and remained in comparative peace and safety for 120 years.

Between 1610 and 1622 the French explorers Etienne Brule and Grenoble traversed this area. They called the lake *le lac superieur,* meaning "Upper Lake," and gradually this was corrupted to become "Superior." Pierre Radisson wrote of Chequamegon Bay: ". . . there is a channel where we take stores of fishes, sturgeons of vast bigness, and Pycks seven feet long."

These first men were followed by a stream of travelers, traders, explorers and missionaries. It is believed that it was some French missionaries who named the island, for an old French map labels them the Twelve

Apostles. Perhaps because there are almost twice that number of islands the "Twelve" was dropped.

As the fur trade flourished, the French built a fort on Madeline Island in 1693 called La Pointe. When the Indian allies of the British—the Sauk, Fox and Kickapoo—blocked the southern routes, all furs on their way to the East Coast came through Lake Superior, and La Pointe became a bustling trading center. It was from here that the great flotillas of forty-foot canoes manned by the legendary *voyageurs* journeyed to Montreal with furs and returned with trade goods and supplies. After the British came to dominate the area, much of the trading shifted further north. Only the aggressive North West Company retained its center of operations at La Pointe. Madeline Island was named for the Indian wife of this company's manager in the 1790's.

With the increasing popularity of the silk hat, La Pointe's decline quickened and trapping ceased by about 1850. Later in the century, logging, commercial fishing—especially for the prized lake trout—and quarrying for reddish-brown sandstone became the primary economic activities. Because of uncontrolled timber cutting and forest fires the logging operations were short-lived, and in the 1950's the sea lamprey destroyed the lake trout, although, aided by scientific management, they seem to be making a comeback now.

Today Madeline Island is the only island with a permanent settlement, and it has several historic buildings open to the public. The other islands are covered with a luxuriant second-growth forest of

The midland painted turtle, or pond turtle, is constantly alerted to danger by sound vibrations and his keen eyesight.

mixed hardwoods and conifers, including some beautiful stands of white birch. Wildlife includes black bear, white-tailed deer, raccoon, fox, mink, beaver, bald eagle, osprey, great blue heron, mallard, wood duck, loon, blue-wing teal, gulls and terns. About the only signs of man are a Coast Guard lighthouse on Devil's Island, some tumble-down fishermen's cabins, overgrown quarries and a few cottages.

As authorized in 1970, the Apostle Islands National Lakeshore includes twenty of the twenty-three islands. Except for Long Island which, until 150 years ago, was part of Chequamegon Point, the islands are the tops of partially submerged sandstone hills of the Bayfield Peninsula's northeasterly extension. They rise above the lake to heights varying from fifty to 480 feet, forming an archipelago about thirty miles long and eighty miles wide, with slightly less than one-fifth of this area in land.

Fortunately, there are few roads either on the mainland or the islands and the water is the lakeshore's main thoroughfare. The only public access today is at Little Sand Bay, at the eastern end of the mainland portion, where there is a campground and fishing dock.

The shores on the northeast side of several of the islands, facing the lake and heavy weather, have many cliffs which average about thirty feet in height but occasionally reach sixty feet. On the south and southwest sides beaches are generally sandy, with a few exceptions. In rocky projections from the cliffs, especially on Devil's Island, the northernmost island, erosion by waves has formed arches, caves and pillars of stone along the shore. This island—called "Evil Spirit Island" by the Indians because they thought the strange sounds made by the action of the water in the caves sounded like evil spirits talking—catches the full force of the storms that hit Lake Superior.

Stockton Island, containing 10,157 acres, is the largest of the islands within the lakeshore and is one of the most beautiful, with its own lake, an abundance of blueberries and long beach known as the Singing Sands—named for the sounds made by the sand as one walks along it. The highest and one of the wildest islands, Oak Island, has deep ravines, clay cliffs over a hundred feet high, occasional bears and rumors of treasure supposedly left there by pirates who called themselves the Twelve Apostles. Raspberry Bay, about midway along the Bayfield Peninsula unit of the lakeshore, has a superb beach, extensive marsh, pine groves, and sloughs and streams along the Raspberry River, a fine sampling of the many elements that make up this place of diverse beauty and history at the edge of Lake Superior—one of the largest and least polluted of the world's inland freshwater lakes.

A white-barked birch tree frames the early summer greenery surrounding a beaver pond in Voyageurs.

VOYAGEURS NATIONAL PARK

During the eighteenth and early nineteenth centuries when ladies of European society demanded the best North American fur for their clothing, these waters in northern Minnesota rang with the singing of French-Canadian *voyageurs*. These rugged adventurers paddled and portaged in their fragile, birchbark canoes thousands of tons of furs and trade goods yearly over the three-thousand-mile waterway extending from Montreal to Fort Chipewyan on Lake Athabaska in what is now upper Alberta.

The movement to create a Voyageurs National Park began in 1891 when the State of Minnesota requested congressional authorization for a national park in the Ontario-Minnesota border wilderness.

Dark evergreens stand out against autumn's light-colored deciduous trees along developed Ash River (above), just outside the southern boundary of the park, which can be seen in the distance. A birch tree (right) is gracefully silhouetted against the Minnesota sky.

After many years of controversy, the park service finally recommended the region east of International Falls around the Kabetogama Peninsula, and in January 1971 President Richard M. Nixon signed a bill authorizing the nation's thirty-sixth national park, just west of the Boundary Waters Canoe Area.

Consisting of 139,000 acres of north woods country plus eighty thousand acres of water, the park includes large Kabetogama Lake and parts of Rainy and Namekan lakes.

Four times ice sheets edged down from the north, grinding the land bare, and each time these spectacular forests grew back. During the last century, many thousands of acres of virgin pine forests in this region were stripped clean by loggers, but the land is now covered once again with large second-growth pines, firs, spruce, aspens and birches.

All of these natural features provide food and shelter for a wide variety of wildlife. White-tailed deer and black bears are common, as are smaller animals such as minks, otters, bobcats and rabbits and beavers. The park service plans to reintroduce caribou and increase the moose population. Hawks, golden eagles and a wide variety of songbirds and waterfowl make Voyageurs their home during season. The lake sturgeon, a rare and endangered fish, lives in some of the larger lakes.

As visitor-use plans are formulated for this newest national park in the coming years, it will be unique in that the waterways themselves will remain the principal means of visitor transportation.

One writer has said of the *voyageur,* "His canoe has long since vanished from the northern waters, his red cap is seen no more, a bright spot against the blue of Lake Superior; . . ." But his land remains, the sky-blue water and north woods forests that he knew, preserved in this park for future generations.

CHIPPEWA AND SUPERIOR NATIONAL FORESTS

Lost in a blue world of clear water below and an endless sky above, drawn back to earth only by the banks on the horizon of whispering birch and pine, canoeists slicing their way through the three thousand lakes and streams of the Superior and Chippewa national forests know wordless appreciation of the peaceful solitude a wilderness experience can bring. Located in central and northern Minnesota, the forests offer three million acres of forested wilderness.

The backdrop seen by travelers of deep green north woods and sparkling waters has not changed significantly for centuries, since white men first began portaging the area in search of fur-bearing animals. Sometime during the seventeenth century fur trappers and traders, rough and independent men of French origin, known as *Coureur de Bois* or "woods runners," plied the network of lakes west and south of Lake Superior. In their wake came the colorful and romantic *voyageurs*. Both groups witnessed the terrible wars during which the Chippewa tribes gained domination over the Sioux in this part of the nation.

Probably the most famous section of the forests is the Boundary Waters Canoe Area, the largest water-

Young balsam fir trees (left) grow beneath aged red pines. The fall color of a deciduous tree (right) contrasts with Eastern white pine. The paper birch (below) has the widest natural range of American birches.

The Boundary Waters Canoe Area, the largest water-based wild area in the country, shows Basswood, Crooked and Iron Lakes.

based wild area in the country. The area abuts Canada's Quetico Provincial Park. So popular is the Boundary Waters region that twenty-five percent of all the recreational activity throughout the national wilderness systems is concentrated there. While many locations are becoming rather well-used, others not accessible by roads remain for the plucky pilgrim to discover. Regulations regarding the use of mechanized vehicles and the maintenance of an unpolluted environment are aimed at keeping the Boundary Waters as clear and charming as when the Indians were the only inhabitants.

In addition to the unbelievable canoeing available, many trails, some of which were formerly old logging roads, lead to top fishing spots where bass and panfish await the patient fisherman, or to glens of blueberries or strawberries or chokecherries. Over the rustlings and scamperings of small rodents can be clearly heard the pileated woodpecker, the yellow warbler, the haunting cry of the Minnesota State Bird, the loon, and the more mundane calls of the mallard. Fungi of an unusual color and shape sprout in moist and dark places for the observant mushroom hunter. Along with the lady slipper, marsh marigolds, wild roses, daisies and dogwoods create a floral arrangement worthy of prizes. Rock hunters will find agates throughout the forests, plus jasper, ironbearing ores and copper-nickel ores.

The habitat in the Chippewa forest at the headwaters of the Mississippi River makes the region one of the most important breeding areas of the bald eagle anywhere in the United States. Water is abundant, and so are dense stands of trees, particularly mature red and white pine, the kind of community eagles favor.

The eagle family builds its nest atop a tall tree high above a marsh within view of a river. Being big birds, they must have a big house, at least five feet across and ten feet deep, sometimes even twice that size. The eagles use mostly sticks and grass in construction, returning again and again to the same site over the years, adding new materials each year, building a bigger and better penthouse.

There is concern over the eagle's future as a species because not all eggs produced are fertile and the numbers of birds is decreasing. In an effort to investigate the cause of the decline, ten years ago the National Audubon Society initiated the Continental Bald Eagle Survey, of which the Chippewa is a part. Many questions vital to complete understanding are still unanswered, such as: Where do the eagles spend the winter? What are the significant factors in adult mortality? What are the ecological factors in selection of a nest site? Unless these questions are answered, the number of eagles will continue to decrease.

Though one might not catch sight of a bald eagle resting atop an aged tree, wilderness experiences of a different nature await any adventurous soul with the courage and spirit of the hearty *voyageurs.*

A flock of swans, subject for both Old and New World legends, spreads out in an irregular line over the Mississippi.

UPPER MISSISSIPPI WILDLIFE AND FISH REFUGE

Of the four basic flyways for migratory birds in the United States—the Atlantic, Mississippi, Central and Pacific—the Mississippi Flyway is the most important. Millions of geese, ducks, swans and other birds spend the winter somewhere along it or move through it to winter further south. One of the most important areas along the flyway is the 194,000-acre Upper Mississippi River Wildlife and Fish Refuge, which has the most extensive boundaries of any inland refuge for waterfowl. Established in 1924, it extends from Wabasha, Minnesota, approximately 280 miles along both sides of the Mississippi to Rock Island, Illinois, where it is adjacent to the Mark Twain National Wildlife Refuge.

Because of its length, covering a number of life zones and differing climatic conditions, the refuge contains an extraordinary number of species of birds, mammals and fish. The extensive marshlands, river-bottom forests, damp slough-grass and sedge meadows and elevated sand prairies provide habitats for 270 kinds of birds, 50 mammals and 113 species of fish. Ranging as far south as Clinton, Iowa, steep wooded slopes of hardwoods with occasional red cedars and precipitous limestone cliffs, some as high as six hundred feet above the valley floor, present some of the most attractive scenery to be seen in mid-America.

The wood duck was on the brink of extinction in the early part of this century because of the drainage of swamps and the overcutting of forestlands. Commercial hunters also killed thousands for the bird's beautiful feathers. His scientific name, *Aix sponsa,*

means "waterfowl in wedding raiment," and without doubt it is America's loveliest water bird. A law passed in 1918 protecting the wood duck and by the 1940's it had regained solid foothold in its native habitat.

The bald eagle, our national emblem (and, to our shame, also an endangered species of wildlife) nests in numbers in the refuge during the winter when the wood duck is further south. Federal law has protected this magnificent bird since 1940 but results, unlike the case of the wood duck, have been far from satisfying. It is abundant today only in Alaska. In the refuge eagles concentrate below the dams or near the mouths of tributaries where in winter they find crippled waterfowl and fish to feed on.

Although not as fierce as its relative, the golden eagle, the bald eagle has long symbolized strength and it is the master of its domain. For instance, it will harass the osprey, an excellent fisher occasionally seen in the Upper Mississippi refuge, and force the smaller bird to drop its catch which the bald eagle will occasionally snatch in mid-air.

Eagles remain with the same mate until one or the other dies. Adults attain a length of thirty-four to thirty-six inches and a wingspan of seven feet. In the first three months of life eaglets grow from three inches to almost their full mature length of three feet. Their dark brown feathers, bill and eyes become the white head, yellow bill and iris of the adult after four years.

Other birds in the refuge include whistling swans, lesser scaups, ring-necked ducks, redheads, canvasbacks, buffleheads and ruddies, found on open pools above the dams, and mallards, widgeons, gadwalls and teals in the shallow backwaters along river banks. Many herons, egrets, bitterns and rails favor the bottomlands, and in spring and fall, hordes of warblers, vireos, thrushes and sparrows add to the great abundance of birds.

Furbearers, such as the muskrat, mink, beaver, river otter, raccoon, skunk, weasel and fox inhabit the area along the river, and an occasional nutria has been seen in recent years. Of course, the lowlands harbor amphibians and reptiles, including two species of salamanders, nine turtles, one lizard and thirteen snakes. Fishing for walleye, sauger, bass, perch, sunfish, crappies and catfish is popular below the dams, in sloughs and in channels between the islands.

This area along the mighty river is rich in history, containing the sites of Indian battlegrounds and villages, former trading posts and the routes of early explorers, in addition to some of the earliest towns in the Midwest and many decades of river traffic. Thus it is all the more remarkable that such a relatively large area, so vital to the migratory birds of North America, has been preserved. It provides a place where we can attain some idea of what the Mississippi must have looked like to the first white men with its untrammeled beauty and wealth of wildlife.

A killdeer (left) stands over its nest of four brown spotted eggs. This species of plover prefers mud flats and open fields near water and is peculiar for its spectacular nuptial flight and its raucous screaming at intruders. The narrow island in the Mississippi (below) lies just south of Wabasha, Minnesota.

FANTASIES IN LANDSCAPE
The Midwestern Plains

In one corner of the midwestern plains, endless patterns of spires and pinnacles fill the horizons in the Badlands of North and South Dakota, fantasies seemingly designed and then forgotten by a mad architect, but now a fascinating item in any traveler's itinerary. Surrounded by wild seas of grass, the raw and arid landscapes hold the fossilized remains of ancient animal kingdoms. To the west stands the huge stump of fluted igneous rock called Devils Tower. In the opposite corner, the Ozark country's limestone bluffs are worn through by clear spring-fed rivers, like the Current and the Buffalo, racing over mossy rocks, then meandering more slowly, banked by oak and hickory forests.

Buffalo, once extremely plentiful in the badlands, were nearly killed off within the last century.

THEODORE ROOSEVELT NATIONAL MEMORIAL PARK

"This country is growing on me more and more," Theodore Roosevelt wrote of the North Dakota badlands. "It has a curious, fantastic beauty of its own." Roosevelt came to love this land of eroded valleys, hills, ridges and gorges in the Little Missouri River basin when he ranched here in the 1880's. It gave him a deep understanding of nature and the importance of conserving it, and Theodore Roosevelt National Memorial Park, the only one of its kind in the country, honors this man, who became our twenty-sixth President, by keeping these badlands he knew so well in their natural state.

At first glance this land seems similar to the more famous badlands of South Dakota, but upon closer observation it is apparent that there are marked differences. Although less spectacular than those in South Dakota, these badlands support more vegetation and are more colorful. The varying shades of tan and gray of the sand and clay layers mix with the greens of trees and the yellows, reds and purples of wildflowers. Erosion played a major role where water has cut away the plains terrain, leaving a rugged land, inhospitable in appearance.

Throughout the area are isolated buttes, the tops of which were once the level of the prairies; because of a protecting layer of rock or the hardness of the clay, they have withstood erosion. In the North Unit of the park are great masses of bluish bentonite, a claylike rock which becomes soft when saturated with moisture during rainstorms and slides down the hillsides.

Another curious feature are the lignite coal beds. Millions of years ago the dense vegetation that grew here was deposited in layers, which in time formed large beds of soft, lignite coal. Occasionally the lignite beds catch fire from lightning or other natural causes, burning for years and baking the nearby clay layers into a bricklike substance locally called scoria (although true scoria is the result of volcanic action). In his book, *Ranch Life and the Hunting Trail*, Roosevelt describes the lignite beds: "A strong smell of sulphur hangs round them, the heated earth crumbles and cracks, and through the long clefts that form in it we can see the lurid glow of the subterranean fires, with here and there tongues of blue or cherry colored flame dancing up to the surface." One such burning vein can be seen in the South Unit.

Plant life in the badlands is varied. The northern slopes, cooler and more moist than the southern slopes because of less sun, support woodlands in which juniper is common. Only semiarid vegetation, such as grasses, yucca and pricky pear cacti, grow on the southern slopes.

During early summer bright splashes of the small prairie rose, the North Dakota State Flower, can be seen along with goldenrod, aster, scoria and mariposa lily, pasqueflower and phlox.

Wildlife has been sharply reduced since Roosevelt's day. Elk, grizzly and black bear and wolf have disappeared from the area, while buffalo, pronghorn antelope and bighorn sheep were "replanted" in the region in recent years. Smaller animals are still found in the badlands, such as the beaver, coyote, bobcat, jackrabbit, badger, red fox, weasel, muskrat and porcupine. As in the South Dakota badlands, many black-tailed prairie dogs scatter their towns on the flats. Prairie rattlesnakes are sometimes encountered along the roads.

There are 116 species of birds in the badlands. Hawks, falcons and golden eagles soar high above the gullies and buttes, while magpies, woodpeckers, sparrows, larks, swallows, wrens and owls congregate in the trees and vegetation.

In the South Unit, as well as in the rest of the badlands, are the petrified remains of a large forest. Fossils of snail-like creatures have been discovered here, and occasionally a rock will break open to expose leaf impressions of ancient oaks, maples, magnolias, sassafras and elms.

Spring and fall are pleasant, summers hot and dry, but winters are severe. Roosevelt writes:

Sometimes furious gales blow out of the north, driving before them the clouds of blinding snowdust, wrapping the mantle of death round every unsheltered being that faces their unshackled anger. . . . Again, in the coldest midwinter weather, not a breath of wind may stir; and then the still, merciless, terrible cold that broods over the earth like the shadow of silent death. . . . All the land is like granite; the great rivers stand still in their beds, as if turned to frosted steel.

On the banks of a stream (left), buffalo find relief from the heat of a warm autumn afternoon. The rugged North Dakota badlands (above) stand out in bold relief at sunset, their varied colors taking on a beauty not seen in midday. An early explorer called this area "hell with the fires out."

Sparse vegetation provides some cover for jackrabbits, badgers, weasels, muskrats and prairie rattlesnakes.

Little is known of the Indian occupation of these North Dakota badlands until the traders and trappers entered the area in the early 1800's. Various Indian tribes, including the Crow, Cheyenne and Sioux (Dakotah), lived along the banks of the Missouri River then.

It was not until 1864, however, that the area first caught the attention of the American people. Brigadier General Alfred Sully traveled through the Little Missouri basin and according to legend, he described the land as "hell with the fires out."

Railroad companies began taking notice of the Dakota Territory because their planned railroad from the Great Lakes to the Northwest lumbering country would have to cross the plains. The Indians did not welcome the "iron horse" or the buffalo hunters that came with it, however, and progress on the railroad construction was slow partly due to the Indian resistance to white incursions.

In 1883 Roosevelt came to the badlands to hunt and then decided to enter into a partnership to set up a ranch there, later known as the Maltese Cross Ranch because of its distinctive brand.

Of his time in the Dakotas, Roosevelt said, "If it had not been for what I learned during those years I spent here in North Dakota, I never in the world would have been made President of the United States." His years in the badlands gave him insights that later made him a conservationist, and his Dakota years made him a Western President as much as an Eastern one. As President, he signed the Antiquities Act of 1906 which empowered Presidents to sign proclamations creating national monuments out of public domain lands. This was a bold innovation for conservation, and "T. R." used this power to create sixteen monuments—more than any other President.

Theodore Roosevelt National Memorial Park was established in 1947 and contains about 110 square miles of the North Dakota badlands in three units: the South Unit near Medora, the North Unit near Watford City, and the Elkhorn Ranch site midway between the two. The park is open all year and there are campgrounds and picnic areas in both main units. Interpretive programs are presented by the park rangers in the summer, and a visitor center is located at the Medora entrance to the South Unit, with the original Maltese Cross Ranch cabin nearby.

The seemingly endless miles of gullies and hills convey to visitors today a sense of spaciousness and forlorn beauty, the same sense that Theodore Roosevelt and Alfred Sully must have felt when they saw these badlands, in Sully's words, "grand, dismal, and majestic."

"Chandelier boxwork" in the Temple Room is a fine example of the unique formations found in Wind Cave.

WIND CAVE NATIONAL PARK

The wind blows east, the wind blows west, and from the other two points of the compass, also. But it doesn't usually blow up through the ground. Yet cowboy Tom Bingham, wandering through South Dakota's Black Hills in 1881, felt the upward draft and stooped in puzzlement, touched with wonder. There he saw a ten-inch natural opening in the limestone rock of the hill—and what could he call it but Wind Cave.

Afterward, explorers got into the cave by digging entrances near the original "blow-hole." Within were the fairyland formations on walls and ceilings, re-

sembling a honeycomb or "boxwork" structure that might have intrigued a Tom Sawyer and Huck Finn into dark and forbidding recesses.

One might first imagine that another aperture higher on the hill would be the air intake. But that is not the case. This strange phenomenon of a breathing hill is believed to be caused by changes in atmospheric pressure. The cave actually completes the cycle of breathing, as it were, by letting in the wind when the outside pressure rises, and by expelling air when the pressure drops.

Once as numerous on the prairies as the buffalo, the pronghorn is slowly regaining in number and can be viewed in the park. A ruminant, the pronghorn is also the fastest of mammals on the American continent.

The weird ornamentation of Wind Cave is unique among famed caverns in that it includes relatively few stalagmites and stalactites. The boxwork was created by a layer of limestone which was sculptured and form-frozen in varied periods of geological uplift and submergence. Then, moisture containing calcium carbonate seeped through and evaporated, depositing the calcium carbonate, forming calcite in the cracks.

More recently the limestone between the fissures dissolved, leaving calcite fins, some lacelike, some broad enough to resemble the sides of boxes and thus called "boxwork." This variegated effulgence is additionally decorated with arresting displays of mineral colors in the form of tiny, sparkling crystals called "frostwork" and formations that look like yuletide arrangements of "popcorn."

The central attraction of Wind Cave National Park, the cavern, is rivaled in naturalistic lure by the wildlife sanctuary surrounding it. Over the park's forty-four square miles of rolling woodlands and plains, graze herds of the historic bison, once slaugh-

tered by callous white men from Pullman car and saddle alike. The bison, more popularly known as buffalo, is rich in legend. Staff of life for the Indians, and the shield against wind and storm in the hides of the red men's teepees, the bison later became a thoroughly American symbol in terms of the settlement of the wild West. Antelope, elk and deer, in herds, also graze among the lush rises and flatlands of the park.

Biologically speaking, east meets west in Wind Cave National Park, where ponderosa pine, typical of the Western mountains, grow on the same slopes with eastern bur oaks. And the animals graze on what is a prime example of mixed-grass prairie, a rich natural blending of medium tall and short grasses, with a sprinkling of wildflowers which lend dashes of color to the scene.

Here, in virginal splendor, is one of the last of the portions of the great Western plains. Here in South Dakota are wonders in number: the breathing cave; the historic, wild sea of grass, rippling in the wind; the mighty buffalo.

Geological formations known as the Honey Combs have been worn smooth by wind and water.

CUSTER STATE PARK

Like a giant mushroom emerging from the soil, shouldering aside anything in its way, a granite dome forced itself into sunlight a billion years ago. The erosive powers of wind and water have sculpted the batholith and the uptilted remnants of what was the covering mantle of sedimentary rock into the spires and tunnels in the Black Hills of South Dakota. Abundant mineral crystals and colors of beryls, feldspars, manganese and bentonite from the once horizontal rock run in concentric rings around the ancient dome's center. Forests, interspersed with lakes and streams, now cover much of the area.

Set in the Black Hills region south of Mount Rushmore National Memorial and north of Wind Cave National Park is Custer State Park, containing the fingerlike projections telling the geologic story of the "island in the plains" that is older than the Rockies, Alps or Himalayas. The Cathedral Spires and Needles regions in the northwest section and the bright red Spearfish Formation in the southeast corner of the park attract admiration and wonder the way gold in the area accrued to itself miners in the late nineteenth century.

One of the largest and best known state parks in the country, Custer remains the prodigy of the late governor and senator, Peter Norbeck, whose wildlife preserve lies west of the park. Formerly a game preserve, Custer was created a state park in 1919. During this era, the construction of the famous switchback and tunnel highway was supervised by Norbeck himself, who drove engineers (and today's drivers) to distraction by constantly modifying plans to take advantage of otherwise missed views. Famous visitors have included President Coolidge who was a guest in the game lodge, his summer White House, in 1927.

Large herds of bison, elk, deer and antelope now roam the hillsides where Sioux and Cheyenne Indians were once promised a lasting home. When the park's namesake, General George A. Custer, led a military expedition through the area two years before his death, he did not see the charming lakes Sylvan, Stockade, Legion and Center that have since been constructed and offer many recreational opportunities. The natural open pine forests have witnessed much activity in the last century — Indian skirmishes, bison hunts, gold rush days, tourists and campers in abundance — but the park still holds caches of pristine wilderness for the earnest seeker, such as in the French Creek Wilderness Area.

BADLANDS NATIONAL MONUMENT

The erosion-scarred landscape of Badlands National Monument has the eerie look of a city that was designed, and later deserted, by a mad architect. The land between the Cheyenne and White rivers in southwestern South Dakota is austere and harsh. Sheer cliffs and jagged peaks form skylines of fantastic shapes.

The Dakota Indians and neighboring tribes called this barren land *mako sica,* meaning "land bad," because it was an area of hardship for travelers. Early French-Canadian trappers appropriately termed it *les mauvaises terres a traverser,* "bad lands to travel across." Settlers later called it simply the Badlands, a name applied later to similar eroded areas in many sections of the country.

Jedediah Smith, perhaps the first white man to visit the area, led a party across the Badlands in 1823. His group noted the absence of potable water, for the few streams are thick with white mud.

Explorers and pioneers ignored the inhospitable Badlands region from the time of Smith's journey until 1846 when Dr. Hiram A. Prout of St. Louis published an account of a fossilized jawbone of a Titanothere found in the Badlands, followed a year later by a report of a fossilized camel described by Dr. Joseph Leidy. Dr. Leidy became an authority on Badlands fossils and by 1869 had inspected fossilized remains of more than five hundred ruminating pigs, called Oreodonts, as well as many other now extinct animals that lived 25 to 40 million years ago.

Early fossil hunters carried away petrified remains by the wagonload. Scientists feared the supply would soon be exhausted, but each new rain unearths new fossils and geologists now believe that as long as the Badlands remain, erosion will continue to uncover them. By far the most common mammalian fossil specimens found are those of the Oreodonts, which chewed cud although they had skeletons similar to a pig. One of the most famous fossils in the world, that of a mother Oreodont and her unborn twins, has been on display in the South Dakota School of Mines and Technology in Rapid City since 1928.

The largest fossils unearthed are those of the Titanothere, a rhinoceros-like animal slightly smaller than today's elephants. These creatures have been extinct for more than thirty million years. Turtle shells, the most common fossil, show that turtles have remained largely unchanged for perhaps two hundred million years. Fossilized remains of prehistoric horses, camels, giant pigs, saber-toothed tigers and other members of the ancient cat family have also been found here.

A unique method for preserving and displaying fossils is utilized by the monument's scientists. They

Constant flux is the only certainty in the Badlands of South Dakota where erosion repatterns the land each generation.

carefully brush the soil from around a fossil and cover it with a transparent domelike shield, thus protecting the fossil and allowing it to be viewed in its natural setting.

Bison, bear, elk, white-tailed and mule deer, pronghorns, Audubon bighorn sheep, gray wolves and beaver were originally native to the area and once plentiful. But the invasion of settlers, hunters and trappers in the late nineteenth century caused a serious reduction of wildlife populations. In 1919 a game investigator reported that inquiries at farms and ranches of the area revealed the fact that not even a coyote had been seen or heard in the Badlands for more than a year.

In an effort to help restore wildlife patterns, the National Park Service reintroduced bighorn and bison into the monument in the early 1960's. Rocky Mountain bighorn sheep were settled there, but difficulties were such that five years later the flock numbered only ten. Bison, on the other hand, adapted readily to their old haunts after being brought back in 1963. The original herd of fifty-three tripled in number in just five years. The bison often can be seen from Sage Creek Rim Road and other places in the grassland areas of the monument.

Because of wildlife preservation, chipmunks, prairie dogs, porcupines, and other rodents are now present, as well as rabbits, skunks, raccoons, badgers, pronghorns, deer and bobcats. On rare occasions red foxes, minks, elk and mountain lions are seen. There are also a few black-footed ferrets, a beautiful small animal now on the national list of rare and en-

rainfall sometimes runs off without soaking into the ground. High temperatures in summer and relatively cold temperatures in winter also limit plant life.

Nonetheless, some three hundred kinds of plants grow here. Although cliffsides and peaks are barren because erosion tears out most plants attempting to root, about half of the monument surfaces are covered with carpets of cactus and other growth.

The light-colored sediments that compose the Badlands were washed in by flooding ancient rivers. This material is now being washed away continually by the White, Cheyenne and Badlands rivers whose waters show thick white sediments, particularly after rains or winter snow melts. This erosion has made the giant mud flat into a jumble of milky waterways constantly reshaped and redirected.

Rocks in the monument are largely mudstones and siltstones so closely compacted they look and feel like stone, although they dissolve in water. Occasional outcrops of resistant sandstone and some thin layers of limestone are found. Nodules and lumps resembling concrete appear in some formations laid down millions of years ago.

The delicately colored saw-edged succession of hundreds of spires and peaks in an unvegetated zone from Cedar Pass to Sage Creek is called the Wall. It

Parching sun (left) glints off the white layers of fragmented material. Sawtoothed ridges of siltstone (above) rise on a plain of whitish mudflats. The long-tailed weasel (right) is notably slender and has a thick, soft coat and a keen sense of hearing.

dangered species. Ferrets are attractive creatures about the size and shape of minks with a white face and black "mask" across their eyes. They are elusive and during the day they usually stay below ground in prairie dog holes, occasionally coming out to sun themselves. At night they are quite active hunting prairie dogs, their principal source of food. It is the severe decline of this food source, primarily attributable to an extensive poisoning program by government agencies, that threatens the ferret. This poisoning is unnecessary, and if the black-footed ferret survives it will be because this national monument is a wildlife refuge where no poisons are permitted.

The Badlands is a harsh and inhospitable environment for all plants because moisture is scarce and

A few members of the pine family find footing among the pinnacles and spires, though grasses are the main ground cover.

divides the upper (northern) grasslands from those on the lower (southern) side. Average elevation difference below these spectacular pinnacles is about two hundred feet. In Cedar Pass and Castle Butte areas, the Wall towers up to 150 feet above the upper grasslands and as much as 450 feet over the lower area.

Sometime in the past several hundred years, a wide part of the towering cliff near Cedar Pass broke loose, slumping down and away from the foot of the cliff. The formerly horizontal layers were split, crushed, tilted and dumped atop each other, disrupting the normal drainage pattern. This type of disturbed area is called a slump, and this particular slump is named Cliff Shelf.

Holes, pits and even seasonal ponds formed as a result of rains and melting snows seeking outlets through the tumbled clay and rocks. Deep pits, located only a few yards south of the Cliff Shelf Nature Trail, are a dramatic illustration of the drastic erosion taking place through slumps. Because of the scrambled formations and the resulting interruption of former drainage canals, moisture is now trapped in the area and creates conditions favorable for the lush growth of grass, shrubs and trees.

Faults—cracks in the earth's crust—intensify the foreboding Badlands aura. Many of these are visible between Cedar Pass and Norbeck Pass further west.

The alternating bands of dark and light sedimentation are broken and exposed, making these faults easily recognizable. Most of this faulting has resulted in vertical movement of only a few feet, but near Dillon Pass the fault is up to forty-nine feet high.

Homesteaders had occupied only half of the Badlands by 1922 and drought caused most of them to leave in the 1930's. The state legislature petitioned the Federal Government to make the area a national park as early as 1909. But it was not until 1939 that President Franklin D. Roosevelt established Badlands National Monument.

Campgrounds, picnic areas and visitor centers are near most points of the monument while private lodgings and camp areas are plentiful in nearby communities. During rainy weather, mud is adhesive and hard to drive on, but many roads are paved. Days are hot in summer but nights are cool and most winter days are warm enough for short hikes.

"Here today, gone tomorrow," has a literal application in this peculiar area of raw and arid landscape called the Badlands, where erosion by wind, water and winter storm holds full sway; some peaks lose height at rates of up to six inches a year. Mudslides, new erosions, slumps and changed drainage patterns continue to tear away the surfaces of this region.

AGATE FOSSIL BEDS NATIONAL MONUMENT

The broadly rolling inclines of western Nebraska near Agate Springs give scant evidence of the vast store of paleontologic treasures just beneath their surfaces. Yet this area has yielded a wealth of fossilized records from prehistoric eras.

Beside the deep slash of the Niobrara River in Nebraska, paleontologists have discovered thousands of fossils of strange beasts that roamed the earth centuries ago. When the first of the Rocky Mountains surged upward ages ago, they created a semitropical savanna which was crossed by meandering rivers where dinosaurs and other animals thrived and would congregate. In the normal course of events, many died along one of the streams, and seasonal floods carried their remains downriver where they were dropped and entombed in the mud. This process probably continued for centuries until a layer of concentrated fossil bones, nearly three feet thick, had accumulated. Later the Niobrara River cut its channel to unearth the fossils.

Thus, this seemingly common hill contains evidence of mammalian ascendency in the animal world of twenty-one million years ago. Among the specimens were remains of Diceratherium, a small, two-horned rhinoceros, and a strange, clawed animal called Moropus, which had the head of a horse, the body of a camel, the front legs of a rhinoceros and the hind legs of a bear. Historically the fossils attracted scientific interest in the late 1880's when white settlers moved into the area, formerly controlled by the Sioux Indians. But it was not designated a national monument until 1965.

Development plans call for Agate Fossil Beds National Monument to be opened to the scrutiny of both scientists and the public. Visitors today can see exposed fossils in their sediment beds at the headquarters area. Because this park is a working outdoor museum, other representative fossils are being exposed so that the exact position of the skeletal remains can be seen as they are reliefed in their beds.

Similar to Agate is Florissant Fossil Beds National Monument. In a gentle valley of the Colorado Rockies, fifteen miles west of Pike's Peak, wildflowers provide a brilliantly colored mantle for sedimentary layers preserving one of the largest deposits of insect and plant fossils in North America. These rich fossil beds have yielded specimens representing more than one thousand species of the plant and animal life of a bygone era.

Scientists studying the formations believe that for many prehistoric centuries the Florissant area experienced periodic volcanic eruptions. These eruptions dropped layer upon layer of volcanic ash which carried birds, leaves and twigs with it to the bottom of the ancient lake in the valley below. Further ashfalls and mud flows covered and preserved the debris.

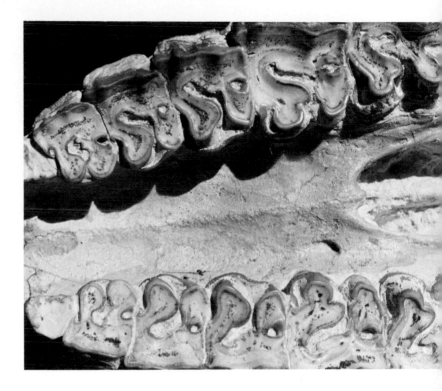

Specimens from Agate Fossil Beds, some over 21 million years old, are in prize collections the world over— like the above set of teeth from a two-horned rhinoceros.

In recent years, scientists have gained much information by excavating portions of that prehistoric valley. The various "digs" have yielded whole petrified tree trunks, often ancient sequoias up to ten feet in diameter, and trunks of trees similar to modern-day elm, along with bark and leaves of oak, walnut, pine, beech, willow and maple. Almost all the fossil butterflies of the New World have come from this site in the Rocky Mountains.

Agate Fossil Beds National Monument is near Scotts Bluff National Historical Monument and comprises 3,150 acres. Visitor facilities and trails are available at Agate the year around, but only on weekends during winter.

Plans include development of a tourist center, museum, interpretive trails and wayside exhibits detailing the area's ancient history. Meanwhile, relatively open terrain and easy access provide an opportunity to view the prairie hills of western Nebraska, as well as space to ponder the eras of earlier history when huge mammals and tiny insects alike fell victim to geological change.

101

The great stump of fluted, igneous rock called Devils Tower has been an object for legends and stunts.

DEVILS TOWER NATIONAL MONUMENT

A mighty laccolith resembling a monstrous petri-fied tree stump thrusts itself eight hundred feet skyward from a rounded hill above the Belle Fourche River Valley in northeast Wyoming. The massive gray and buff stone—a dramatic natural landmark northwest of Sundance, Wyoming—has a startling appearance from all sides.

A geological prodigy, this rock upthrust had a place in Indian legends of the region. The Kiowa Indians called the place *mato teepe,* meaning "bear's lodge." The Cheyenne legend termed it "bad god's tower." Explorers used it as a guide point, and this landmark came under intense scientific interest at the end of the nineteenth century. It was set aside as Devils Tower National Monument in 1906, the first U. S. national monument to be authorized by a presi-dent under the Antiquities Act of 1906.

Volcanic activity, deep inside the earth, caused an explosive upsurge of magma here about fifty million years ago. Devils Tower was created when the vol-canic thrust pushed this particular mass of molten materials only to the surface—or perhaps somewhat below the surface—where it cooled. Erosion in the intervening millions of years, possibly during some ancient deluge, gradually eroded away softer forma-tions of surrounding earth and rock, leaving the fluted sides of this gigantic stone standing 865 feet above its base on a hill.

Devils Tower is more than a thousand feet in diameter at its base. Its top, measuring 200 by 400 feet, is 1,280 feet above the Belle Fourche River and 5,117 feet above sea level. It is the tallest rock forma-tion of its kind in the United States, and geologists continue to study its strange origin and peculiarities.

Because it is comprised of crystallized molten rock and some sedimentary forms, the composition of the towering rock has a strikingly multicolored appear-ance as seen from various vantage points in its forest-green and grassy setting. Looking from near the base, the giant pillar has a curiously fluted look, appearing as though the middle part of the tower is made of col-umns bound by well-developed, open joints. These open, smooth joints, however, seem to join in a weld nearer the top as they taper together at the higher points.

Gravity, along with moisture, heating, freezing and thawing, has been responsible for splitting off huge sections of the columns, and a rubble of talus has been formed at the base of the tower. Colors range from dark igneous porphyry to the bright buffs and reds of colorful sedimentary formations at the base.

The legends of the Indians indicate that the rock was a fascination for the first Americans. The Kiowa story detailed how several flower-gathering Indian maidens, being pursued by an angry bear, jumped onto this rock (then normal sized) which was quickly elevated to its present height by their powerful god. The Cheyenne legend, in which young braves were principals, was somewhat similar in that it also in-volved huge bears. Attempting to scale the heights, the bears were supposed to have left claw marks— the flutings—along the tower sides.

On July 4, 1893, at a celebration, two ranchers, William Rogers and Willard Ripley, climbed the tower and unfurled a United States flag. Since then, more than a thousand climbers have made the ascent.

Today, with new roads and bridges across streams easing travel hazards, a visitor center, furnished camp and picnic grounds, this geological phenomenon is a fascinating place to visit.

MARK TWAIN NATIONAL FOREST

The forest is a community, or complex of communities, of interdependent plants and animals. The foundation common to all is soil, sunlight and water, plus influences of climate, weather, erosion and reproduction cycles. The food chain is the tie that binds all life forms together, and plants provide the basic food. Thus the making of a forest environment begins with simple plant forms. One can witness the early process of plant succession in an area where a glacier is retreating—the start of a new virgin forest—or where fire has left its mark. When the soil has acquired sufficient texture and nutrients, it develops green plants capable of manufacturing food by taking carbon dioxide from the air and water from the soil.

If the soil is good, and the plants can produce proteins, fats, sugars, starches and vitamins, chances are good for the health and prosperity of the entire forest community.

An acre of healthy soil is densely populated with millions of insects and tiny animals, diligent architects and engineers, who sift air and water and when they die return valuable minerals to build the soil to support higher life forms, including the highest form of plant life, the tree.

Missouri was formerly almost completely covered by magnificent stands of hardwoods. Intensive logging depleted the tree supply to less than a third of what it was. Two national forests nurture much of what

Greer Spring in the Mark Twain forest helps to make the Eleven Point River a remarkably clear stream.

remains—the Clark and the Mark Twain in the southern part of the state, along the edge of the Ozark Plateau. The second-growth forests of hardwoods spreads throughout the half million acres of the Mark Twain forest.

A tree, any tree, is a thing of beauty in its own right. The sturdy, stately sugar maple, for instance, may be seen in spring sending forth myriads of greenish-yellow clustered flowers, from which bees obtain pollen and nectar. In early summer, seeds mature and fall to the ground on papery wings. Later, in autumn, sugar residue in heart-shaped leaves produces the most striking orange-yellows and reds of the hardwood landscape. The quaking aspen is an almost universal friend of the traveler—this white-trunked, fluttering-leafed tree greets one wherever he goes, from Labrador and the southern shore of Hudson Bay northwest to the Arctic Circle in Alaska, south through the mountains into lower California, then scattering eastward across the northern plains to New England and the southern Appalachians.

Rivers are the living arteries of most forests, and in the Ozarks, there are about twenty streams spring-born and spring-fed. Some have been dammed to form lakes of tremendous size—arenas for motor-boating, water skiing, bass fishing and resort camping. To some, however, true Ozarkiana is still to be found in a float trip down a clear, swift-running stream like the Eleven Point, which bends and winds between steep hollows and towering bluffs of the Mark Twain forest.

The Eleven Point is a favorite in southern Missouri for float fishing and camping. Such travel is in the Ozark tradition, recalling the days when each farm had a landing with a skiff or two (known as a flatboat, Long John, or just plain johnboat) tied to a handy tree root and when it was easier to get around on the back streams than on the back roads.

The Eleven Point River meanders without hurry or concern through the picturesque Ozark hills east of Thomasville, its course cut in the shadows of steep bluffs, through forested sloping valleys and low-lying pasturelands. Springs gushing from the rocky cliffs and rushing up from underground reservoirs provide a continuous source of crystal-clean water. Varying stretches of rapids and clear pools wind beneath shading hardwoods of birch, oak, hickory and sycamore.

Intermittently the trees lean far over the river, forming a green canopy, and deep recesses in the surrounding hills contain caves large enough to bring out the spelunker in any visitor, although dangers exist for the visitor untrained in cave exploration. Foxes, raccoons, beavers, muskrats, turtles and water snakes are common near the waters, as are wild turkeys, great blue herons and bobwhite quail. The Eleven Point is primarily a float river. Three float camps, or primitive campgrounds accessible only by river or trails, have been built and more are planned.

The Eleven Point is a river where man can forget his machines and contemplate the goodness of the earth.

Many who float the river start at Greer Crossing, floating down through rushing rapids and alternating deep tranquil pools, passing Turners Mill, the last vestige of an old settlement called Surprise. The roads of today normally follow the ridgetops rather than the stream valleys, so that canoers can insulate themselves from everyday pursuits and thoughts. Along its course the river borders the wildest and least accessible area in the Eleven Point area called the Irish Wilderness. It was settled by a hardy band of Irishmen, but they were dispersed by bushwackers in the Civil War.

The rivers shaped the land. When man arrived the rivers became avenues of destiny, first to the birch-bark canoe, then to the raft, flatboat and barge. In the advance of history the rivers were clogged with logs, and afloat with pioneers, traders and warriors, while their banks became lined with cities and industries. Always there seemed more streams untapped, waiting for a young Huck Finn or Tom Sawyer to get his small share of natural heritage close to home.

It is said that some three million miles of river channel flow across the face of the United States. Today almost all of this vast watery network has been harnessed to serve the material needs of people.

We need harnessed and developed rivers. But we need other kinds of rivers, too. The nation has undertaken over the years to protect parks and forests, to establish refuges for wildlife and reservoirs to conserve water. Most of the rivers, though woven into the romance, literature and soul of the surrounding land, had been sacrificed to progress. Only a small number of streams remain untamed, unspoiled, approaching the natural conditions in which man found them. Now Congress has established the National Scenic Rivers System. The concept of this system recognizes the need of pleasant scenic rivers, close to big cities, that can be viewed by car, and semiwild and wild rivers that must be reached by footpath or horse trail and are removed from the smells and sounds of mechanized civilization. We need them all, in balance, to assure survival of a society that is truly civilized.

The Eleven Point is one of the rivers that became part of the system. Like the others, the Eleven Point is a special place to visit and enjoy, where young men test their hardiness by running the rapids and older men can find their contact with nature in a float trip and camp-out on a gravel bar, where artists of all ages can find inspirational source matter, and where natural scientists, whether of the Boy Scout or professional variety, can pursue the miracles of life.

This free-flowing river survives with natural shoreline borders of trees, bluffs or open meadows. It is really for all people, preserving a quality of the true America that future generations deserve to know.

Graceful swans are among the birdlife seen near rustic Falling Spring Mill in the Mark Twain forest.

OZARK NATIONAL SCENIC RIVERWAYS

This is a place of quiet relaxation and gentle beauty: just two swift-flowing Ozark streams which are undammed, unspoiled and unpolluted.

Ozark National Scenic Riverways protects the Current River, its tributary, Jacks Fork, and their riverbanks as they meander through a portion of the Ozark foothills in southeastern Missouri. These were the first rivers in the country to be specifically preserved as part of the National Park System as scenic rivers. Included within the boundaries are large, natural springs, riverfront caves, limestone bluffs and a great variety of flora and fauna.

The Ozarks are among the oldest mountains in the country. Uplifted and then eroded by wind, water and frost, little remains of their once-spectacular heights. Water, turned into carbonic acid as it seeped into the ground ages ago, dissolved the limestone overlaying the basic granite and formed a honey-combed series of underground caverns. Some of the cave roofs have collapsed, causing sinkholes, a striking example of which is the Sunkland along the upper portions of the Current River, a great hollow several hundred feet across and nearly a mile long produced by the successive fall-in of several interconnected underground chambers.

In many areas here, groundwater drips into the caverns, collects and circulates through the underground conduits and emerges as springs. At Big Springs, one of the largest single-outlet springs in the country with a maximum flow of 840 million gallons a day, the water rushes with great force from the underwater base of a cliff to the surface, then flows into the Current River several hundred feet downstream.

The streams themselves are strong and transparent, varying in color from sapphire blue to many shades of green, according to depth and the hour of the day. Quiet waters alternate with chutes or rapids as the streams flow through green forests and under rocky bluffs.

A variety of 1,500 plants are found along the riverways. Most of the upland forest is a combination of oak and hickory, but shortleaf pine, maple, sycamore, sassafras, blackgum and birch also grow here.

The wildlife along the riverways nearly disappeared because of early hunting and lumbering, but in the last thirty years deer, beaver, bobcat, opossum, skunk, mink, fox, muskrat and wild turkey have begun to return. One species, however, the rare red wolf, may have left the area permanently. This is unfortunate, for the red wolf is so rare that it does not live in any other unit of the park system.

About two hundred species of birds have been seen in the riverways, even an occasional great blue heron and osprey. The Current and Jacks Fork rivers are among the best smallmouth bass streams in Missouri, and there are ninety-two other species of fish in the rivers, from brilliantly colored darters to largemouth bass.

Indians roamed this area for thousands of years, leaving behind arrowheads and mounds where they buried their dead. French trappers later named one of the rivers in the area *la riviere courante,* "The Running River."

Lumbering in the late 1800's proved the need for a boat suited to the needs of the Ozark rivers, and a long boat with square, upturned ends and a flat bottom was developed. Called the johnboat, it is still used today.

Ozark National Scenic Riverways was authorized by Congress in 1964. It was a pioneering concept for conservation which led to the enactment in 1968 of the Wild and Scenic Rivers Act. Ozark contains 113 square miles along 140 miles of free-flowing streams. Many public and privately operated campgrounds and picnic grounds are within the riverways' boundaries. A visitor center is located at Powder Mill in the center of the riverways. Canoes and johnboats may be rented within the boundaries and in nearby towns. Love the pure waters of these hills—and keep them that way for others who follow.

The still waters of a millpond reflect in perfect detail the haunting atmosphere a gray day leaves in the upper Buffalo valley.

BUFFALO NATIONAL RIVER

From high in the Ozarks of northwest Arkansas trickles a tiny, almost hidden stream that grows and meanders through hill country for many miles until it merges with the larger White River. Clean and free flowing, the Buffalo remains one of our relatively untouched wilderness rivers. It ribbons through canyons and valleys whose layers tell the geologic history of the building and erosion of the Ozark Dome. The sedimentary rocks in the Buffalo watershed were laid down in an ancient marine basin which in its 300 million year history, has changed frequently and drastically.

The river winds past hillsides and bluffs sprouting innumerable varieties of plants and trees, including six species of oak—white, black, blackjack, chinkapin, post and northern red—and three of hickory—

mockernut, black and shagbark—amidst more than forty other species of trees. The highest free waterfall between the southern Appalachians and the Rockies is found misting down in Hemmed-in-Hollow. Beauty Cave, although quite difficult to reach, offers a collection of gypsum formations outstanding in variety and size.

Though its banks are now largely unpopulated, the river has murmured through the dreams of Indians for nine thousand years. Hunters and gatherers lived there in bluff shelters. Gradually, as they learned agricultural arts, they set up semipermanent villages in the bottom lands. After the Osage and, later, the Cherokees established their hunting grounds in the Buffalo area, the first white men visited there.

At Hemmed-in-Hollow the water showers down to a small plunge pool.

From before the Civil War until the turn of the century, immigrants homesteaded all the available bottom land, benches, hollows and ridges. When resources were depleted more than fifty years ago, another wave of migration swept the area, and almost everyone left. Now wildflowers again bloom amidst log cabin floors and tender saplings crowd along the timber cutters' decaying tie slides which were constructed along the bluffs.

The Buffalo is the only major stream left undammed in the Arkansas Ozarks. It is unpolluted because neither industry nor large numbers of people have settled along its banks. The lower part of the river was protected from development in the 1930's when Buffalo River State Park was established. Twenty years later, action was initiated to preserve the entire stream, and in 1972 Congress authorized it as a national river, one of the first of its kind in the United States. The Buffalo differs from rivers in the wild and scenic system in the amount of land scheduled for Federal control, nearly twice as many acres per mile. Access routes along the narrow strip of park land encompassing 132 miles of the Buffalo lead to many types of adventures for the individual, including the hiker, horseback rider, canoer, or the casual drive-through visitor. The rugged tunnels of Lost Valley to the south and the shallow caves called "Bat House" hollowed into the limestone bluffs in the center of the park await to entrance the eye.

The favored theory explaining the hot springs' mechanism is seeping rainwater, shown as icicles at Dripping Springs.

HOT SPRINGS NATIONAL PARK

A few months before he died, Hernando de Soto, bold Spanish explorer and conquistador, passed through what is now Hot Springs and possibly bathed in its waters. He was searching for gold and he probably never got closer to his impossible dream than his immersion in the warm water which springs from vents in the gray, volcanic tuff at the base of Hot Springs Mountain near the center of Arkansas.

That was the year 1541. Before the arrival of the white man the Indian was reportedly attracted to these hot waters where the "Great Spirit" dwelled. The Dunbar and Hunter Expedition in 1804 mapped the water route from Natchez to the springs and made chemical analysis of them. Soon after, a permanent settlement developed which by 1820 included an inn and several crude canvas-shack bathhouses.

Today's national park of 1,035 acres is visited annually by several hundred thousand tourists. The park's primary significance is probably that it is this country's most important example of man's centuries-old romance with and affinity for the thermal and mineral waters of the world. The magical liquid minerals boil and bubble up from the west slope at the base of Hot Springs Mountain in forty-seven springs with an average daily flow of almost a million gallons and an average temperature of 143 degrees Fahrenheit.

"The springs are now the property of the people," the superintendent of Government bathhouses wrote to the Secretary of the Interior in 1915. "They are free from monopoly and extortion, and within the reach of all." Yet the area did not become a national park until 1921.

There is no certainty about what causes the hot springs. The currently favored theory is that the springs are formed when rainwater sinks into the ground between Sugarloaf and West mountains, then rises along tilted layers of rock to emerge finally through the geological fault at the base of Hot Springs Mountain.

The heated water is variously attributed to inordinately deep and uncooled underground rock, chemical reactions near the bottom of the wells, friction from sliding rock masses at profound earth-depths or compression from overlying rock burden and radioactive minerals far beyond the range of the discerning instruments of geologists.

Not all visitors take the waters. Below the mountain is the gay winter resort city of Hot Springs where horse racing and golfing rival the waters. And in the park itself, one of the nation's oldest national preserves, are five rugged little mountains and oak-hickory-pine forests which consistently bring their own special rewards.

Perhaps the late President John F. Kennedy best summed up the twin beneficence of a preserve like Hot Springs when he declared in 1962: "We must have places where we can find release from the tensions of an increasingly industrialized civilization, where we can have personal contact with the natural environment which sustains us."

SPLENDID GIANTS
The Northern Rockies

"Room—glorious room in which to find ourselves" capulizes a feeling for the peaks in the northern Rockies where one can meditate in subalpine meadows, on granite cliffs and near looking glass lakes. In Rocky Mountain National Park, the "roof of America," one can view the plains stretching far to the east and in every other direction, the serrated edges of other mountain ranges. In the hewn earth of Glacier National Park, flowers bloom a few feet from the icy fingers of snow fields. The same region offers the startling landscapes of Craters of the Moon and the wonders of Yellowstone.

Snake River, Grand Teton National Park, Wyoming

Monkey-flowers bear their showy blossoms in late summer below the Garden Wall, a long cliff face.

GLACIER NATIONAL PARK

Upper St. Mary Lake in Montana is a sphere of blue—a sapphire of water worn like a jewel, mirroring wisps of cotton clouds and wearing the sharp lines of surrounding mountains as the hands upon the face of a clock. The massive peaks, sheer, sharp walls of stone, are the rulers of this empire of trees and water and wildlife, flower-strewn meadows and living glaciers existing almost side by side in paradoxical enjoyment of their environments.

Here there are the seekers of this extraordinary beauty, the "Crown of the Continent," which includes more than a thousand miles of trails which lace through nearly 1,600 square miles of wild loveliness.

The ice-fingers of earth-evolution are not far from the velvety grass spread of hills and valleys sprinkled with summer flowers, one of the four biological life zones found here. Above are the spruce and fir, and surmounting them are subalpine plants, while still farther lie the colors—green, white and pastels—

which hint at life in the most improbable places. Snow-capped peaks touch the limits of the sky a mile or more above the looking glasses of over two hundred lakes.

The joyous sound of rushing water fills the spectator's ears, the pounding of diamond-blue streams cascading over moss-strewn stones and the never-ending roar of waterfalls tossing dancing crystals into the air above, defying time to stop their existence.

The geological history of the land is the foundation upon which this extraordinary beauty rests; plants and animals, fish and fowl are here because of the chain of events which evolved to form this panorama, from its rugged peaks mantled with snow to the green spread of meadows and valleys.

The heights arrived when the Rockies came into being sixty million years ago, but while that great stretch of peaks rose, new forces vised this Canadian-border region, bringing it sharply together, forcing

Flinsch Peak (left) is an excellent example of a cirque or amphitheater caused by ice erosion. The potholes are also from glaciation. In early summer, yellow glacier lilies (above) dot Logan Pass with color below the Garden Wall, seen to the north.

the infant mountains sideways until finally the folded earth broke under the strain. The pressure continued, edging the land to the east for almost forty miles.

Sedimentary layers—silts, sands, clays and muds—started it all a billion or two years ago in the shallow arm of a prehistoric sea. Chemical changes coupled with time and pressure solidified the layers, and they submerged, then emerged.

A million years ago, the valley floors lay beneath great glaciers which relentlessly ground downhill. They gave way years ago to smaller masses of ice, but not before the park's valleys were filled with ice three-fifths of a mile high. Then the earth became warm again, and magically the ice disappeared, then returned in lesser fury to cover the earth once more.

There is still preponderous evidence of the glaciers here, despite the warming trend. Nearly three hundred acres are still covered by Sperry Glacier, about four hundred feet deep, a latter-day, and comparatively miniscule, sample of what helped shape this region. Those flowing rivers of ice of a million years ago grabbed particles of sand and massive boulders, edging them along to rasp at the landscape and form today's rugged spectacle.

The hewn earth is a natural habitat for 57 species of animals and 210 bird species, some of which rest here a day or two twice a year during migration.

The Rocky Mountain goat uses its soft-centered, splayed hooves to grasp the precarious cliffs, along with the pika and marmot and an occasional wolver-

ine. In the deep, green depths of the forests live moose, elk, white-tailed and mule deer, and black and grizzly bears. Above them wheel hawks and eagles, their telescopic eyes seeking food, and grouse escape in a thunder of wings from underfoot. Thrushes sing anonymously from the thick undergrowth, while the slaty-gray dipper flits along swiftly flowing streams. Harmonizing with the cacophony of bird sounds is the angry shriek of the jays preaching from the pulpit of treetops over the steady tree-drumming of the scarlet-crested pileated woodpecker, pausing only to vent its feelings about insect-hunting expeditions deep beneath tree bark. Beneath the surface of rushing streams and the translucent mirror of lakes live twenty-two species of fish: trout, salmon, whitefish, grayling.

It is little wonder Indians found their way here and chose it as a place to live for about ten thousand years. The Kootenai were displaced by the Blackfeet more than two hundred years ago, and it was possibly their hostility that kept the Lewis and Clark expedition from the region. The Blackfeet received $1.5 million for their lands in 1890 when a copper strike was announced, and thus the region became open to a new generation of explorers.

Their reservation, an attraction in itself, adjoins the park to the east where some of them sometimes gather in the colorful garb and feathered headdresses of their ancestors.

But color is not confined to the dyed feathers, for here is an area south of the Canadian border where a

(continued on page 117)

Under the brooding storm clouds a sunrise reflects on Little Chief Mountain to the left and Citadel Mountain in the rear on the shore of St. Mary Lake.

114

Beargrass, which is not a grass but a lily, blooms along the slope of 9,604-foot Going-to-the-Sun Mountain above Logan Pass Road. So common and showy is the beargrass that it is generally considered to be the park flower.

subarctic climate exists, giving life in short but magnificent splendor to alpine flowers. Up and down the great expanses of land are glacier lilies, their yellow blossoms contrasting with the blue of gentians and the scarlet of monkey-flowers. The lower landscapes are dominated by the cone-bearing trees, sometimes dripping needles upon Lake McDonald, the largest of the bodies of water, nestled in the loving grasp of Western red cedar, with its fernlike leaves, and hemlock and yew. The most common tree in the park is the lodgepole pine, which occurs on both slopes of the park, growing in pure stands or mixed with spruce, fir and Douglas fir. The needle-losing "evergreen" is the Western larch. In autumn, its golden-yellow needles stand out in bright contrast against a background of forest greenery.

During the brief summer, sudden rain squalls or thundershowers may occur, and the higher elevations are cool at all times of the year. Even at the lower levels it is chilly after the sun sets.

The hasty traveler will see a part of this by driving across the park on the Going-to-the-Sun Road, the only road to cross the park. But this is only a hint of what lies beyond the long stretch of modern creation. A mountain never truly unfolds until one has stood at its feet or feasted upon the valleys below its peak; a green forest does not reveal its unique charms unless one stands under its pyramid spires; nor do nature's charms become fully apparent until one takes a few moments for silent appreciation. Glacier was meant to be felt, not idly viewed.

117

NATIONAL BISON RANGE

At the southern end of the beautiful Flathead Valley, in the shadows of the majestic Mission Mountains in western Montana, is the home of one of the premiere herds of American buffalo or bison. This herd in the 18,540-acre National Bison Range varies in size from year to year but is generally between three hundred and five hundred.

This huge beast once ranged from Great Slave Lake in Canada to Mexico and from Nevada and Oregon to Tennessee and Pennsylvania, numbering perhaps sixty million animals. What occurred between 1840 and 1880 was a saga of wildlife slaughter that is one of the most savage in U.S. conservation history.

A few buffalo were killed for meat, but millions of others were stripped for their hides and tongues. By the 1870's a widely advertised "sport" was shooting buffalo from the open windows of trains as the animals raced along beside them. The carcasses were left to rot in the prairie sun. The herds were almost completely wiped out by 1882-1883, but the ruthless buffalo hunters apparently did not realize the extent of the massacre for many insisted the herds had gone to Canada and would return. By 1900, only twenty wild bison were known to exist in the United States, with about 250 more in Canada.

Largely through the efforts of the American Bison Society, under the leadership of naturalist Dr. William T. Hornaday, the National Bison Range was established in 1908. In the fall of the following year the first buffalo were released on the range. The bulk of this first herd of thirty-four had been purchased by the Bison Society from the Conrad herd at Kalispell, Montana, which descended in part from four young calves brought back from a hunting expedition in 1873 by Walking Coyote of the Pen d' Oreille Indians.

A member of the cattle family, American bison are cloven hoofed and chew their cud as do their close relatives, domestic sheep and cattle. Their closest wild relative is the European bison. Both sexes have a set of hollow, curved horns and the bulls may weigh a ton or more. Their huge heads and great humps are covered with dark brown wooly hair in fall and winter but they begin shedding their winter coat in spring. To accelerate the shedding and to relieve itching, buffalo rub against large stones and trees. By late spring only the long hairs on head, forelegs and hump remain, and during this period, they are especially vulnerable to harassment by insects. To escape these pests buffalo wallow in dust or sand.

Buffalo are hardy animals with surprising speed and agility. In deep snow they can outdistance a man on snowshoes and in powdery snow they can outrun a dog team. They are excellent swimmers, and their bones have been found on rugged mountain summits. They can root through deep snow with their muzzles and head to find grass for food. In the national refuges they feed primarily on buffalo grass, gramas, bluegrass, bluestems, wheatgrass and fescues.

Buffalo mature at seven or eight years and may live to be twenty-five to thirty years old. During the breeding season in mid to late summer, bulls bellow loudly and become quarrelsome. Many fights occur but they are brief, and much time is spent pawing the earth pugnaciously.

Calves are usually born in April or May, and at birth there is only a hint of the hump they will develop later. Buffalo travel in small herds which, in the nineteenth century, sometimes merged into the great herds occasionally observed then. Only when panicked did these smaller groups lose their identity. Although playful and easily handled as calves, mature buffalo are unpredictable; men who know them best are always wary of them.

As with the buffalo, the other large animal herds on this range are maintained at a more or less constant number: fifty to seventy-five elk (wapiti), two hundred to three hundred mule deer, the same number of white-tailed deer, forty to eighty bighorn sheep and eighty to two hundred pronghorns. All of these animals, except the bighorns, can be seen at headquarters exhibition pastures. For those with more time, a nineteen-mile self-guided tour over graveled road can be taken which includes Headquarters Ridge, Pauline Creek, Elk Creek, Red Sleep Mountain Viewpoint, Trisky Creek, St. Ignatius, Antelope Ridge and Mission Creek.

The range is made up of grasslands, steep hills and narrow canyons. In winter, snow piles deep in nearby hills, but the bison range is so located that it is scantily covered. The grasslands are composed largely of Palouse Prairie vegetation, including the grasses the buffalo feeds on. The area near Pauline Creek is typical of the grasslands and the range generally. Among the species of birds favoring such open areas are rock wrens, horned larks, short-eared owls and many hawks such as the red-tailed, marsh and the prairie falcon. Pronghorns, introduced into the range in 1951 for research purposes, are often seen here also. Mission Creek, frequented by white-tailed deer, is typical of the bottomlands in the range. Trees such as alders, junipers, aspens, birches, cottonwoods, thorn apples and willows are plentiful along such streams, providing habitat for various warblers, thrushes, swallows, woodpeckers, flycatchers and orioles.

The upper hills are in a montane forest zone containing small parklike stands of Douglas fir and Western yellow pine. Here are found several interesting birds, including Western tanagers, Clark's nutcrackers, Lewis' woodpeckers, blue grouse and the spectacular golden eagle. Mule deer inhabit the

In a herd of 300 to 500, the American bison roams the National Bison Range in the Flathead Valley of western Montana, a grass and timberland of 18,540 acres preserved for this great species.

higher slopes and ridges where the vegetation includes paintbrush, clarkia, several penstemons and bitterroot, the Montana State Flower.

Rocky Mountain elk and gray, or Hungarian, partridge can sometimes be seen at Headquarters Ridge, but the best place to see elk is on the upper reaches of the Elk Creek drainage. Rocky Mountain bighorn sheep, brought into the range in 1922 from Banff National Park, Alberta, are occasionally viewed in the lower reaches of the Trisky Creek drainage. The mountain bighorn is a subspecies of the American bighorn, and its average weight is 185 pounds. The record span for their impressive, corkscrew horns is forty-nine and a half inches. The northern species tend to be grayish brown, while those in southern deserts are pale buff.

During fall and winter wild ducks gather along Mission Creek and ten thousand mallards have been counted there. Furbearers throughout the range include badgers, mink, beavers, muskrats and weasels.

St. Ignatius is the focus of historical interest. Jesuit Fathers founded a mission there in 1854, and the original log-cabin building constructed by them still stands. Before the mission was founded, the site was known as "The Rendezvous" because it was where the Kalispell and Kootenai tribes gathered for bartering and gaming.

Located forty-eight miles north of Missoula, the range has no facilities for camping, but there is a picnic grove inside the main entrance at Moiese, and public fishing is provided on the part of the Jocko River that flows along the southern edge of the range. But perhaps the choicest spot in the range is High Point Lookout on top of Red Sleep Mountain, at an elevation of 4,885 feet the highest point in the range. The lovely valley stretches out below, justifying its Indian name meaning "Land of the Shining Mountain."

CLEARWATER NATIONAL WILD AND SCENIC RIVER

From the time of the earliest settlers, America's rivers have been an integral part of our history, serving as avenues of commerce, sources of municipal water, and providers of electric power and irrigation for farmlands. They continue to nourish our growth, but these rivers, once also used for recreation, have become increasingly polluted and stripped of their freshness and appeal by all manner of intrusions.

In an attempt to preserve many tributaries and sections of rivers in an unspoiled condition, a new and different concept of conservation was launched on October 2, 1968, with the passage of the National Wild and Scenic Rivers Act. In this act Congress declared: ". . . That certain selected rivers of the Nation . . . shall be preserved in free-flowing condition, and that they and their immediate environments shall be protected . . . ."

Rivers in the system are classified as wild, scenic or recreational and are administered by various governmental bureaus. It is contemplated that many other rivers will be added to this new system of parklands in the years ahead.

The sparkling waters of the Middle Fork of the Clearwater River in northern Idaho and its tributaries, the Selway and Lochsa rivers, became a part of this system. Within the Clearwater, Bitterroot and Nezperce national forests, the streams are under the management of the U. S. Forest Service. Running westward from the Bitterroot Mountains to the town of Kooskia, the rivers are the most accessible of any in the system. The Lewis and Clark Highway parallels the Middle Fork of the Clearwater and the Lochsa rivers, and another road follows the lower Selway River, but the upper Selway is still quite primitive.

Cutting through heavily forested and partly barren mountains, the rivers alternate from swift rapids to smooth, slow-flowing currents, providing variety for the canoeist or rubber-raft floater. Elk, moose and otters may frequently be observed near the Lewis and Clark Highway, and the Rocky Mountain goat is a common sight in the Black Canyon area.

Among the stately evergreens of Kooskia, Idaho, the Middle Fork of the Clearwater winds its blue waters, rippled white from underwater rocks.

CRATERS OF THE MOON NATIONAL MONUMENT

A desolate landscape of unyielding blacks, chocolate-to-golden tans, and sometimes, rusty-reds, has made another world of an eighty-three-square-mile sector of south-central Idaho. Ebony-colored rock rivers, glinting bluish purple in strong sunlight, are guarded by peculiar open cones, startlingly red inside with side slopes of tawny brown shadings.

Characteristics of this strange land on the northern reaches of the Snake River Lava Plain between the Pioneer and the Lost River mountains bears striking resemblance to the craters and darkened valleys of the moon as viewed through telescopes. Therefore, in 1924, when President Coolidge set aside 53,545 acres of this barren wasteland, it was named Craters of the Moon National Monument.

Volcanic eruptions resulting in extensive lava flows during at least three different time periods are responsible for this foreboding wasteland. The molten, gaseous rock killed all growing things in its path, leaving one of the harshest environments known. Time determinations, made from the life span rings of pines found growing in the newest lava flows, indicate the last eruptions ended at least two thousand years ago.

Early westbound settlers avoided the area, but in the 1880's, two venturesome cattlemen, J. W. Powell and Arthur Ferris, explored this wasteland hoping to find a permanent water supply for their livestock. Later studies by the U. S. Geological Survey caused wide-spread interest resulting in the national monument designation.

The era of volcanism responsible for Craters of the Moon perhaps encompassed a million years. Although the monument resembles a gigantic, cataclysmic convolution, most of these lava flows and cinder cones rose through what they called the Great Rift— a fissure in the earth's crust that can be traced through the monument—in relatively mild fashion. Cinder cones, both large and small, show that the eruptions occurred along a definite line pattern.

A marvelous view from atop Big Cinder Butte reveals two distinct forms of basaltic (black) lava involved in these eruptions. The *pahoehoe* (pronounced pah-HO ay-HO-ay) and *aa* (ah-ah) are the two. *Pahoehoe* is a billowy, ropy type of lava having many caverns and covers about half of the monument area. Its shiny blue, glassy crusts make some of the flows darkly beautiful in brilliant sunlight. The ropy, wrinkled surfaces are caused by the hardening of a thin crust on the lava flow while the underlying molten rock continues in motion.

In contrast, the *aa* lava is rough, jagged and spiny— apparently having the same chemical origin, but made up of a different combination of gas and heat. When it is flowing hot this kind of lava is a doughy mass and escaping gas pulls out stringers of lava, causing the spines. The whole flow resembles slush ice on a river in springtime. Flows of *aa* lava is the monument are twenty-five to one hundred feet thick and some of them extend miles into the plains nearby.

A variety of cinder cones, spatter cones and lava domes are seen in the monument. Cones are formed by lava froth or spray from fire fountains at the time of eruptions. Big Cinder Butte is the finest example in the area, with rich browns and tans and undersides composed of smaller cinders which are sometimes a brilliant brick red.

Spatter cones were built by smaller fire fountains when clots of lava were hurled from the eruption hole and moved so slowly in the air for such short distances that they failed to cool, and thus were literally "spattered" when they landed. Lava domes have smooth domelike shapes rising from ten to fifty feet high in the monument. These interesting formations came from continuous, slow-welling lava from the same vent opening along the Great Rift.

One of the strangest landscapes in America is the unearthly wasteland contained in the Craters of the Moon National Monument, where volcanic formations, like these black spatter cones, are bounded by distant mountains.

SAWTOOTH NATIONAL FOREST

"Solitude," according to James Russell Lowell, "is as needful to the imagination as society is wholesome for the character." For people who like solitude, Idaho offers acres of it, particularly in the newly established Sawtooth Wilderness Area, declared such after a long and bitter battle between mine and commercial developers and conservationists. The Sawtooth, located in southern Idaho, the potato capital of the world, and partly in Utah, has all the earmarks of a national park and will probably be declared so shortly.

A region of natural beauty that is Idaho's pride, extending from cattle and sheep rangeland up through highland lakes and streams to eleven thousand-foot snowy pinnacles, received Congressional approval as a national recreation area in 1972. An hour's drive north of Sun Valley, it embraces the Sawtooth Primitive Area, over 200,000 acres in the Sawtooth and Boise national forests, where the Salmon River is born in snow crevices and cascading waterfalls. The Sawtooths are the home of deer, elk, mountain goat, bear and mountain lion, and were a special favorite of Gary Cooper and Ernest Hemingway.

The Sawtooths are popular today with hikers, climbers, trail riders and fishermen. In the valley,

Redfish Lake, the largest lake, is noted for two species of salmon–the chinook and landlocked kokanee. The visitor center at the lakeshore interprets broad phases of natural and human history, including the lusty mining days of the late nineteenth century. Elsewhere in the recreation area, remains of mining camps—Sawtooth City and Vienna—are being preserved to tell their story for themselves.

Gold was first discovered in the north of Idaho, then a part of Oregon Territory, by E. D. Pierce in 1860. Although gold did not significantly play a part in the development of the Sawtooth area, golddiggers searched with axe and pick in various parts of the mountains. Significant amounts of molybdenum, an element resembling chromium and tungsten and used in strengthening and hardening steel, have been located in the Sawtooths, but the market for molybdenum is oversupplied at the present time, conservationists joyfully proclaim.

Though few stopped to settle, many pioneers traveled through the lonely valleys of Idaho, for the famed Oregon Trail passed through the Snake River Valley and left the state west of Boise. For a long time Idaho was thought to be as common, good and

Big Redfish Lake (left) is noted for two species of salmon–chinook and landlocked kokanee. Mount Cramer (above) in the Sawtooth Wilderness Area looms with gray and mighty splendor.

unobstrusive as her most well-known product, the Idaho potato. The Rocky Mountains of the surrounding states seemed to dwarf the natural beauty the Sawtooths and some of the smaller mountain ranges had available. Adventurers, however, are beginning to acknowledge the wonders of the area, and are hiking and camping with abandon and in numbers. The deep gorges, deep crystal basins and almost two hundred alpine streams in the recreation area also characterize the rest of the national forest. For wholesome adventure for the imaginative, the Sawtooths are the answer.

YELLOWSTONE NATIONAL PARK

It is like the creation of the very devil himself: Angry forces of the underworld locked in combat beneath the earth with the sounds and visible fury of their struggle seeping through fissures to enthrall the curious above ground who come to see what the forces of fire and ice have spawned.

This is Yellowstone National Park in the northwest corner of Wyoming (and narrow strips of Idaho and Montana), where nearly all that nature has to offer has been concentrated in a spectacular display unmatched anywhere on earth. Boiling springs, steam vents, mudpots spewing mud and, as a climax, the great geysers hurtling tons of water hundreds of feet skyward—these dot the otherwise pastoral land to make a strangely beautiful if not sometimes forbidding world.

The park's strange landscape had its origin some twenty million years ago when Yellowstone, then a mountain-rimmed basin, became the seat of violent volcanism. Clouds of dust and ash filled the air. Settling shroudlike over the land, it buried entire forests. Fiery cascades of semimolten rock rolled down the mountainsides, and great fissures belched forth enormous volumes of highly fluid lava. Some six hundred cubic miles of this molten rock was spewed out onto the land. The mountain-rimmed basin filled; it was a basin no longer, and Yellowstone became a high plateau.

But a few scars remained, as did a handful of open wounds which could never quite heal because of the cancerous fury far beneath. The heat of these prehistoric volcanoes remains, much like a storage battery to provide power for the sights which greet the visitor today.

Old Faithful is aptly named, for it is prompt, appearing about once an hour, day and night, hurling fifteen thousand gallons of hot water in a single, magnificent unleashing of force. There are few other places in the world where such phenomena exist—New Zealand, Chile and Iceland.

Old Faithful has two hundred cousins at Yellowstone, among them the Riverside, Grotto, Castle and Beehive geysers, all sustained in the same way. Cold water from the long winter's melted snows finds its way through the hard volcanic rock around the geysers. Thousands of feet below the surface it is heated by hot rocks and also by gases and natural steam escaping from still deeper molten rock. Soon the cool water begins to boil, building pressure as steam forms, forcing the water higher into the geyser column. Then

The thermal activity of the Norris Geyser includes a variety of small geysers plus the violent and unpredictable Steamboat Geyser which has hurled steam and water as high as three hundred feet into the air.

Sunlight captures the power of steaming water as it erupts from Castle Geyser. The geysers, located in the western end of the park, are part of a series of natural geothermal exhibitions, including springs and pools.

as the pressure is relaxed, huge quantities of steam are formed within the underground chambers, forcing the column of water to the surface in a pulsating, continuous finger of dancing liquid, pirouetting on the surface for four or five minutes. Suddenly the mad ballet ends, the crown of vapor floats skyward and the water recedes as the energy of the steam dissipates. Then, it begins again in the mighty flexing of muscles which has become America's best-known natural wonder.

With this fire which has shaped the face of Yellowstone, there is also ice—the great glaciers which formed on the mountains to the north and east when the fires cooled and died, on the surface at least. These unyielding masses, some a thousand and more feet thick, began to move downward, bringing with them the inorganic scrapings of the land over which they passed. Small valleys were deepened and widened, some mountains were sharpened and others ground level. The ice melted, leaving lakes which have long since disappeared.

The rest of Yellowstone is not quite so forbidding, but has a rugged loveliness all its own: A cliff of obsidian, or black volcanic glass, overlooks columns of lava rock; a steady flow of the hot springs is seen a few miles beyond Obsidian Cliff; fossil forests exist in silence not too far from craggy mountains caressed with the green of conifers; a multitude of wildlife roams fearlessly through great forests of pine; roaring waterfalls plummet into a yellow rock canyon, the sun forming a rainbow above its splashing waters.

The stories of the early travelers to Yellowstone, such as John Colter in 1807-1808, were looked upon with skepticism. But the tales continued, and finally in 1870 Yellowstone was officially "discovered." Two years later it became the nation's and the world's first national park.

Even after it became the first of the great park system, it was not a safe place for tourists. While some Indians possibly lived in fear of the geysers, the Bannocks, Shoshones, Blackfeet and Crows raided and murdered hunters, trappers and explorers. In 1877 the Nez Perce turned to violence, killing some visitors, then burned a ranch north of the park.

Yellowstone's noises of the twentieth century are not those of war-painted red men, but those of winds brushing tree limbs, the rumble of water crashing to far-below canyons and the whisper of rain on the high plateau. It is the sound of deer and American elk (wapiti) browsing on the deep green carpet of

(continued on page 131)

Laced with snow, the dark ridges of the Absaroka Mountains (left)
extend for 175 miles into northwestern Wyoming. Trumpeter swans (above)
stay at Yellowstone all year because the water is heated from hot springs.

meadows, the rattle of stones under the feet of the majestic bighorn sheep clambering up a steep wash, the frightened snort of the pronghorn antelope fleeing into the wind, the earth-shaking rumble of the great and shaggy buffalo racing red-eyed across a flat plain, the mournful cry of the coyote and the angry roar of the grizzly bear.

These creatures, one of the greatest concentrations of native American wildlife in the nation, roam about the park in impressive numbers, joining to drink in spring and fall at the pools where great flights of migrating waterfowl pause to rest. They each have found their environmental niche at Yellowstone, wading in the marshes, flitting from tree to tree or browsing on tender green shoots in the forests where there is a cool respite from the summer sun.

High above much of the park is Yellowstone Lake, a body of water stretching twenty miles in one direction, fourteen in the other. Its mirrorlike sur-

Calcium carbonate deposits terrace colorfully at Mammoth Hot Springs, forming a quasi-frozen waterfall. The gradually growing terraces hold small reflecting pools. Park headquarters are located nearby.

face can be broken into giant whitecaps within minutes as storms blow in from the snow-capped Rockies beyond, or great bolts of lightning are discharged between the surface and the sky.

Travel this lake in a boat to its outlet where the Yellowstone River begins its course, a clear, swift-running stream knifing through green forests and past grassy meadows. Then the soft but persistent stream becomes more determined as it shoots out in a straight line to the base of the Upper Falls 109 feet below. A deep gorge holds it fast until the burgeoning water pours over the lip of the Lower Falls through a narrow notch, dropping more than three hundred feet accompanied by a thunderous crash and gale of wind. It is here, where the river has cut over a thousand feet into the highly colored rocks, that the Grand Canyon of the Yellowstone begins. This, one of the most beautiful of canyons in the world, is best viewed from Artist's Point, Inspiration Point or Grandview.

The weather, like the park itself, has great contrasts. Winters are fierce and snow falls relentlessly to fill great earth cavities. Storms make cruel blows at the plateaus, bringing awesome amounts of snow and ice. It melts slowly, but fortunately it arrives each year, for without this ponderous volume of water the geysers would fail, the hot springs dwindle to a trickle and then die and finally the two spectacular falls would become but a dribble and streams would dry, upsetting the ecological balance of all that lies to the south.

But fortunately, it seems nothing will change in Yellowstone for the forces of nature are not easily swayed. Here there is no man-made edifice or unnatural changes by machine. There is no skyscraper, except some of rock, or hole torn in the earth, except the slowly evolving depression caused by water and wind today and the volcanoes or glaciers of yesterday. There is peace and ultimate grandeur in Yellowstone, a legacy left by nature and administered for all the heirs of tomorrow.

GRAND TETON NATIONAL PARK

Vast, snow-covered graph lines of gray are etched upon the spring-breath blue of sky, mirroring their mighty heights upon apparently miniscule lakes below; giant shadows are cast across already-dark forests of deep green.

The Tetons of Wyoming give no hint of their ascension, no foothills lead the viewer's eye to this grandiose essence of all the beauty that the mountains of the West have to offer; for here there is a glassy lake, a stand of conifers and suddenly there are those incredible peaks.

Through the great valley pours the Snake River, a wide and rushing stream flowing clearly across a deep bed of sand and stones where gamefish dart in cool depths and to which adventurous man escapes for a few moments to ply the current in a fragile rubber raft.

Lakes lie among the green like a cool morning's dew on a field of newly mown grain, glistening in the sun between the natural fist of the Tetons on one side and wind-whispered forests of conifers on the other. Here and there are sun-splashed meadows, a crown of green wearing the royal jewels of complacent wildflowers and streams trickling through rich, black humus where the colors of spring blooms push their way through the floor of last autumn's fallen leaves. This forest is not silent, for there is the pleasure grunt of the moose with newfound food, the chattering of thousands of birds feeding and the scrape then crash of a long-dead tree as the black bear uncovers a delicacy of insects burrowed beneath. There is the hoof of the deer as a doe leads her fawn to shoots of green ready to burst through the carpet of the forest.

The graceful mule deer pick their way down mountain trails in fall, seeking vegetation in the valleys below. High above are a few bighorn sheep, laboring among the rocks finding forage, while thousands of American elk (wapiti) move through the park in herds. In autumn, the big-chested bull elks trumpet mightily, the sound echoing and re-echoing as they lead their harems through the forest.

There are some birds here in winter, but in summer more than two hundred species from bee-sized hummingbirds to eagles and soaring falcons congregate. This peaceful place even attracts the rare trumpeter swan.

Each season unfolds something new; yellow masses of buttercups spring forth shortly after the snow

(continued on page 138)

The Episcopal Chapel of the Transfiguration at Moose Entrance Station is one of many religious centers at the national parks. Overleaf: Jackson Lake at the foot of the Tetons in the central section was formed from the waters of melted glaciers.

melts, followed by violets, spring beauties, yellow fritillaries, mariposa lilies and shooting stars. Calypso orchids hide their delicate beauty in damp and dark corners, while late-blooming gentians begin to unfold as summer's heat wanes. On the peaks, where the warmth lasts but a few weeks, alpine flowers bud, blossom and go to seed in a matter of days.

The mountains are hard, crystalline rock, hugging, in part, Cascade Canyon where a trail rims beaver-built ponds and crosses meadows, skirting great slashes of boulders on hillsides. The valley of Jackson Hole is filled with rock and gravel too porous to hold water, and is therefore covered with the tenacious sagebrush, common to semi-desert regions.

The Tetons' beginning was nine million years ago when a chunk of earth was thrust up along the west side of Jackson Hole. The crack in the surface, Teton fault, divided the masses of rock. To the east, they sank, and to the west rose slowly. The high country formed the Tetons, then perhaps some twenty thousand feet above sea level. Erosion worked upon the peaks, sending showers of rock and stone into the valley, then glaciers completed the task in the Ice Age as the sandpaper effect wore away sharp ridges, filling gorges, then water put the finishing touches on these great natural works.

Grand Teton National Park was established in 1929, and in 1950 Congress added another fifty-two square miles to it, the gift of John D. Rockefeller, Jr. It brought the total to about 473 square miles, a spectacular corner of the United States where nature is the great equalizer, enthralling all who reap this majestic scene with their eyes.

The Teton Range (left) is a gigantic block uplifted along a forty mile long fault and then carved out by glacial action. Mount Moran (right), reflected in Buffalo Fork of the Snake River, is flat-topped because sediment covers jagged rock beneath.

ROCKY MOUNTAIN NATIONAL PARK

High over the mile-high city of Denver, Colorado, fifty miles to the northwest, is the "roof of America." The four hundred or more square miles of craggy heights which we know as Rocky Mountain National Park, in the Rocky Mountains, contains 107 named peaks over eleven thousand feet in skyward reach.

What has been aptly called an alpine tundra is predominantly a terrain of few trees. Beyond the treeline ranges one third of the park area, with rolling, grassy slopes softening the panoramic onslaught of granite cliffs and spires.

In the two brief months of the highland summer the park is a land of enchantment, the atmosphere heady with the fragrance of tiny alpine wildflowers. In other seasons it is often bleak and desolate, windswept, with gales of arctic intensity swirling the snows into multiple hollows and crevices amid great peaks.

Far to the east, breathtakingly beautiful as seen from the uplands, the leveling edges of the Great Plains give one a literal sense of the immensity and variety of our continent. To the north, south and west, the skyline is broken by the serrated crests of other mountain ranges.

This is obviously the prime attraction for visitors: the view, as it were, from the top of our land. Unparalleled in its accessibility, because of the Trail Ridge Road, which winds through these uplands, tourists find themselves positioned, without need for the skill and strain of mountain climbing, at an elevation of 12,183 feet.

Historically, a route roughly following the Trail Ridge Road was used by the Utes and Arapahoes in crossing the Continental Divide. It was called *Taieonbaa,* the "Child's Trail," because it was so steep in places that children had to dismount from their horses and walk. Archeological research reveals that the Ute-Arapahoe Trail may have been in use for the past eight thousand years.

Unlike many of the Western national parks, there is little historical evidence that the area was extensively used by either Indians or whites in the ex-

ploration and winning of the West. Hunting parties from the tribes on either side of the Divide visited the area in summer on hunting trips. Berry-picking and just plain recreation were not unknown in these calming haunts. Trappers assessed the fur-bearing potential of the region—these, the informal explorers, must have been familiar with Longs Peak, awesomely viewed from the plains below. Two more formal parties, Lt. Zebulon Pike in 1806, and Major Stephen H. Long in 1820—for whom the peak was named—charted the uncharted for future generations.

In 1859 Joel Estes discovered the valley which was to bear his name. He moved his family to the "gorgeous gorge" and thus initiated further settlement of the town and valley now familiar as Estes Park.

The tremendous potential of the expanse of glaciated landscapes, as a national park, was grasped and articulated by surveyor and conservationist Enos Mills. At the tender age of sixteen he had built a home in the Longs Peak valley in 1886. In 1891 he had filled his spirit enduringly working with a survey party in the Yellowstone. With a ferocity born of dedication to, and belief in conservation, he fought unceasingly for the ultimate establishment of Rocky Mountain National Park in 1915. Mills died in 1922, but some of his statements seem to have a touch of the immortality of the Rockies he loved and fought for: "Room—glorious room," he wrote, "room in which to find ourselves."

Today, about two million visitors annually enjoy the rugged and untrammeled beauty of the area. Meadows resplendent with wildflowers; forests of pine, spruce and fir; a variety of wild creatures in their natural habitat: American elk (wapiti), mule deer, black bear, coyote and cougar can be glimpsed throughout lower and higher ranges of the park.

The solemn and symbolic bighorn, largest of American wild sheep, can be sighted—sandy-brown in summer, grayish-brown in winter—at Sheep Lake and on lonely promontories near Milner Pass in the northwest section of the park. The methodical beaver,

(continued on page 144)

Hallett Peak in the Bear Lake area is one of 107 named peaks over eleven thousand feet in the park.
Overleaf: Trail Ridge Road is often above timberline where one can stop to view unusual rock formations.

141

lord of his dams, can be observed at several locations, including Horseshoe Park or Moraine Park, near the visitor center. In immaculate, pebble-bottomed streams, astringent with shallow, crystalline waters, stingingly frigid, fish trend toward anglers awaiting them in the lower levels. Trout is the resident of Rocky Mountain waters: brook, rainbow, cutthroat, with the latter native to the area. One of the principal lakes is Bear Lake in the south-central section.

Winter programs, the ski run and the ski lodge, are active around Hidden Valley, eight miles west of park headquarters. But springtime is the season of the Rockies, the season of bright wildflowers on the sunny slopes; and the meadows are a painter's heaven. Snow flurries with the sun's decline but does not endure under the heavy glare of the noonday sun. Summer in the park's tundra region doesn't really begin until July, but it is always summer in the spirit when the peace of the mountain grandeur descends upon those who seek its benisons.

In the northern section of the park, the Mummy Range, with worn and aged-looking mountains, appears as mellowed as the Appalachians a continent away.

Capitol Reef National Park, Utah

WILDERNESS OF ROCK
Wonders in Colorado and Utah

Flanked by mountain ranges, the bequests of ancient forgotten seas lie unearthed along the Colorado Plateau. The time-worn rock, sediment and lava form a gigantic three-dimensional mosaic in vermilion, buff, black and shades of red. Striking monoliths, crystalline-textured granite gorges bisected by unnavigable torrents, huge rocks balanced on fragile pedestals, and multicolored barrier cliffs characterize the region. Harsh yet delicate, the rock country is permeated with an air of mystery that proves irresistible to visitors.

ARCHES NATIONAL PARK

The Colorado Plateau contains the most colorful, varied, sculptured land on the face of the earth, and Arches is one of its masterpieces. In this 137-square-mile national park in southeastern Utah, sedimentary rock, formed in lakes and floods before the memory of man, has been shaped gloriously by the carving tools of wind-blown sand, frost and moisture. The result is a superb display of eroded formations that together form a collection of stone arches, windows, spires and pinnacles unequalled in this country.

Established in 1929, the size of Arches, then a monument, doubled in 1969 when President Lyndon B. Johnson signed an enlargement proclamation. Three years later Congress declared the area a national park. Inside the park are eighty-eight natural arches carved from Entrada sandstone, layered above the hues of Navajo and Carmel sandstone formations.

These huge sandstone masterpieces, formed near the confluence of the Green and Colorado rivers, are surrounded by picturesque canyons, tall, snow-capped mountains in the distance, and an azure desert sky floating above the red, yellow, buff and brown layers of time-worn rock. Elemental forces have produced beautiful land forms in a surprising number of ways. Giant monoliths tower above all else. Balanced rocks teeter unbraced on fragile pedestals and daring arches symmetrically connect the cliffsides.

Perhaps the most fascinating of these arches is Landscape Arch. Thought to be the longest natural span in the world, it is 291 feet across and towers to a height of 120 feet, with the smallest point in the arch now eroded to less than six feet in diameter.

Other splendid natural arches in all stages of erosion may be seen in the park with rock strata standing out in bold colors. These Jurassic Age formations begin near the valley floors with the Navajo Formation sweeping upward in a rounded, sloping mass of light-colored sandstone. In this area, the Navajo Formation has become pock marked allowing enough silt to accumulate for rooting juniper trees, which seem to grow from solid rock.

Above the Navajo is the Carmel Formation, identified by its thin strata of red and bands of wavy sedimentation. The Carmel Formation wears away easily and this erosion is responsible for some of the spectacular park. Above the Carmel is the layer of Entrada sandstone where most of the arches have been formed. The dominant Entrada is a massive three-hundred-foot-thick, orange-red sandstone that originated as wind-deposited sand.

The basic shapes of these rocks are created naturally through the freezing and thawing of moisture which has seeped into vertical cracks in the sandstone formations. Pressure of freezing water causes slabs to fall from the sheer sides of the cliffs until eventually a single vertical slab of resis-

A granite monolith towers above a plain of stunted Utah or desert juniper and pinyon pines which together form a pygmy forest.

tant rock remains—a formation known as a fin. These slabs, in turn, are carved into windows, arches, monoliths, coves, caves and towers in constantly changing patterns.

A length of these eroded vertical slabs near the south end of the park, looking like rugged spires, reminded early visitors of a city skyline—hence the name for the mile-long series of towers called Park Avenue. Other resistant patches of rock in the Courthouse Towers area, called monoliths, have assumed recognizable shapes and are named the Three Gossips, Sheep Rock and Organ Rock.

The prodigious power of nature is evident at Balanced Rock where a magnificent Entrada boulder caps a puny pedestal of Carmel Formation, apparently in defiance of the laws of gravity. This, the most famous balanced rock in the park, is 128 feet high and weighs as much as 1,600 automobiles.

The full splendor of Arches National Park is best appreciated by hiking. Delicate Arch, for example, which has become the principal symbol of the park, can be seen in the distance from a turnout near Garden of Eden. But a drive up an unimproved road to Turnbow Cabin, followed by a mile hike to the arch itself, provides a magnificent close-up view of this splendid work of erosion and a series of "slick-rock" shapes beyond.

Late afternoon is the best time for a look at the Fiery Furnace area, just north of Salt Valley. A westering sun turns this entire area into a red, glowing mass of odd-shaped slabs etched from the age-old layers of sandstone from a forgotten era. This section, only recently explored, is near Devil's Garden where a jumble of fantastic shapes in sheer cliffs justifies the name.

The shifting angles of sunlight through the day cause captivating changes in the appearance of some of the monoliths as light and shadow play across the texture of the rock faces. Erosion still causes a constant change in the cliff walls and sandstone facings. Occasional rockfalls occur when a formation splits under the forces of freezing, thawing and gravity, and add variety to the appearance of the valley floor.

Lovely lakes and aspen glades in the northern portions of the La Sal Mountains outside the park provide contrast with the red rocks of the valley. On the stark escarpments in the park, stunted Utah juniper and pinyon-pine forest communities furnish most of the larger vegetation. Indians used these trees to make medicinal preparations and rope and used the bark for making sandals and matting. A special variety of plants, including ferns, columbine and orchids, are found around springs and areas of seepage. A lack of vegetation means there are few birds; yet mammals and reptiles do survive. Deer, foxes, coyotes and snakes are rarely seen, but white-tailed kangaroo rats, ground squirrels, rabbits and lizards are relatively common.

A visitor center at the southern entrance, not far from Moab, Utah—the gateway city of this park —provides maps and descriptions of the formations as well as biological information on wildlife and plants. a picnic and campground area is located within the park.

The profusion of massive erosion sculptures varies with time of day and season, but Arches National Park from end to end and beyond offers a lesson in humility as one contrasts the ephemeral works of man with the works of nature.

Double Arch displays twin bows, a perforated fin and a pothole formation, and is located in the Windows section, an area ideal for studying the rock strata which stand out in bold relief.

A morning sun brightens sandstone pinnacles (above) towering into a dark sky. The mile-long Entrada sandstone walls (right) are a series of thin, vertical fins weathered to appear like a great city skyline.

CANYONLANDS NATIONAL PARK

This is a land where rock is master. It is everywhere in every form and shape imaginable, as if other objects had somehow been changed into it. You can see the sheer, vertical walls of a building, the swirls of a giant vat of rippled ice cream, the spires of a grand European cathedral, a Roman viaduct's arches, a waterfall's cascades, the pyramids of Egypt, the towers and columns of a Spanish castle—all are rock. The names of these fantastic rocks are as imaginative as the shapes themselves—Washerwoman Arch, Six-Shooter Peak, Silver Stairs, Spanish Bottom, Candlestick Spire, Dead Horse Point, Peekaboo Arch, Paul Bunyan's Potty.

Harsh yet delicate, this weather-streaked, time-worn Utah rock country has an aura of mystery about it. Natural forces, the erosion of wind and water and the expansion of minute slivers of ice, sculptured these forms—this much we know. Desolate as they are, the "Canyon Lands," as they were called a few years ago, have a fascination and visitors keep returning.

The center of Canyonlands is where the Green and the Colorado Rivers come together. And all around the confluence of these streams, the land is laced with tangles of small gorges down which, after a sudden cloudburst, a raging torrent will smash its violent way for an hour and then leave a dry and soon-dusty creek bed for perhaps another year, or even longer. Since the beginning of time this cut and slash of water has eaten away the land into a complex mass of sand and sagebrush and sandstone that is unmatched for variety. The heavier and constant flow of the main rivers, the Green and the Colorado, have scooped out three large intersecting areas, between which it is difficult to move.

Some people have been lucky enough to sight-see Canyonlands from a helicopter. Light, low-flying airplanes have given others a sweeping panoramic glance at all of its treasures. With daring, experienced skill and special boats it is possible to run through the now lazy, now rasping, tumbling, terrible waters of Cataract Canyon. Other waters can be traveled by rubber rafts, pontoons or motor boats. But for most of the park's modern vacation-explorers transportation is a tough, well-sprung car. And then there are some places one can only reach by walking, and yet still others to which you have to climb.

Coming in from the north, between the Green and Colorado rivers, the visitor moves along the skyline plateau to Grandview Point, on the southern tip of Island in the Sky, from which a great sweep of the park's high desert wilderness may be seen. Looking back to the north and west one can see the red round lift of Upheaval Dome which seems to bubble out of the earth's crust; and looking forward below him, the esplanade of White Rim, in a southern semicircle, puts a catwalk around the inner gorges. From there one looks down into a smaller arroyos, embayments and basins of lesser canyons.

West of the meeting of the rivers is the Land of Standing Rocks and a network of little-known, interlocking gullies and buttes called The Maze. Most of this area is broad upland plateau made up of vast, wild, overlaying, twisted and broken layers of rock—worn away by wind and occasional rain into shapes that would seem to be the work of a madman.

The southeast section of the park, known as The Needles, is perhaps its most exciting part. Here the sandstone has been broken and eroded and pushed about into a jumble of pillars thrust-up, arches thrown-out and valley stamped-down into shapes so unusual that the visitor must learn new words to describe them.

The Grabens (from the German word for "ditch") are places where the land seems to have dropped down an elevator shaft, leaving behind them immense flat-bottomed valleys of stone bordered by vertical walls. And as the visitor comes upon these Grabens in this section of the park, such is the immensity of the surrounding distance, that what are deep faults in the earth's crust seem much smaller than they are.

Famous Druid Arch is also in this southeastern section of the park. Squarer than other natural-span formations, this arch looks like three balanced druid stones taken from England's mysterious Stonehenge on the Salisbury Plain—except that these rocks have been multimagnified many times: instead of the menhirs being twice as high as a man can reach, these are about 220 feet high.

In this part of Canyonlands long departed Indians, or their predecessors, have left their mark. Storehouses of grain, with the corn still in them and dried iron-hard by a thousand summers, are still standing almost as they were left. Palm prints of prehistoric man are still visible on the walls of some caves. And at Newspaper Rock (outside Canyonlands' boundaries, at Utah's Indian Creek State Park, on the approach road to The Needles) the visitor can read the pictographs that someone scratched there on the "desert varnish" of the cliff. Here are man and animals, houses and hunters, circles and snakes, and symbolic rivers that must have meant something once to those who could read what was written here. But now these simple scratches on the canyon wall add to the wonderful solitude of Canyonlands' great empty space, another mysterious dimension of silence in the dim, forgotten past.

The view south from Grandview Point shows variety in the canyons from mesas to spires.

In some cases, the approaches to a national park are as interesting as the park itself. Dead Horse Point, just north of the park, provides a mighty view of the Colorado River winding among the multihued and eroded rock faces as it heads into Canyonlands.

The view north of Round Top takes in a serpentine section of the Yampa River Canyon and a few sparse clouds.

DINOSAUR NATIONAL MONUMENT

Straddling the Colorado-Utah border just south of Wyoming is an ancient burial ground containing the world's largest known deposits of petrified skeletons of dinosaurs. Here also are deep canyons cut by swift-flowing rivers, and sculptured land contours carved by centuries of erosion.

Dinosaur National Monument is not all fossil beds, but these remnants of past ages are remarkable in their extent and number. Mostly found in a sandstone ledge in the southwestern corner of the monument, the bones were first discovered in 1909 by Earl Douglass of the Carnegie Museum. From then until 1922 the museum unearthed tons of fossils of ancient animals, from the Nannosaurus, which was about the size of a chicken, to the huge Apatosaurus (Brontosaurus), with a length of seventy feet and a weight of thirty-five tons. These skeletons were shipped to museums in this country and in Europe. Paleontologists thought all discoveries had been made, but others were found, and reliefing work continues even today. Visitors to the unusual Dinosaur Quarry Visitor Center, which is built directly on the quarry face, can see a working archeological project in progress as workmen use jackhammers, chisels and ice picks to cut away the rock and expose more fossils.

Other dinosaur remains unearthed here included the Coelurus, which was about the size of an ostrich; the Ceratosaurus, a large animal with a horn on its nose; and the Camarasaurus, a heavy-bodied dinosaur which probably browsed on the lower branches of the gingko tree. Fossils of two types of crocodiles and three turtle species have also been unearthed in this quarry.

Vegetation has adapted admirably to the semiarid environment. At lower elevations sagebrush, shadscale, rabbit brush and greasewood predominate; mountain mahogany, serviceberry and other shrubs grow at the higher elevations.

Several hundred species of wildflowers have been found here. Although the slopes appear barren from a distance, closer examination reveals a covering of pink trailing phlox in early spring, followed by sulphur flowers. Patches of bright red Indian paintbrush, yellow and purple beeplants, balsamroots, lupines, penstemons, sego lilies and evening primroses mix with this color blanket.

Larger mammals, such as deer, coyote and bobcat, range in the low country, and rodents—beaver, muskrat, porcupine, marmot, chipmunk and prairie dog—are found throughout the region.

The Whispering Cave is located in Echo Park near the junction of the Green and Yampa rivers.

The great range in elevation accounts for the more than eighty species of birds. During the day a turkey vulture or Say's phoebe may be noticed, but it is at dusk when many of the birds come out of their nests, including the gray-brown rock wren, robin, Western fly-catcher, Audubon's warbler, red-shafted flicker, cliff swallow and white-throated swift.

Two campgrounds with facilities are near the visitor center and Dinosaur Quarry; two picnic areas are located near Echo Park. Other accommodations may be found just outside the southwestern entrance at Vernal and Jensen, Utah. Numerous primitive river camps on both rivers provide night stopping points for the river runner, and scheduled float trips are made by guides. The rapids in the monument are many and fast, and only the experienced should try a river trip without local authorized guides.

This greatest of the world's fossil finds may have named the monument, but the rivers, scenic canyons and eroded mountains are equally worthy of preservation for the present generations and those to come.

America's most common feline, the bobcat is an awesome lightweight hunter known for his powerful springs.

COLORADO NATIONAL MONUMENT

Wind, water and frost have exposed millions of years of geologic time in the vividly colored cliffs and towers carved from the Uncompahgre Plateau, which rises 1,500 feet above the Grand Valley of the Colorado River in southwestern Colorado. Great cross sections of rock displayed in deep canyons portray eons of formative periods. Nearby, in Grand Valley near the city of Grand Junction, agricultural fields stretch a dozen miles like a checkered carpet on the valley floor. This region of semiarid climates and peculiar geologic formations provides an interesting habitat for a surprising array of wildlife and plants.

Geologists read a progression of more than 225 million years here, from the hard, crystalline rocks on the floor of the valley, through layers of greenish, sedimentary limestone, to brick-red siltstone and buff-hued sandstone. Changes of climate, periods of flooding, deep oceans, shallow lakes and marshy bogs are recorded in these formations.

Scientists have found the records of ancient men in pictographs and in the sites of prehistoric villages, while paleontologists have learned about the age of dinosaurs from skeletal fossils discovered in the area.

Sedimentation found in depths of up to three miles show that the original Uncompahgre Highlands were gigantic mountains. About 100 million years later a prodigious upheaval occurred in the terrestrial crust. Mountains crumbled and ocean floors were raised thousands of feet to put a new look on the face of the Western United States. From Artists Point above the valley, visitors can see the red, green, gray and brown silty shales that once were shallows in an ancient sea. Ripple marks in the formation indicate that a shallow lake or inlet may have done part of this lamination.

These colorful cliffs and towers have been set aside as Colorado National Monument. To the north across the valley, Book Cliffs form the skyline; to the east, Grand Mesa looms on the horizon.

Dramatic names label the formations—Coke Ovens, No Thoroughfare Canyon, Monument Canyon and Red Canyon. Great rock displacements of an earlier era caused a fault during the uplift period of the region's development. Now this fault is an escarpment hundreds of feet high paralleling the monument. It is one of its most striking sights.

Average rainfall is only about eleven inches annually, yet the natural forces are still at work forming fantastic monoliths, open caves, windowed walls and other forms as they erode the cliffs and highlands sand grain by sand grain, weakening the heights and undercutting huge, delicately balanced rocks. Sentinel Rock, Independence Monument and Balanced Rock all are examples of the results of these weathering processes.

Artifacts, burial grounds and habitations of prehistoric basketmakers have been found throughout the monument. Evidence shows that at an even earlier time the Brontosaurus and the eighty-ton Brachi-

Monument Canyon was the area settled by John Otto, the energetic visionary who determined to make this area of wildly colored cliffs and fascinating wildlife preserved for the future.

osaurus, the largest dinosaur ever discovered, once lived here.

Ute Indians resided here when a small group of Spaniards arrived in 1776, led by Father Dominguez and Father Escalante. Antoine Robidoux, a St. Louis Frenchman, set up a trading post a short distance to the south in 1830, and fur trappers probed the area during the same period. Modern-day history of the monument began with a pioneer named John Otto, who "discovered" it about the turn of the century and became an enthusiastic road builder and trailblazer. Not satisfied with word-of-mouth advertising of the sights and thrilling experiences he found here, he began to write letters. Otto's dream came true in 1911 when President William Howard Taft signed a proclamation establishing Colorado National Monument, and John Otto was named its first custodian.

Park visitors catch fleeting glimpses of wildlife and the brilliant displays of red, purple, pink and white desert and mountain wildflowers suddenly blooming after spring rains.

Plants and animals share a habitat of unusual interest. Three kinds of lizards may share the same locale without friction: One hunts for food in crevices and niches, a second gets his food on the tops of flat rocks, while the third eats food found at the bases of cliffs and in the shade of huge rocks. The yucca, with its creamy white blossoms, depends entirely on a moth for reproduction. The moth burrows into the bloom to lay eggs in the ovary (seed capsules), and while the fruit furnishes food for several larvae, the moth carries pollen to another plant to fertilize it as she burrows to plant more eggs. Tiny birds build nests in the spiny thorns of the few cactus growing here to protect their nests from marauding predators, while the birds themsleves protect the cactus from devouring insects.

Forest cover is comprised mostly of Utah juniper and pinyon pine interspersed with some grasses and shrubs, such as sagebrush, serviceberry and mountain mahogany. Deer, foxes and bobcats are plentiful, but cougars and elk (wapiti) are only infrequent visitors. Bison, introduced into the monument in 1926, are limited by forage supply to a herd of not more than ten. There is scarcely a pinyon pine in the monument that remains unscarred by the sharp teeth of the yellow porcupine, which eats the inner bark of the pines.

Only the quick-eyed see most of the desert birds. Rock wrens, magpies, blue-gray gnatcatchers, sage sparrows and green-tailed towhees sometimes are heard without being seen behind special camouflaging markings. The few broad-leafed trees such as cottonwoods, however, attract many birds including red-tailed hawks, ravens, blackbirds and owls. The turkey vulture and the golden eagle nest on the higher crags.

A visitor center, campgrounds and picnic areas with tables, water, fireplaces and firewood are provided in the monument by the National Park Service. The twenty-two-mile Rim Drive, plus interior drives, hiking trails and scenic viewpoints, make the monument's attractions easily accessible.

As ages pass, leveling forces of weathering continue to reshape this area of sheer cliffs and precarious cap-rocks. But glimpses of an environment made by nature and ignored by man leave a memorable impression of the vastness and changeability of the earth's crust.

CAPITOL REEF NATIONAL PARK

The violent upthrust of multicolored barrier cliffs stretching one hundred miles across the south-central Utah desert looks like a huge ocean wave suspended between the Fremont River and its two tributaries. These interruptions in the striking shale and sandstone escarpments resemble the clustered buildings of a city—hence the appellation Capitol Reef given to this area by Captain John C. Fremont, who viewed the area from Thousand Lake Mountain in 1854.

This magnificent escarpment is the western face of a folding of the earth's crust that occurred in some ancient upheaval. Major John Wesley Powell, a geologist who first explored this region in 1869, called this upthrust the Waterpocket Fold. Capitol Reef National Park preserves a quarter of a million acres of the most picturesque parts of this geological museum. Here the term "paintbrush of nature" takes on special meaning with vermilion-hued shale layers and walls of glowing pink and white mixing with splatters of orange and ocher. The brilliance deepens to "a land of horizontal rainbows" as day wears on.

The surging and folding of the earth's surface caused the eastern segment of the fold to top the western side and erosion has exposed the stratified crust formation. Cliffs range from one thousand to two thousand feet high, making an almost impassable barrier to crossing the desert from west to east. At the base of the cliffs natural cisterns called potholes catch and retain the only fresh water to be found for many miles across the desert. These water catchments caused Powell to call it the Waterpocket Fold.

Petroglyphs chipped into the walls of the scarp or in caves hollowed into the sandstone provide a record of prehistoric eras. Small bands of Indians grew corn on the valley floor, and artifacts, including bone tools, pottery stone implements and rough fabrics, are kept in a museum at the park's visitor center.

The peculiar geographic isolation of Capitol Reef caused it to be one of the last areas of Utah to be explored and settled. It was, however, scarcities of both water and arable land that kept settlement sparse.

Thin soils in the valleys and gorges, plus the paucity of rainfall, have maintained Capitol Reef's ecology as a typical sample of the plants and wildlife of the Colorado Plateau. Pinyon-juniper communities, along with sage, saltbush and squawbush are dominant. Deer, foxes, bobcats and porcupines as well as small rodents and numerous lizards comprise the wildlife. Upland species of birds also inhabit the area.

At Capitol Gorge early settler Cutler Behunin decided to make a wagon trail in 1880. He entered the gorge with tools and wagons, but eight days later he had progressed only three and a half miles. Yet until recent years, his trail was the only traverse of the fold in that area.

The loneliness of Capitol Reef is captured by the view across the desert to the Henry Mountains in the distance. This was the last major mountain range to be named in the United States.

Isolated and desolate, this part of the mile-high land of southern Utah was first set aside in 1937. In 1969 President Lyndon B. Johnson extended it by more than 200,000 acres to preserve the most spectacular parts of the Waterpocket Fold. In late 1972, Congress changed the status of the area from a monument to a national park. A visitor center, public camping and picnic areas, plus two private motel and lodge areas inside the park, assist travelers in seeing this out-of-the-way sector of North America.

Capitol Reef today remains almost exactly as it was when geologist C. E. Dutton said of it a century ago: "The colors are such as no pigments can portray. They are deep, rich and variegated; and so luminous are they, that light seems to flow or shine out of the rock rather than to be reflected from it."

The remarkable "slickrock" garden (left) is a part of the Waterpocket Fold. Overleaf: A great dome of erosion-sculpted rock towers above a river bed.

Cedar Breaks in southwestern Utah is outstanding for its splendid natural amphitheater.

CEDAR BREAKS NATIONAL MONUMENT

A gigantic natural amphitheater, carved from multihued stone, slopes steeply westward from two-mile-high Markagunt Plateau in southwestern Utah. This is a spectacular example of the deterioration of limestone formations uptilted by ancient shiftings of the earth's crust. The gently rolling rim of this grotesquely eroded area is covered by a verdant growth of trees interspersed with lush meadows which display mountain wildflowers soon after the retreat of melting snow. Color, both from various metallic mixes in the limestone and from the lush plant growth, is probably the dominant characteristic of this dramatic area only two and a half miles from Brian Head Peak, the highest point in southwestern Utah.

Early Mormon settlers called the area "breaks" or "badlands." That early name became Cedar Breaks because settlers mistakenly identified the mountain juniper of the area as cedar. This scenic display of erosion became part of Dixie National Forest in 1905, and about ten square miles was established as Cedar Breaks National Monument in 1933. From the rim of the plateau at 10,300 to 10,400 feet above sea level, the amphitheater drops almost half a mile to its lowest point.

Bold rock shapes and cliffs carved from stone layers two thousand feet thick are revealed from outlook points along the rim. Sidewalls are furrowed, corroded and broken into massive ridges that seem to radiate from the center like spokes of a wheel. This geologic display of color starts at the top with white or orange limestone ranging downward through rose and coral tints. Yellows, lavenders and even purples and chocolate hues are seen in many sections of the

(continued on page 164)

Overleaf: *Patches of snow mix with the golden orange on the limestone walls to give an abstract effect.*

161

prodigious natural bowl. The Indians called it "circle of painted cliffs." An artist once counted forty-seven different tints in the stones of the monument.

Even the brilliant coloring, however, is surpassed by the grotesque sculpturing of wind and water in the monument. Formations of columns, pinnacles, standing walls, gateways and terraces suggest structures ranging from cathedrals to tombstones. An outline of a woman with a baby at her breast is shaped in one area. In another spot, erosion has carved the rock into the appearance of a group of people kneeling to pray. Solitary spires, knife-thin walls and crumbling towers seem like the desolation of an ancient city of giants. At sunset the colors soften, and twilight shadows lengthen into blues and purples, making ghostly shapes of the giant obelisks.

The layers of rock from which the amphitheater was eroded were formed some fifty-five million years ago as limy ooze at the bottom of shallow lakes in the region, then near sea level. In the past thirteen million years, the lake bottoms were uplifted to a height of more than ten thousand feet, and a westward-facing escarpment of limestone was created.

With the lifting of the plateau, erosion began, and during intermittent volcanic activity, lava boiled through fissures in the earth adding to the variety of scenes in the area. Many of the newer lava beds still do not support vegetation. Here, in a region where summer heat on the desert below is nearly unbearable, temperatures are cool in July, with snow flurries occasionally taking place in midsummer.

From mid-July through August, mountain wildflowers compete with the desolate beauty of the amphitheater as a major attraction of the monument. Marsh marigold, mountain buttercup, green and fringed gentian, columbine, larkspur, monkshood, mountain bluebell, lupine, sunflower and fields of Indian paintbrush grace the hills.

Some of the true ancients of the forest world, bristlecone pines, are found in sizable groves along the rim. Many of these patriarchs of the wilderness, clinging tenaciously to the near barren soil at the upper edge of the amphitheater, are more than 1,600 years old. Alpine fir and Engelmann spruce are in thick stands in the alpine meadow areas near the rim, and heavy forests of pine, fir, spruce and quaking aspen cloak large sections of the rim and spill down into the formations.

Mountain snows, nearby lakes and the lush vegetation support many wild animals. This is one of the few places the cony, a rodent-like creature mentioned in the Bible, can be seen frequently. Native to the area, these hardy little animals, also called pikas and similar in size to small rabbits but without the ears, eke out their living near the rim. Chipmunks and red squirrels gather pine cones for their winter feeding; but the conies cut grass, cure it in the summer sun and then store it for their winter use. Mule deer are the largest mammals in the monument and can be seen often at morning and evening grazing quietly in the meadows. Weasels, badgers and porcupines are common throughout the area.

Birds find this region a good habitat, better than most sectors of the Western mountain-desert country. Perhaps the most conspicuous is Clark's nutcracker, a handsome bird with a light gray body and bright white patches on its black wings and tail. It is a regular guest at picnic tables and pecks away at campground crumbs. Two species of birds, the violet-green swallow and the white-throated swift, seen to flit untiringly near the rim with never a pause.

Camping is allowed in the monument, usually from June through early September, although no utility connections are available for trailers. A visitor center is located on the rim near Point Supreme. The Utah Parks Company operates a snack bar, lodge, dining room and cabins in the area. Motels and hotels are available at Parowan and Cedar City, each about twenty miles away. Roads and rim trails provide good scenic views.

The amphitheater at Cedar Breaks is always spectacular, with its eroded limestone cliffs cutting into the Markagunt Plateau. This monument offers an unusual array of attractions with its lush meadows, forests, alpine lakes, wildlife and dramatic landscapes.

Cycles of geology for 150 million years are responsible for such fascinating formations as the Three Patriarchs.

ZION NATIONAL PARK

"Canyonland in color." That is Zion National Park in Utah which Mormon pioneers, in 1858, called a place of "peace and comfort," articulating the grandeur of infinite being which its 135,256 acres overwhelmingly suggests.

Ranging across the plateau and canyon region of southwestern Utah, the park's sheer-wall formations in color are unique among the world's geological phenomena. Over 150 million years of natural processes formed this beauty. Here, visitors can actually follow the path of the large three-toed dinosaur and discern his huge footprints in hard sandstone rock layers. His distant cousins in the form of reptiles and amphibians still abound, yet the only deadly survivor

of ages past, in the park, is that dramatic insurgent of pioneer life, the rattlesnake.

Thirteen million years ago, the area, long a bottom for surging and subsiding seas, was lifted thousands of miles through phenomena such as mile-high deposits of sediment. The erosion of this uplifted plateau formed the domes, peaks and canyons that now have become familiar.

The native inhabitants of this region, the peaceful Paiute Indians, first looked upon the white man during the Escalante-Dominguez explorations in 1776. Fifty years later, Jedediah Smith led a party of trappers and fur traders into previously inaccessible reaches near this region, prowling and plodding in quest of pelts from Great Salt Lake south through the valleys probably to the Virgin River.

The gallant and intrepid Captain John C. Fremont, in his 1843-1844 explorations of the great Southwest, garnered the geographic certainties of primeval wonder which were to excite the imagination and determination of dedicated Mormon pioneers in 1847. Within a decade the Mormons had settled around the Virgin River and named the region, appropriately, Zion, "the heavenly city of God."

Greenery tumbles richly about the banks of the Virgin, contrasting breathtakingly with the majestic red of Navajo sandstone precipices and the intense blue of the skies overhead. To the northwest can be seen Horse Ranch Mountain, 8,740 feet high, towering above all the great cliffs of the park.

East of the highway, driving north along the effervescent north fork of the Virgin River, the Watchman, 6,555 feet, glows like a vast reddish-brown jewel in the glints and starts of a remorseless sun. The driver-distracting panorama continues up Zion Canyon, a distance of eight miles, to the Temple of Sinawava. To the left, in succession, are the reverently named heights: the Towers of The Virgin, the Altar of Sacrifice, the Beehives, Sentinel Peak, the Three Patriarchs, Majestic Mountain and Angels Landing; to the right, East Temple, Mount Spry, the Twin Brothers, Mountain of the Sun, Red Arch Mountain and the Great White Throne.

Beyond the Great White Throne, river and road twist to the west at The Organ, behind which Angels Landing rises 1,500 feet above canyon bed. Cable Mountain is on the right, now. A 6,496-foot peak, it takes its name from a 2,136-foot cable, used by lumbermen in 1900 to transport lumber from the east rim into the canyon. To the west is Cathedral Mountain with Observation Point and The Pulpit, soaring to the right and left.

Zion Canyon has well been called a threshold or point of departure. It is only a beginning, for trails lead out of the canyon onto the highland plateau and far into the back country where unviolated wilderness is supreme. Paramount, and especially unique to Zion and its far reaches, is the instant understanding of Henry Van Dyke's phrase: "A national park should be as sacred as a temple."

Trails lead to overlooks, too, such as the one atop Angels Landing or to Observation Point at the end of the East Rim Trail. Here, as almost everywhere in Zion is what Enos Mills called "glorious room—room in which to find ourselves, in which to think and hope, to dream and plan, to rest and resolve."

From here the view of Zion Canyon offers a unique geologic insight into the whole Zion region. Far below lies the meandering Virgin River, tortuous in its windings around each bend of rock on its way to Lake Mead of the Colorado.

The Virgin River is responsible for the inch by inch, eternal and incessant carving of Zion Canyon. The river has never been much larger than it is today and this is a clue to the fact that the river and its tributaries are not a fisherman's paradise—although fishing is permitted in the park. Frequent flooding and shiftings of silt and sand are not kind to the survival of trout in the stream and its offshoots.

Animals indigenous to the mountains and arid areas survive in this region, and the cough of the cougar, the chilly plaint of the coyote can be heard on the land. Bobcats, foxes, weasels, squirrels and chipmunks are numerous. Here the golden eagle and hawk are king and princeling among the feather-bearers. The wiry species of roadrunner, spurred towhee and Rocky Mountain nuthatch are extremely deft in avoiding the two aforementioned "dive-bombers" of the peaks.

The pinyon pine, gnarled juniper, deep-green forests of Douglas and white fir flourish. And the golden aspen of autumn flourish when moisture and soil are plentiful. Here are found the magical night-flowers, the jimson weed (or thornapple), the white evening primrose and the ferns and grasses rich along the river and trickling streams.

In winter only the higher trails are unnegotiable because of snow. The contrasts of red sandstone amid blinding sun glancing off snow drifts can be productive of bizarre loveliness to behold. And in spring the cascades plummet in foaming furies over the sheer faces of the cliffs.

Such is Zion, the bequest of forgotten, prehistoric seas. "A great reservoir," as Donald Culross Peattie once wrote, "of the serene order of nature."

Rising above the Virgin River is Angels Landing, a sandstone monolith which is representative of the name Zion, the heavenly city of God. A stiff climb there on foot and horse trails provides an excellent view.

*Queen Victoria stands in the Queen's Garden below
Sunrise Point. Variations in the weather and erosion resistance
of the rock layers account for the unusually interesting
forms at Bryce Canyon. The varying intensities
of red are the result of the iron content of the rock.*

BRYCE CANYON
NATIONAL PARK

To enter Bryce Canyon is to come upon a unique world set in the middle of an already spectacular country. Its pinnacles and spires, in their strange, almost Gothic delicacy, create an impression that they are related to rock as lace is to fabric. The canyon is weird and other-worldly and at the same time inescapably an elemental, sculptural part of Earth. There *is* creation in destruction, and Utah's Bryce Canyon National Park is a silent, slowly evolving example of the forces of water seeking lower levels.

Stretching for about thirty miles along the eastern edge of 8,000-foot Paunsaugunt Plateau are the famous Pink Cliffs, one of the finest of Utah's eroded landscapes. Primordial forms (sometimes called "castles" and "temples") have been constructed by the relentless forces of water rushing down the slopes of the plateau.

From atop the plateau rim, one looks out over the Bryce Amphitheater and the Silent City, or into the narrows of the canyon called Wall Street, or over the vast expanse of land to the east and southeast where the Paria River for millenniums has capriciously cut, gouged and torn away layer upon layer of rock. The river and some relatively pencil-thin streams are now nibbling away at the rate of two feet every century.

The plateau is the edge of a bowl of color—oranges, reds, whites, pinks, yellows and purples interspersed with gentle browns, reflecting the changing light, from sunrise to sunset, from storm to sunshine, from summer to winter. Hardy visitors get a different and exciting glimpse of one of the superlatives of nature's handiwork, while hiking below the rim among the eerie but beautiful erosion remnants of the Wasatch-limestone formations.

Bryce Canyon's history began long before the Paiute Indians gave Paunsaugunt ("home of the beaver") Plateau its name and called the area, "red rocks standing like men in a bowl-shaped canyon." It was sixty million years ago that inland lakes and seas started to lay down on this area deposits of silt, sand and lime in beds as much as two thousand feet thick. The deposition of the Bryce strata ended about

169

*Natural Bridge (above) was cut from the famous
Pink Cliffs. Standing rigidly above the spires of
Campbell Canyon (left) is Boat Mesa.*

twenty-five million years ago and the lands of southern Utah began to rise slowly. During this gradual elevation produced by pressure within the earth, beds of rock were broken into blocks many miles in width and length. Some blocks were raised more than others, producing seven plateaus.

One of the area's early settlers was Ebenezer Bryce for whom the park is named. He pastured cattle here in the late 1870's and made the famous remark that it was "a hell of a place to find a stray cow." But it wasn't until the early twentieth century that the remote canyon began to gain recognition as a potential park.

Today the park is everywhere enhanced by the trees, shrubs and flowers that nature has so expertly placed. Stately ponderosa pines, very old weather-beaten bristlecone pines, spruce, fir and junipers all abound. These in turn give a setting for the colorful birds, deer, foxes and many other forms of wildlife. Bryce is geologically the youngest of the trio of truly great Southwest canyons, as unique in its own way as its older brothers, Grand and Zion.

RAINBOW BRIDGE NATIONAL MONUMENT

Navaho Indians called it *nonnezoshi,* meaning "rainbow-turned-to-stone." Today it is known as Rainbow Bridge, but no matter what name is used, it remains the same—a soaring, massive pink arch between two cliffs near the Arizona border in Utah.

The dimensions of the bridge are staggering. It is the largest, most spectacular natural bridge in the world—278 feet long, nearly the length of a football field. At a height of 309 feet, the Capitol Building in Washington, D. C., would fit underneath. It is 42 feet thick, more than the height of a three-story building, and 33 feet wide, enough to accommodate a two-lane highway.

Unlike most natural bridges, which are straightened and flat at the top, Rainbow Bridge is a true symmetrical arch. It was formed by a stream, Bridge Creek, which meandered through canyons in Utah's red "slickrock" country. One of the sharp bends was nearly a complete circle and ages of slow erosion wore away the thin piece of canyon wall separating the two sections of stream until the water broke through and gradually enlarged the opening to its present size.

The bridge is composed of salmon-pink Navaho sandstone, with dark stains caused by iron oxide and hematite. During rainstorms hematite in the sandstone is washed down the sides of the arch and deposited by evaporation, leaving streaks of reds and browns.

While on a field trip in 1908, Dr. Byron Cummings of the University of Utah heard rumors of a great stone arch somewhere in the ten-thousand-square-mile wilderness along the Colorado River. A Paiute Indian, Nascha Begay, said he knew where it was and offered to guide a small party to it. The next year they were joined by John Wetherill, a local trader, and W. B. Douglass, a Government surveyor, and they climbed in and out of numerous "slickrock" canyons until finally they stood beneath Rainbow Bridge. Their enthusiastic reports gained national attention, and only a year later, in 1910, President Taft proclaimed the bridge a national monument.

For fifty years the bridge proved too inaccessible for any but the hardiest hikers and riders willing to traverse the fourteen rough miles from Rainbow Lodge. The Rainbow Trail has been called one of the most rugged in the United States because it breaches deep chasms and zigzags over the rock formations.

In 1962 the Glen Canyon Dam was completed downriver from Rainbow Bridge, and the Colorado backed up (forming Lake Powell) to within a half mile of the bridge. It is now easily accessible by a short trail from the Lake Powell docks in Rainbow

Bridge Canyon, but there are no facilities except for a campground.

Although mostly barren, small springs exist in gouges of sandstone around the bridge and support a variety of plant life. Maidenhair fern and wild orchid

Rainbow Bridge is the largest and most spectacular natural bridge in the world. The soaring arch of nonnezoshi *or "rainbow-turned-to-stone" rises above the creek which carved it.*

thrive in the shade, and growing on the drier slopes are Indian paintbrush, lupine, aster, daisy, yucca, sunflower, evening primrose and sego lily.

Early travelers claimed Rainbow Bridge was one of the great wonders of the world, ranking as high in esteem as Grand Canyon and the Yellowstone geyser beds. The present-day visitor, arriving via boat on Lake Powell as the evening sun sets the pink arch afire, finds it easy to see why the Indians called it a "rainbow-turned-to stone."

Owachomo Bridge is the oldest of the three natural bridges in the monument. Only nine feet thick, it is flat on the top.

NATURAL BRIDGES NATIONAL MONUMENT

Southern Utah is renowned throughout the world for its fantastic landscape of sandstone arches, pinnacles, towers and natural bridges. Three of the most impressive bridges are the principal features of Natural Bridges National Monument.

Located in rugged country, the mammoth stone wonders were formed like most natural bridges: A meandering river gouged out a canyon and gradually wore away the canyon wall of the inside part of a sharp bend. The waters then flowed through the hole and created a natural bridge. Although similar in looks, arches differ from natural bridges in that they were not formed by river erosion, but by wind, rain and frost erosion.

A Government surveyor, W. B. Douglass, explored the monument region and tried to find out the original Indian names for the bridges. The latter proved difficult because there were no Indian names. Paiutes, who still live in the region, called all bridges, natural and man-made, *ma-vah-talk-tump,* or "under the horse's belly." At the time it was thought that the cliff ruins of southern Utah were once the dwellings of the ancestors of the Hopis, so it was natural, since Paiute names were not forthcoming, that the bridge's names should be Hopi. Thus in 1909 President William Howard Taft enlarged the monument that had first so been declared a year before and officially assigned Hopi names to the stone wonders.

In White Canyon, the Sipapu Bridge stretches 268 feet across at a height of 220 feet and is the largest and most graceful. The symmetrical arch suggested to those who named it the *sipapu,* a hole through which the Hopis believe their ancestors emerged from a lower, dark world into the present one.

Kachina Bridge, at the junction of White and Armstrong canyons, reaches 210 feet above the stream bed and 206 feet between the cliffs. On one of the abutments are numerous pictographs, some of which resemble Hopi masked dancers or *kachinas.*

The last and smallest bridge, Owachomo, is located in Armstrong Canyon. It is the thinnest (nine feet thick) and the oldest bridge of the three, no longer being eroded by stream waters. Named for the large rounded rock mesa near one end, *owachomo* means "rock mound".

Although the monument roads are paved, the approach roads are dirt and sometimes impassable during heavy snows and rainstorms. An eight-mile loop road links the bridges with the visitor center and the campground at the east entrance.

It is fitting that these bridges were given Indian names, for this is an unspoiled, solitary landscape, and its natural wonders in a wilderness setting has much appeal to those who are attracted to this region and its Indian history.

174

Under summer clouds, the La Plata Mountains provide a background for scenic views along Mesa Verde park road.

MESA VERDE NATIONAL PARK

About 250 years before conquistador Coronado's ruthless and romanticized quest in 1540 through Arizona and New Mexico, seeking the illusory wealth of the "Seven Cities of Cibola," the cliff-dwelling Indians of southwestern Colorado's Mesa Verde had disappeared into archeological history.

For eight hundred years the Indians of the Four Corners country cultivated their beans and maize, lived and prospered—then vanished.

The empty homes of these departed people remain behind today, preserved in protective rock-shelters by the mild climate of this country. Those who come today to wonder at the majesty of Cliff Palace, the largest cliff dwelling of them all, must feel much as the cowboys did in the late nineteenth century when they stumbled onto it while looking for grazing cattle from atop the mesa.

News of the discoveries spread rapidly, and before long a great many curious people began to wander among the ruins, ferreting out their secrets. Unfortunately these people included careless tourists and callous curio-seekers, and some serious damage to the ruins resulted. Even though this was not an altogether bright period in the history of the Mesa Verde, the work of these early explorers began to attract the attention of more serious scholars. One of these was Gustaf Nordenskiold, a Swedish scientist who in 1891 directed the first scientific excavations in several of the cliff dwellings and published his findings. By 1900 a women's organization, the Colorado Cliff Dwellings Association, was incorporated and began working for the preservation of the ancient buildings. In 1906 their efforts attained fruition and Mesa Verde National Park was established by act of Congress on June 29. One result of this act is a regulation stating that all visitors to cliff dwellings must be accompanied by a National Park Service employee.

So successful has been the excavation and repair of the early damage to these precipitous Indian mansions that Cliff Palace, Balcony House and Spruce Tree House are now considered to be the best examples of cliff dwellings to be found in the continental United States. These citadels of man, built like the eagle's aerie in inaccessibility to enemy attack from below, are an everlasting tribute to how primitive man mastered the enduring craft of masonry.

In the Mesa Verde museum are restored fragile artifacts of cookery, agriculture, jewelry and pottery which tell the history of a vanished cliff-dwelling civilization in graphic detail.

Although the story of Indian life on the Mesa Verde has been preserved so clearly, the sudden departure of these people from their homeland remains a mystery. As one gazes at the cliff dwellings, perched in the cliffs high above the canyon floors, they may seem to him impregnable castles, often guarded by towers. Perhaps a persistent enemy finally overran the farmers of the mesa, but there are other possibilities. The narrower growth of tree-rings in the late thirteenth century suggests to some that drought may have driven the Indians from this region. It may be that after eight hundred years of farming the mesa tops the Indians had exhausted the soils. Nevertheless the visitor who lets his imagination play over the spectacle of the cliff houses generally departs with a memory of the defensive refuges of a harassed people.

The quest for clues to these ancient people continues. The mystery may soon be solved in concrete scientific analysis. The National Park Service completed a five-year archeological study of Wetherill Mesa in the undeveloped western section of the park and possibly will come up with certain key answers.

When the new area under study is opened to the public, the number of cliff dwellings accessible to tourists, archeologists and anthropologists will double. Long House, Mug House and Step House specifically will be added to the park's houses of ancient wonder. And a new museum on Wetherill Mesa will fill out the gradually focusing jigsaw puzzle which gives a quaint, unique, historical picture of a vanished American people.

The 400,000 people who visit Mesa Verde annually are thus given an extraordinary opportunity to be grateful for the forces of preservation and conservation which enable them to reflect on both the intrinsic perishability and immortality which is the life and time of man.

The imposing Square Tower House (left), dating from the eleventh century, was discovered by settlers in 1888. Shadows move across Mesa Verde country (right) as Ute Peak stands snowcapped in the distance.

BLACK CANYON OF THE GUNNISON NATIONAL MONUMENT

From the rim, this gigantic slash in the mountains of southwestern Colorado appears like the jagged jaws of some natural cataclysm. The Gunnison River has carved forbidding rock walls that rise almost perpendicular for more than two thousand feet above the river's surface as it slices its way from high in the Rocky Mountains to its confluence with the Colorado River.

A mist frequently hangs over the river, and the sun, even in summer, strikes the bottom of the dark, tortuous gorge for only a few minutes each day. Here and there, the towering walls have zigzag patterns of white where molten rock has pushed its way into the formations. Huge, angular slabs of rock lying in the river attest to the continual collapse of the walls.

A feeling of wildness and uncontrolled power pervades this cleft between the Uncompahgre and West Elk mountains. Fifty miles in total length, the canyon's most spectacular section is within the boundaries of Black Canyon of the Gunnison National Monument, proclaimed by President Herbert Hoover in 1933.

The monument sector of the river has walls as close as 1,300 feet and as wide as 3,300 feet at the rim. Narrowest point in the gorge bottom is about 40 feet. The erosive force necessary to channel this deep path through solid rock formations can be partially conceived in hearing the roar from the depths. Occasionally sounds of rock slides add a reverberation to the din.

From either the north or the south rim, the geologic story of the river becomes plain. Gentle slopes above the gorge prove a much wider, slower river once flowed here. Sediments show these upper layers are 180 million years old. However, as the level of the area rose during an upthrust, the river—already in its earlier channel—had no choice but to cut through the hard core strata beneath its former bed.

The rock in the walls is mostly crystalline-textured granite in which feldspar, quartz and mica form an intricate tracery. The various formations are stained black and streaked by the elements, thus the name Black Canyon.

The Painted Wall area in the western end of the monument shows how eroding water, channeling its way through bedrock that is uniform and unbroken, leaves nearly smooth, vertical cliffs. But dramatic differences occur upstream in the fractured areas where "block" islands and pinnacles have been left. In this area, differential weathering has caused the softer sectors of the rock to be eroded away, leaving the harder parts standing clear of the walls.

The Gunnison River eroded through the rock more rapidly than its tributaries, leaving many side valleys literally "hanging" high above the river surface. Since the tributaries lacked the sustained flow and steep incline of the Gunnison, the valley facing at the Gunnison juncture gradually was shorn off. A few of these tributary valleys, however, extend to the valley floor.

Some spear points ten thousand years old were discovered in the Uncompahgre Valley, and ancient pictographs and petroglyphs are seen in other nearby valleys. These findings lead archeologists to believe the area was once the home of ancient Indians. But by the time the first non-Indian explorers came, only small numbers of Ute Indians roamed this region.

The first modern history of the canyon originated with Juan Maris de Rivera, who visited the area under orders from the Spanish governor in 1765. Eleven years later, two Franciscan priests tried a trip down the river but gave up. In 1853, after the area became U. S. territory, Captain John W. Gunnison came looking for a likely railroad route. He shied away from close exploration of the canyon, but put his name to the river.

Finally, in 1881, a Denver and Rio Grande Western railroad engineer, Byron H. Bryant, led a small party through the canyon. He wrote later, "It was like feeling one's way blindfolded through an interminable Inferno."

His party found that the bare walls above the narrow confines of the river channel amplified sound so harshly that the noise of the water and the sound of the falling rocks were nearly unbearable. Midway in the length of the chasm, they discovered that their greatest danger was from falling rocks and landslides. Huge slabs of rock were balanced precariously the length of the canyon, they reported, and any sudden sound would cause them to tumble down to the bottom of the gorge. They found the sound of an avalanche either nearby or far away to be a blood-chilling, fearful experience.

Two decades later, a two-man team traveled down this canyon in the only other recorded tour, even today, of its dangerous, dismal length. A. L. Fellows of the Bureau of Reclamation and W. W. Torrence, his guide, were looking for a likely spot to dig a tunnel to release some of the river's life-giving water into the plains nearby. Although the two men found a spot for their irrigation tunnel, which was completed in 1909 and is outside of the monument, they very nearly did not get out alive to tell about it:

> *The river at the bottom is icy, wild and raging, filled with rocks and sucks like no other river.... There are only two hours a day, at best, when vision is unimpaired. During the afternoon the canyon fills with a chilling mist that doesn't dissipate entirely until sunshine time the next day—and if it be a cloudy day, the mist stays on.*

Black Canyon winters slightly modify the wild depths of the Gunnison River's gorge with snow scattered on the dark walls.

Both plant life and animals in this wilderness are intensely interesting. Deer and smaller kinds of wildlife are often seen and cougar, bear, bobcat, fox and coyote exist here in small numbers. Amphibians, many lizards and birds, including both golden and bald eagles, also inhabit the region.

Eight miles of scenic drives, plus hiking trails and numerous overlooks on both rims, provide ample opportunity to view this panorama. A ranger station and campground are maintained on each rim. Access to the 13,176-acre monument is sometimes limited by heavy snowfalls in winter.

The folds and veins of Black Canyon's walls vary in thickness, texture, color and direction from vertical to horizontal. Formations are bent and arched like a gigantic web, cut by the roaring fury of the Gunnison River charging through the chasm below.

Stands of aspen for which the area is famous are dwarfed by the barren slopes of Maroon Bells. This striking wilderness area in the White River forest encompasses over seventy thousand acres and is a family favorite for hiking.

WHITE RIVER NATIONAL FOREST

Located west of the Continental Divide and Denver in some of the best skiing country, White River National Forest covers over two million acres of Colorado's most rugged and exciting mountain regions. White River conservation history can be traced to 1891 when it was declared one of the first national forests. It is named for the White River which headwaters in it, and because of its rugged character could easily be classified as a wild and scenic river. The White River forest holds the very popular Maroon Bells-Snowmass Wilderness as well as the Flat Tops Primitive area.

Most of the Maroon Bells area is above timberline, and is noted for its jagged granite cliff faces and rockslides. The red beds of the maroon formations were laid down 200 million years ago when tropical streams carried coarse gravels to the inland sea. The multicolored formations were exposed about seventy million years ago when upheavals bulged the granite with its overlying sedimentaries of igneous and metamorphic rocks to its present twelve thousand foot elevation.

The magic of wilderness is many things to many people. To the ghetto dweller, it may be compressed into the sight of a blade of grass. To a suburbanite, it may be the perfume of honeysuckle in a woodland not yet subdivided, to the farmer it may be the fragrance of an open field after a spring shower.

In the National Forest System, lands designated as wilderness, such as the 68,000-acre Maroon Bells-Snowmass region, no mechanized equipment is permitted (except in emergency and when necessary for administration). Trees are not cut, nor permanent roads built. Virtually all developments except trails and shelters—simple facilities necessary to allow use without damaging the wilderness resource—are prohibited. The emphasis is on keeping (and restoring) wilderness in its natural state for those who journey beyond civilization.

It offers refuge and roving room to big animals who might otherwise be lost, including the grizzly bear, mountain lion, mountain goat and elk, as well as deer, fur bearers, birds and small creatures. It furnishes sportsmen opportunities for some of the most challenging hunting on this continent and for fishing in clear, free-flowing streams and lakes carved out of the earth by its own forces.

As a scientific resource, the fifteen million acres of wilderness and primitive areas serve as a living laboratory, a control plot, where the biologist, botanist, ornithologist and ecologist can measure the behavior of plants free of human intervention.

Wilderness is a many-sided recreational resource. Some come to travel the long trails, others to climb the formidable mountains, to camp in the fullness of night, to exercise the body and stimulate the mind, to contemplate the shape and substance of wildflowers, to follow the arc of the eagle, to luxuriate in solitude, to feel the summons of adventurous times.

Almost everybody uses wilderness in one way or another. The family that camps in a developed area nearby feels it as a warm and welcome neighbor, an unscarred scenic backdrop. The motoring family sees it as a sweeping vista on the landscape. The airplane passenger can look down and tell that the varied physiography of the land is not all cleft and carved from the same standard mechanical patterns. The person who stays at home and goes nowhere can know that a fragment of the original America still endures for the benefit of pioneers unborn.

As one views any wilderness unit of the national forests, he sees that it is national document inscribed in the land for all those who enter its portals, for as short as a day, or even for a fleeting hour, wilderness provides a quality of enjoyment and refreshment found nowhere else. One can walk only one hundred yards to feel the unconquered land that once possessed America. Here even invalids can thrill to the rare wonder and beauty. It is not how much distance one covers, but what he perceives—slowness, indeed, expands the dimensions of time; it encourages one to absorb the fullness of what lies close at hand. So wilderness touches the heart, mind and soul of each individual in a way known only to himself.

John Muir adequately pointed out the values of land where the earth and its community of life are untrammeled by man: "In God's wilderness lies the hope of the world—the great fresh, unblighted, unredeemed wilderness. The galling harness of civilization drops off, and the wounds heal ere we are aware."

GREAT SAND DUNES NATIONAL MONUMENT

In sharp contrast with the snow-capped peaks of the mountains nearly surrounding them, the dunes of Great Sand Dunes National Monument stand at the edge of a grasslands valley in southern Colorado, a thousand miles from the nearest ocean or sea. The highest inland dunes in the country, they rise over six hundred feet from the San Luis Valley floor and are shifted, sorted, piled and repiled by winds.

Three conditions are generally necessary for the formation of sand dunes—sand, wind and a natural trap. Here streams fed by melted snow carried sand, silt and gravel into this basin for thousands of years. Most of these streams dropped their loads of material and sank into the valley floor.

The floor itself had little vegetation, and there was not much to hold the sand in place. Once in the valley the sand and silt were exposed to prevailing southwesterly winds which blew and bounced the sand grains toward the Sangre de Cristo Mountains on the east and northeast of the valley. On reaching the abrupt mountain barrier, the wind swept over and upward through the mountain passes with a subse-

quent loss in velocity. The sand was then too heavy to be swept through the passes and was dropped at the foot, caught in the curvature of the range. The sand gradually piled up and these dunes were born, stretching ten miles along the base of the mountains.

Few streams enter the valley, the principal flows occurring in spring when the mountain snow melts. Medano Creek follows the eastern boundary of the dunes for several miles until it suddenly disappears into the sand to appear again five miles away as an immense spring. An area of smaller dunes, formed from sand which blows across the stream bed during dry seasons, is east of the creek. Here are skeletons of a pine forest, called the Ghost Forest, which was covered by these smaller dunes and then uncovered when they moved elsewhere.

The sand dunes and Medano Creek provide a variety of living conditions. In addition to the flora and fauna of the valley, foothill slopes and forested mountains, there is the distinctive but sparse vegetation of the dunes themselves. A lack of water and the moving grains of sand prevent plants from gaining a

Near the campground and Medano Creek is the Ghost Forest, all that remains of a large stand of trees covered over with sand and then uncovered by wind. Here grasses grow sparsely where once these ancient trees stood tall.

Rising over six hundred feet from the grassy San Luis Valley floor in Colorado, the Great Sand Dunes appear as foothills to the snowy peaks of the Sangre de Cristo Range. The highest inland dunes in the country, they stretch ten miles along the range's base.

foothold, except in depressions where small patches of grass, a species of low pea plant, and sunflowers find conditions suitable to their growth and stabilize the sands.

In 1806-1807 Lieutenant Zebulon Pike, on assignment to explore the lands acquired through the Louisiana Purchase, entered the valley by way of the Medano Pass and wrote a description of the dunes in his journal. Other men later visited the dunes, including Captain John W. Gunnison in 1853, about the time permanent settlement of the valley began. The dunes were made a national monument in 1932.

A campground, picnic area and visitor center are located on the southeastern edge of the dune mass. Visitors may walk anywhere on the dunes; a walk to the top and return takes about three hours. In summer the sand is usually hot during mid-afternoon, but mornings and evenings are pleasant.

These delicately sculptured but massive sand dunes look out of place in the midst of forested, snow-capped mountains. Sunlight plays bizarre games with them, changing their color, texture and shadows every hour, and these misplaced dunes take on a strange beauty not shared with their seaside cousins.

An ideal combination of beautifully curved lines and soft shadows make the dunes a pleasing composition for both the professional and amateur photographer.

SCULPTURES OF WIND AND WATER
The Great Desert I

View from North Rim, Grand Canyon, Arizona

"Whoever stands upon the Grand Canyon beholds a spectacle unrivaled on this earth." The nine-mile wide sloping and vertical desert has an unforgettable and wonderful grandeur that Theodore Roosevelt further defined as a "great loneliness." The desert around the Grand Canyon, for instance, at Death Valley, provides unending variations in color, form and texture as light and shadow cast different spells on the scrambled convolutions of stone and stretches of rippled sand. The Painted Desert displays a kaleidoscope of colors and the Petrified Forest holds the fossilized contours of an era claimed by the mists of time.

After a passing rain storm that cooled the endless hot buttes and precipices, dark clouds rise above the North Rim.

GRAND CANYON NATIONAL PARK

The wind blows gently down this vast wound in the earth, rippling the surface of its creative force, the river, and carrying occasional small puffs of red dust from the awesome walls. The breeze wanes and the eerie silence fans out in four directions, held captive within the impenetrable fortress nature spent nine million years to create.

The Grand Canyon is true to its name, yet a mere, momentary glance prods the beholder's mind, searching for a word more expressive than "Grand." The majestic, water-wrought stone sculpture in Arizona is 217 miles long, averages a mile deep and spreads nine miles across in a panorama of pastels, each a page in the book of the canyon's continuing evolution.

In places where the bottom can be reached, the long hike or ride on muleback gradually unfolds in a geological layer cake—gray limestone walls formed when a long-forgotten sea shimmered in the prehistoric sunlight; green shale holding primitive fossils; pastel layer upon pastel layer, until finally millions of years have been passed in a drop of three-fifths of a mile. In the Inner Gorge are sheer walls growing progressively darker as they plunge toward the rushing Colorado River, walls so ancient they were formed before life on the earth, their fossilless bulk existing in the dark centuries when creation was building its foundation.

The river is still building the Grand Canyon, widening it and deepening it an unmeasurable, infinitesimal fraction of an inch each year. Until the closure of Glen Canyon Dam in 1963, the pulsating red torrent of water carried half a million tons of soil downstream each day, each abrasive bit gently, imperceptibly wearing away at the captive walls, loosening other particles in the interminable process of erosion. Today it carries approximately one-sixth as much sediment.

In 1869 its vastness lured John Wesley Powell, the great explorer, here to lead a long and daring expedition through the treacherous canyons and gorges. The Spanish conquistadores stood upon its edge in the mid-1500's, and American trappers visited it in the eighteenth century, but it remained for Powell to conquer the Colorado.

A topographer, Lt. Joseph Christmas Ives, viewed the canyon in 1858, and later wrote, "It seems intended by nature that the Colorado River, along the greater portion of its lonely and majestic way, shall be forever unvisited and undisturbed." A geologist with Ives, John S. Newberry, did not share Ives' gloomy thoughts, and later interested Powell in the expedition. To Powell, the dangerous trip was a labor of unbridled joy. "Past these towering monuments,

past these mounted billows of orange sandstone, past these oak-set glens, past these fern-decked alcoves, past these mural curves, we glide hour after hour, stopping now and then as our attention is arrested by some new wonder," Powell wrote.

The splendor of the canyon has changed little since the Powell expedition. There are still the sheer walls, tiny rills tinkling across the red stone and patches of green here and there, sprinkled in improbable places, defying gravity and the elements.

Hardy Indians wrested a livelihood from the forbidding land, but each day must have been a supreme effort. Evidence of primitive hunters three thousand and more years old has been discovered in dry caves. Twigs were cut, split and twisted into semblances of animals, as if the ancients created them in hope they would materialize into living creatures for food.

The hunters sought more fertile lands, and in their place came the Basketmakers, followed by the Pueblo tribe and its intricate culture. They lived in the area for about six hundred years and their villages are among the more than five hundred Indian sites found within the 1,050-square mile park.

The Navajo and Hopi live on reservations to the east of the park while the dwindling Havasupai dwell in a small area in the western section of Grand Canyon. The two hundred Havasupais, whose tribal name means "people of the blue-green water," farm a small valley irrigated by Havasu Creek.

This lush valley, with its docile, sequestered people, is in sharp contrast with much of the canyon where a forbidding desert spreads beneath the rims. The bighorn sheep has found survival difficult here, and its barren stretch has isolated on the Kaibab Plateau to the north a tiny colony of tufted-eared tree squirrels, the rare Kaibab.

South of Grand Canyon are the San Francisco Peaks, which reach 12,670 feet, the highest in Arizona. From their peaks to the depths of the canyon is a range of plant and animal life encompassing the identical varieties a traveler would find on a track

(continued on page 192)

At the South Rim, one can stand at the brink of grandeur. Overleaf: Prickly-pear blossoms bloom with the dark wall of the South Rim in the background.

189

from the Arctic Circle to northern Mexico, each having found its ecological niche in this relatively small section of a wild and free place.

The spectacle of the canyon from the air is indescribable; flat stretches of unbroken stone suddenly turning ninety degrees and dropping thousands of feet to the silvery knife of water appearing as a line of indolent mercury beneath the noon sun.

Within the canyon, the insignificance of man is realized with the first uplift of the eyes to rims above, dark shadows creasing the walls in the foreground and blue-hazed peaks beyond the next bend in the river. Here and there are wide places where the river's current has slowed a bit, depositing sand and silt on a narrow bank where a little green flourishes.

To those who find their greatest appreciation of the canyon from within it, rather than standing on the rims and looking below, Theodore Roosevelt was moved to say when the century was only three years old: "In the Grand Canyon, Arizona has a natural wonder which, so far as I know, is in kind absolutely unparalleled. I want to ask you to do one thing in connection with it in your own interest and in the interest of the country—to keep this great wonder of nature as it now is. I hope you will not have a building of any kind . . . or anything else to mar the wonderful grandeur, the sublimity, the great loneliness and the beauty of the canyon. Leave it as it is. You cannot improve on it. The ages have been at work on it, and man can only mar it."

Left: *Views on the South Rim are those seen most often by park visitors.* Above, top: *Late sunlight illuminates the walls of Deva, Brahma and Zoroaster "temples" near the North Rim.* Above: *The late afternoon sun illuminates red limestone formations of the Inner Gorge of the Colorado River.*

While snow falls on the rim, the temperature may be fifty degrees at the bottom of the canyon. After Theodore Roosevelt's visit in 1903, he described it "as the one great sight every American should see." Two billion years of geologic history are exposed at the mile-deep Grand Canyon. Its width of nine miles came from tremendous landslides.

194

The polychrome fairyland of Zabriskie Point in the Black Mountains lies in an ancient lake bed into which silt was washed.

DEATH VALLEY NATIONAL MONUMENT

Heat waves shimmer in the scorching sun as it beats down upon the flats and crags of this barren valley situated between severe mountain ridges rising from a distant desert. It is a heartless master, this valley, unchanged by the softening touch of time. Man's efforts to tame this wilderness seem puny, dwarfed by heaps of lava, burst stone and many-hued clays cast up from beneath the earth's crust in some ancient cataclysm.

Indians who once dwelled in nearby mountains and attempted to harvest a little food from the sparse vegetation called the valley *tomesha,* meaning "red earth," because it yielded a fire-colored clay that

warriors used to produce warpaint for their bodies. Sourdough mountain men claimed the Indian word meant "ground afire." But the name that finally attached itself unshakeably to this harsh valley is Death Valley.

The name is inappropriate, for this is a land of light, color and considerable beauty. Each shift of light, shadow or perspective casts a different spell because of the infinite variations of color, form and texture.

Pioneers in the westward movement of the nineteenth century bypassed this valley, believing—as its name implies—that it would sustain no life. Yet, in the vivid contrasts of this landscape, there is abundant desert life—wild animals, birds, insects and plant life. Although the annual rainfall is scant, only 1.66 inches, if there is enough rain in November, mountain and desert wildflowers provide a burst of color in spring.

The old sourdough prospectors are gone. But the wry, sometimes grim, humor with which they named the ghost towns that remain in the valley recalls the period when an ore strike would stampede thousands to raw frontier areas in a single day. Panamint City, said to have been started by a band of thieves high in the Panamint Mountains, was the roughest of the boom towns in the United States for a few short months. A surging flood from a desert cloudburst washed it away. Greenwater is a litter of rubbish and old bottles today. Ryan was moved en masse to a new location when boom became bust and a new strike was made. Cloudbursts, vandals and dust storms are completing deterioration.

Although the days of the "desert rat" prospector are over, their burrows, now wild and abundant, have added to the animal life of the area. These hardy, scruffy-looking creatures roam the mountains and flats, surviving and increasing on the sparse grass and bushes, searching out their own watering places. Sometimes called "rocky mountain canaries," these little beasts, with their ornery antics and braying calls, recall the ribald impudence of those who pioneered Death Valley.

Few of the men who loved and fought the elements in Death Valley became wealthy. But Walter Scott, later known as Death Valley Scotty, was able to combine his love for the valley and a comfortable living in his last thirty years. In 1924, Scott and a wealthy Eastern friend, Albert Johnson, built a huge Moorish castle at about the three-thousand-foot level in Grapevine Canyon. This monstrous spoof, patterned after European castles, had eighteen fireplaces and the added touch of a 185-foot swimming pool. The place Scott called his "shack" remains as a monument to the eccentricities of some who once called Death Valley home.

Seeing Scotty's Castle perched halfway up a stark canyon is no more surprising than the sight of wildflowers blooming in the desert after an early spring rainfall. Golden primroses shine like newly minted coins. Some bright cactus flowers blossom for several days, while others burst into bloom, lose their petals, and drop their seeds in a single day. Because of the unique abilities of desert flowers to adapt, they bloom and seed only when conditions of moisture and temperature are correct. Sometimes, they bloom only at intervals of several years. As late as 1920, many believed Death Valley sustained no life, yet there are actually some six hundred species of plants in the monument.

Out on the broad mud flats and sand dunes, as well as in the specialized ecological communities of cacti, arrowbush and mesquite brush, the life cycles

A stark contrast exists between brightness and shadows in the sunrise reflections on Badwater, a pool of bitter water formed by a seepage of spring water that collects Glauber and epsom salts on its way to the surface of the valley.

From an oasis of palms (above) fed by natural springs at Furnace Creek, to land so dry that it looks like rubble of broken pottery (right), Death Valley is a varied terrain made up of three basins split by ridges.

of birds, plants, animals and insects continue in historic patterns. The plants are capable of withstanding the scorching heat and drought through use of peculiar narrowed leaves, broad, deep root systems and unusual seeding methods. In addition to cactus flowers and many mountain wildflowers, botanists have found two species of orchid in this desolation.

Mesquite bushes sift dust from blowing storms, forming a layer of fine silt around them. Here packrats, pocket mice and other small animals burrow. Insects come to the animals and plants. Then birds become predators of the insects and the smaller animals. Last in the chain of life are predator kit foxes, bobcats and coyotes which feed on the small creatures of this area.

An early morning inspection of sand dunes reveals tiny prints of many feet which scampered across the dunes the previous night. Small markings in the sand trace the path of an antelope ground squirrel, a mouse, rat or perhaps some insect. But here and there these tiny paths are interrupted, obliterated in a flurry of talon and wing scuffs where some nocturnal bird of prey, possibly an owl, has dropped from the sky on silent wings to continue the cycle of life and death. The rare pallid bat is also found here joining the insect hunters in evening forays.

Peculiarities of wildlife in this desert wilderness are apparent in the flocks of saltwater marsh birds and coots that regularly wade and search for food in Salt Creek and other salt pools. They find "desert sardines," the sourdough name for small minnow-sized, silvery blue pupfish found in the saltwater pools of Death Valley. These rare and endangered fish

Aguereberry Point was named for a prospector, Pete Aguereberry, who became known here after the '49 goldrush. Death Valley is not a true valley, but a graben or block of earth's crust bounded by faults and dropped down in relation to the surrounding walls.

are believed to be descended from an ancestral species originally living in a prehistoric lake of which the valley was bottom. Saline water holes at Slat Creek, about three times as salty as the ocean, contain some of these fish.

Cloudbursts are a dangerous summer phenomenon in the monument despite the mountains that serve as a barrier to Pacific Ocean moisture. High rising thunderheads occasionally dump torrents of rain in the mountains and create flash floods.

These flash floods cause a rushing wall of water to race down the narrow twisting canyons. The pressure of the water carries huge boulders, silt, gravel and chunks of mountainside with the flood. Suddenly, the gorge opens into the broad valley and the flood waters discharge their load of rocks and silt in a gentle incline at the mouth of the canyon.

The erosion caused by these pell-mell floods from the mountains have gradually filled the valley with silt and rock particles. There is nearly as much "fill" below the surface of the valley now as there is height to the mountain ridges above. Bedrock has been estimated to be nine thousand feet below the surface.

Winds, too, are active in the ever-changing appearance of Death Valley. The fourteen square miles of sand dunes near the north end never appear exactly the same, although varying crosswinds always keep the sand dunes in the same location. These dunes are spectacularly tinted purple and gold by the play of early morning sunlight and shadow.

From Aguereberry Point and from Dante's View in the eastern heights, the Devil's Golf Course in the valley below looks like a smooth salt flat. But at floor level one realizes the "flat" consists of crystalline salt which remains when water seeps up to the ground's surface, evaporates and leaves spiked pinnacles as much as two feet high. As the salt pinnacles form, a breaking sound is clearly discernible in the heating and cooling of the valley floor.

Off the 250 miles of paved roadway in the monument, terrain is still raw, wild and threatening. But the rare combinations and complexities of this land beckon many year-round. There are twelve campgrounds in the monument, and other accommodations are available at Furnace Creek and Stove Pipe Wells. A visitor center is located at Furnace Creek.

Although austere and awesome, Death Valley National Monument has a strong attraction for both naturalists and historians. Here, evidence of the ebullience of the frontier period remains alongside the harsh terrain that appears to threaten the fragile beauty of the isolated patches of wildflowers. However, this strange and foreboding landscape with its mysterious beauty makes an impression on the senses and the imagination that is as enduring as the valley itself. Death Valley qualifies in every respect to be a true national park. Someday soon Congress should act to give it this status.

199

DESERT NATIONAL WILDLIFE RANGE

The people trying their luck at the gaming tables in Las Vegas are probably little aware that less than ten miles north is a spectacular, vast desert wilderness used primarily for the preservation of one of nature's most intriguing animals, the desert bighorn sheep.

Found in a number of scattered spots in the arid regions of the Southwest and Mexico, the desert bighorn is similar to its cousin farther north, the Rocky Mountain bighorn. Stocky and heavy-bodied, the desert bighorn averages about three feet in height at the shoulder and weighs between 120 and 200 pounds. They are light buff in color with a large white rump patch around the short tail and are one of the most prized hunting trophies in the world because of the massive, curling horns of the rams. These horns may have a circumference of up to sixteen inches at the base and taper sharply to the tip, sometimes measuring nearly forty inches around the outer curls. The ram's horns grow steadily from birth, while the ewe's horns generally do not exceed twelve inches.

Beautifully adapted to their dry desert environment, the sheep go without water for weeks or months during the cooler season and for as long as three to seven days in the hot summer months, sustaining their bodily moisture from food alone. Ewes give birth to a single lamb between February and April when new plant growth is available for the newborn offspring. Twin lambs occur rarely, and only the hardiest of the lambs can survive the rigors of this desert climate.

Grass seems to be their preferred food, but the succulent parts of shrubs and trees are also eaten. Long migrations are infrequent, but seasonal movements resulting in gradual shifts of elevation are common.

Desert bighorns are extremely sure-footed and fast, bounding between rock ledges at speeds up to twenty-five miles an hour. Their only natural predators, the coyote, bobcat, cougar and golden eagle, do not get much chance at the bighorn because of its speed and its superb eyesight. It is reportedly able to see things five miles away. If cornered, it lowers its head and angrily charges, which is usually more than enough warning for an opponent. Predators are not a limiting factor on bighorns on the range.

The battles between bighorn rams are among nature's fiercest spectacles. Somewhat similar to the battles between elk bulls, two rams challenge each other by rising on their hind legs and letting out a trumpeting, bellowing sound. Then they lower their heads and charge into each other with a force that would kill most other animals. The sound of the head-on collision echoes up and down the canyons, sounding something like a two-ton boulder crashing off a cliff. The charge is repeated again and again for hours on end. But it is never a battle to the death,

for after they have become tired, they lie down side by side in the shade of a cliff or rock, contentedly chewing their cud as if nothing had happened.

The Desert National Wildlife Range, established in 1936 and containing over a million and a half acres, is the largest Federal refuge in the forty-eight states and one of four ranges whose objective is to protect these sheep in their natural environment. Once numbering about three hundred, the sheep in the range have now increased to one thousand head through the management programs of the Fish and Wildlife Service. The Cabeza Prieta and Kofa game ranges in Arizona and San Andres National Wildlife Refuge in New Mexico also have vigorous herds of bighorns.

The Nevada refuge has a number of mountain ranges, notably the Sheep Range whose highest crest, Hayford Peak, is 9,912 feet high. Vegetation varies with elevation, with saltbrush, creosote bush and mesquite in the lower valleys; yucca on the flats; and forests of juniper, pinyon pine, mountain mahogany, ponderosa pine and fir in the mountains. Some bristlecone and limber pines are found at higher elevations.

Water is scarce on the range. Small springs and slowly dripping seeps are the only running source of refreshment. A few catchments have been constructed to hold infrequent floodwaters, and many sheep rely on them for sustenance.

The range is habitat for a large number of other mammals also, such as mule deer, coyotes, bobcats, foxes, badgers and occasional cougars, desert tortoises and gila monsters. Antelope ground squirrels, kangaroo rats, mice, cottontails and jackrabbits are widely distributed.

Over 250 species of birds can be found in this desert region, and about fifty are permanent residents, including Gambel's quail, the roadrunner, pinyon jay, Clark's nutcracker, pine siskin, the cactus and canyon wrens and the burrowing and horned

Magnificent, curling horns have made the desert bighorn a sought-after game animal (above), but here in Desert Wildlife Range the Nelson variety of the species flourishes on the preserved range. Coyotes on the range (left) provide the essential service of predation on small rodents.

owls. Some migrating birds are Canada geese, mallards, teal, gadwalls, pintails, herons, egrets and ibises. Several species of hawks live here also.

Indians, Spaniards and early settlers lived, of necessity, off this land using precious supplies of water, desert plants and animals. Ruins of old corrals, a sawmill, crumbling cabins and old mines are mute testimony of man's former presence. A number of fossils can be found along Fossil Ridge in the range's southern portion.

Because this area is maintained to preserve the habitat of these animals, roads and trails on the range are limited. The best way to see the country and the bighorn is to hike or ride horseback along mountain ridges, up steep-walled canyons, over dry lakes and through drifting sands. About three-fifths of the range is used by the U. S. Air Force as a bombing range and

is closed to the public, and the Atomic Energy Commission uses the land just west of the refuge boundary as a testing center. Studies are continuing on the adverse effects these agencies have on the ecology of the range, and hopefully these activities will be phased out soon. A small wildlife interpretation center is located at Corn Creek Field Station on the southern boundary.

Afield in this strange land, the newcomer sees barrenness, but gradually the desert's beauty is disclosed. The glaring sun and shimmering heat of day give way at dusk as shadows dull the sharp angles of rocks and the soft colors of the desert at sunset create a special kind of peace—the only occasional interruptions coming from far down the canyon, where bellowing sounds can be heard as two bighorns once again match horns in battle.

LEHMAN CAVES NATIONAL MONUMENT

Lehman Caves National Monument is in the foot-hills on the eastern slope of towering Wheeler Peak (13,063 feet), the highest point of the Snake Range of eastern Nevada. It is surrounded by a forest of pinyon pine and Utah juniper that overlooks the sage-covered Snake Valley. This square-mile monument, established in 1922, has an average elevation of seven thousand feet.

Absalom S. Lehman moved into the area in the late 1860's and established a large ranch about a mile and a half from the cave. He guided parties through its underground galleries from about 1885 until his death in 1891, showing them a variety of colorful and curious formations—including columns twenty feet high.

On opposite sides of the monument are Baker and Lehman creeks flowing out of the glaciated canyons. Wheeler Peak has been carved into its present shape by mountain glaciers (the southernmost in the United States) at the heads of these creeks and by the rushing waters of the streams themselves.

This quartzite peak was originally sandstone and its eastern slopes are covered with layers of lime-stone. The heat from a granite intrusion changed some of the limestone to its metamorphic state, marble. Lehman Caves was formed from this marble.

Hundreds of thousands of years ago, when the climate was more humid, the formation of the caves began. Water charged with carbon dioxide filled the cracks and joint planes in the marble and gradually widened and enlarged them. The more soluble rock dissolved, leaving large, vaulted rooms, and the joint planes widened into connecting passages. These eventually formed a labyrinth of corridors and small winding tunnels between the larger chambers.

The second stage of cave formation began as the water table lowered, draining the underground cavities. Seeping down through the overlying rock, the calcium-laden water gathered as drops or spread out in thin films on the ceilings and sides of the chambers. Carbon dioxide escaping from the incoming water allowed the mineral to come out of its solution as calcite crystals, gradually forming stalactites on the ceilings. Water dripping from the stalactites built up stubby stalagmites on the floor. In places, water trickling down sloping ceilings has built grace-ful "draperies" and translucent, ribbonlike "bacon strips." Particularly curious formations are the thin, round disks of calcite, called shields or pallettes, which occur throughout the caves in angular positions on the walls and floors. They are an uncommon phenomenon not yet explained by geologists.

Water pools on the floor have built miniature rim-stone dams around their edges that are beautifully terraced. The huge, fluted columns, with their many "nodes" or terraces, reach from floor to ceiling. Strange-looking mushroomlike lumps, twisting helic-tites and frosty incrustations grow on many formations, walls and ceilings in a variety of colors—creamy white, buff, chocolate, orange and red.

Trips through the caves, lasting about one and a half hours, are conducted over a two-thirds-of-a-mile paved trail with several stairways. Temperatures average fifty degrees.

Wherever one goes in these caverns he will see in the myriad of unusual formations shapes resembling animals, tom-toms and figurines, even a "cypress swamp." These outlines of shapes, color-splashed ceilings and enveloping shadows stimulate the imagination as only treasure caves such as Lehman can do.

In Cypress Swamp, one of the beautifully sculptured rooms in Lehman, thousands of small calcite stalactites hang from the ceiling like Spanish moss. Stalactites have sometimes joined with stalagmites on the floor to make a solid column which grows with each drop of water.

JOSHUA TREE NATIONAL MONUMENT

These trees that grow up, down and out in every possible direction are called Joshua trees, said to have been named by the Mormons who saw the crooked, asymmetrical branches as a symbol pointing to the promised land they were seeking, just as the Biblical Joshua pointed the way into the promised land of the Israelites.

In spite of its prickly appearance, the Joshua tree is not a cactus, but a kind of yucca *(Yucca brevifolia),* a member of the greatly varied lily family, and is one of the most spectacular plants of the Southwestern deserts. They grow mostly in southern California, but are also found in a few areas of Nevada, Utah and Arizona. The Joshua tree may attain a height of forty feet and during March and April bears creamy white blossoms in clusters eight to fourteen inches long at the ends of the branches. However, every tree does not bloom every year.

The Joshua tree is often confused with the Mojave yucca (or Spanish dagger) whose leaves are much longer than the Joshua's and also grows at lower elevations. Joshua trees are normally found between three thousand and five thousand feet.

Its sharp, ten-inch-long leaves grow in clusters and when they die, they droop downward and dry into thornlike needles. The branches' strange contortions are caused by the death of the terminal buds after they blossom. Thus each elbow of the crooked arms was at one time the end of the branch where the blossoms died. The twisted arms are also caused by the yucca boring beetle: The tree builds a material over the hole made by the insect, forcing the branch to grow in a different direction.

One of the best stands of Joshua trees in the world is the focus of Joshua Tree National Monument, one hundred miles east of Los Angeles. Located on the border of the California Mojave (mo-HA-vee) and Colorado deserts, the monument is rich in species of cacti and other desert plant life.

It is phenomenal how these plants survive in the desert with its extreme heat and lack of rain. They give themselves plenty of room to develop extensive root systems, some of which may reach fifty feet from the trunk. The little moisture they do receive— eight or ten inches a year—is strictly rationed by the use of thin, hard bark with few pores to let the moisture escape, or soft, spongy bark which holds water inside.

Jumping cholla (CHOH-ya), also called teddybear cholla, is quite conspicuous along the Cholla Cactus Garden Trail in the center of the monument. It is considered the most handsome of the cactus family, but it has many sharp, barbed spines which can easily penetrate the skin. Its name is based on the impression that the spines jump out at anyone who gets too close. The cholla are more friendly to animals, and cactus wrens build their nests in their branches, even adding extra spines for safety against predators. Lizards, crickets, mice and snakes also find haven in jumping cholla.

The short, flat cactus with the magenta blossoms visible in the monument is called the beaver tail cactus. Although this plant looks quite smooth from a distance, it has many sharp, tiny spines which readily penetrate the skin.

Rocks of several geologic eras are found in the region, but two types dominate—Pinto gneiss (pronounced "nice") and quartz monzonite. Dark-colored Pinto gneiss makes up the bulk of the mountains, while boulders of light gray or pinkish quartz monzonite are found scattered in heaps, especially in the monument's northern portion.

Most of the monument's animals are nocturnal, but antelope ground squirrels scurry over the sands in the hottest of temperatures. Coyotes are often seen prowling at the outskirts of the campgrounds, but the largest mammal, the desert bighorn sheep, is only occasionally observed.

The brownish kangaroo rats have become so adapted to the dry environment that they can go through their entire lives without ever taking a drink of water. They manufacture water out of their staple diet of dry seeds, grain, and some foliage. Easily recognized by their long, tufted tail, they are neat appearing, unlike some of their cousins living in other areas. Their average size is eight to fifteen inches, but five to nine inches of this is tail. These burrowing rodents make very good pets if they can be caught (not permitted within the monument), for they bound around rapidly and can jump six feet if startled. However, they also have fleas which can carry diseases.

The most commonly seen reptile is the side-blotched lizard (little brown uta), one of many species of lizards in the area. One of the largest, the chuckwalla, can be observed basking on warm rocks in the cooler mornings and late evenings. Most of the 250 species of birds that have been sighted in the monument are migrants, and those that remain the year round are usually found near oases.

Many of the trails in the monument, established in 1936, are self-guiding. Eight campgrounds without water are available for use. A visitor center is located at Twenty-nine Palms on the north and there is a visitor contact station at Cottonwood Spring on the south. Temperatures are variable with hot days and cool nights.

The outstanding scenic point is Salton View at 5,185 feet. Here in one sweep is an impressive panorama of deserts, valleys and mountains, from the hot, barren Salton Sea, 241 feet below sea level, to the snow-capped summits of San Jacinto and San Gorgonio Peaks, both above ten thousand feet. Thus, Joshua Tree country is also a land of contrasts.

Mormons called this species of yucca the Joshua tree because the branches seemed to point to the promised land.

Overleaf: *The San Gabriel Mountains in the background lie northwest of Joshua Tree monument.*

A morning sun brightens the various colors of Marble Canyon as a raft floats down a calm section of the Colorado.

MARBLE CANYON NATIONAL MONUMENT

If this canyon were in any other part of the country, it would have been made into a national park many years ago. But Marble Canyon has the dubious honor of being located adjacent to even more spectacular Grand Canyon. Linking Grand Canyon National Park and National Monument with Glen Canyon National Recreation Area, it was the last major Colorado River canyon to be Federally protected. Under the shadow of a dam proposal for many years, the fifty-two-mile stretch was proclaimed a national monument by President Lyndon B. Johnson the day he left office, January 20, 1969. Two hundred consecutive miles of Colorado River canyons from Utah through Arizona are now preserved from man-made developments.

This chasm has remained so wild that Major John Wesley Powell would immediately recognize it as the place that he named Marble Canyon in 1896. The only way to see the canyon is to ride the rafts through its dangerous rapids. It is an unforgettable experience. Some of the rapids are no more than seventy-five feet wide with a consequent violent churning of water. Leaving Glen Canyon at historic Lee's Ferry, the adventurous modern visitor must traverse Badger Creek Rapids, Soap Creek Rapids, Cave Springs Rapids, President Harding Rapids and Nankoweap Rapids before he reaches the junction of the Colorado and Little Colorado rivers, where the Grand Canyon begins. Whirlpools in the wide chan-

nels are very strong and large, but large rafts are able to navigate through them safely.

The rock walls support little vegetation, only a few varieties of yucca and cactus, and it comes as a shock to the river runner to come across Vasey's Paradise. Named by Major Powell for his friend, botanist Dr. George Vasey, it is an oasis in a canyon of emptiness. Beautiful streams gush from holes in the rock walls, which are in turn covered with maidenhair fern, vines and watercress. In front of this green background are willow trees, their leaves flapping in the breeze.

Stanton's Cave, a half mile upriver from Vasey's Paradise, has become an important archeological site in the past thirty years. Robert Stanton, for whom the cave was named, was an engineer who surveyed a water-level railroad route through the Colorado River canyons in 1889, a venture which luckily did not succeed. In 1939 over sixty split-willow twig figurines were discovered just under the dirt cover of Stanton's Cave. Many of them were ritually pierced by tiny wooden spears, leading scientists to believe they were part of some kind of imitative magic. Immediately beneath the figurine level were numerous bones of birds, including the extinct giant vulture and condor, and evidences of an extinct sheep or goat that sought shelter in the cave thousands of years earlier.

This deep canyon is secure from human intrusions, and it is hoped that it will soon be added to the Grand Canyon National Park.

PETRIFIED FOREST NATIONAL PARK

Fossilized contours of an era claimed by the mists of time, and a vast horizon of alternately mingling, emerging reds, blues, browns and yellows—this is the Petrified Forest and Painted Desert combine of east-central Arizona. The "forest" of stone tree logs and trunks, coupled with the sweep of the desert's rainbow-like proscenium, constitutes a national park paradise which can be motored over, using the thirty-four miles of roads.

The stone forest emerges from a prehistoric period called the Triassic, over 180 million years ago, when pine-like trees grew beside streams which flowed through a seaside desert, similar to the present-day deserts of northern Chile. As best we know, the trees died of the same natural causes—fire, insects and old age—that decimate forests today. Some of the trees found in the park show signs of having been carried long distances by the early streams; others appear to have been buried where they grew.

Then the wondrous process of petrification took place along with patient sculpturing by nature. After the trees fell, they were buried by stream-carried mud and silt containing volcanic ash. In successive ages mile-thick deposits of similar material accumulated above the logs, mountain building lifted the logs far above sea level, and, comparatively recently, the logs and multicolored layers of the Painted Desert were exposed by erosion. During the time the trees were buried silica laden waters percolated into the air and pore spaces of the logs, filling these openings

with multicolored quartz. Also during this period, earth tremors broke some of the logs into sections; others were fractured as erosion wore away the supporting earth.

The waters of the earth, which cyclically claim many of man's civilizations and landmarks, will, according to science, ultimately siphon away the color-charged clays, through erosion. Thus, we know that the Painted Desert will inevitably be sluiced away, as tons of silt, into the Gulf of California. Nevertheless, both the petrified logs and the wild, mixed colors of desert murals will be seen for many generations. Actually, only a part of the Petrified Forest is currently exposed. There are many other petrified logs scattered along substrata of the earth to a depth of about three hundred feet.

In addition to the natural wonders preserved within the park, there exist about three hundred archeological sites, spanning the period from about 300 A.D. to 1400 A.D. The pueblo (or cliff-dwelling) and other Indian cultures left in this area clear marks of their passage through time.

The unique wonder of the Painted Desert, especially for the tourist, is the titillating kaleidoscopic effect of changing colors. After rainfall, and following the shift of cloud shadows, the most stunning and varied suddenness of color combinations takes place.

Although visitors are not always conscious of the elevation of the park, it nonetheless ranges in height from 5,300 to 6,200 feet. The entire area receives less

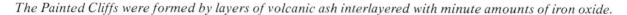

The Painted Cliffs were formed by layers of volcanic ash interlayered with minute amounts of iron oxide.

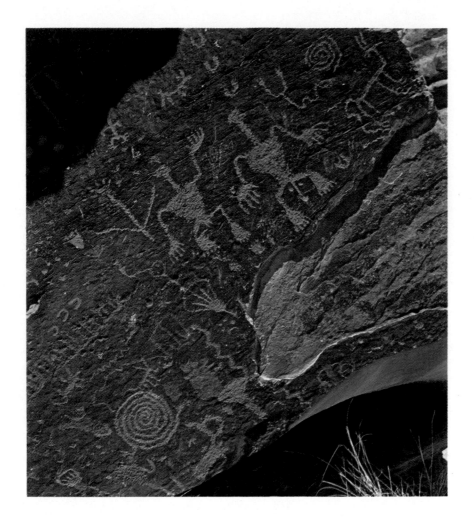

Newspaper Rock (left) is a series of petroglyphs believed to depict the events in the lives of Indians there long ago. Brilliantly colored, the petrified logs (right) receive their mottled patterns from oxides of iron and manganese.

than ten inches of moisture annually and thus only hardy varieties of flowers add their smaller combinations of color to the phenomena above them.

The emphasis is upon delicate beauty with the blossoming of the yucca, mariposa-lily and cactus in the spring and the aster, painted-cup, or "paint-brush," the rabbitbrush and sunflower in bloom during the summer.

Birds, mammals and reptiles survive adequately in this barren museum of marvels. The jackrabbit, cottontail, squirrel and coyote are seen here as in other desertlands. The bobcat, porcupine and pronghorn antelope are more elusive, but omnipresent. Bird watchers know the diverse haunts of horned lark, house finch, rock wren, phoebe and sparrow in these wastes. And in this happy habitat of aridity are nearly

three dozen species of snakes and lizards, including the prairie rattlesnake.

In the 1880's serious threats to the petrified wood through commercial exploitation and sheer vandalism aroused strong public protest and adroit Government action. At one point, logs were being blasted open for the amethyst crystals to be found within. Finally, on December 8, 1906, President Theodore Roosevelt created Petrified Forest National Monument by proclamation. In 1962 the area officially became Petrified Forest National Park, under the executive direction of the late President John F. Kennedy.

The park, in our own lives, and those of many future generations, exists, and will exist, for the interest and edification of the poet and beauty-lover in each of us, rather than for careless exploitation.

SUNSET CRATER
NATIONAL MONUMENT

In 1065, one year before William the Conqueror and his bands of Normans landed on the British Isles, a few farming Indians called Sinagua lived in the present Little Colorado River basin in north-central Arizona near the San Francisco Peaks. Because of the lack of moisture, these people located their farmlands near the edge of old cinder beds which had the best soils for growing crops.

One day they were startled by a sudden volcanic eruption in their fields. A small earthquake caused a minor break in the earth's crust. Steam and gasses hissed from the hole, and as the vent grew, the increased pressure ripped chunks of rock and dirt from the edge and sides of the vent. Ashes and cinders from deep within the earth were tossed skyward, and the roars and rumbles of the blast could be heard for miles.

The Indians, doubtless fearful of this evidence of some god's anger, must have fled for safety. Turning around, they would probably have seen the pieces of red-hot lava blowing from the eruption vent and a huge black dust cloud blocking the sun from view.

Heavier particles, cinders and lava built up around the hole, forming a small cone which continued to grow as days passed and the eruptions increased with intensity. Boulders, red-hot from within the earth, rolled and bounded down the steep slopes, creating a wider base. Sudden flashes lit up the column of smoke rising from the cone's crater, and heavier ashes and cinders continued to spread a black carpet for hundreds of square miles, covering the Indians' homes and farmlands.

For six months this activity continued as explosive outbreaks were interspersed with outpourings of molten lava from new vents near the base of the cone, creating rivers of lava which hardened in mid-flow. Steaming spatter cones and crusted lava lagoons were formed, and the cinder cone reached a height of a thousand feet before activity slackened.

For years after, hot springs and vapors seeped out from fumaroles around the main vent, and minerals from the vapors stained the cinders at the crater's rim so that the summit seemed to glow with the colors of a sunset.

Gradually vegetation took a tenuous hold in the immediate vicinity of the cone, and some of the hardier Indians moved back to their ash-covered lands, finding that the volcanic materials held the moisture in the soil, and crops grew tall with a much greater yield than before. Word of this productive farmland spread and the Sinagua area became a melting pot of Indian culture—Pueblo, Hohokam, Mogollon and Cohonimo. Continuous farming and winds, however, soon removed the protective layer of ash, and, archeologists believe, by 1225, only a few

Indians remained in the region and villages were left to the elements.

This volcanic cone is now the Sunset Crater National Monument. The sparse vegetation consists mainly of dwarf ponderosa pine and small quaking aspen trees. At the base of the cone is the Bonita Lava Flow, and nearby, visitors may see rare "squeezeups," where putty-like lava was forced through the earth at fantastic pressures. Small caves exist in the west base of the cone, and ice formed

in them during winter remains throughout the summer. The monument, a short distance north of Flagstaff, has a visitor center, and an eighteen-mile road connects Sunset Crater with Wupatki National Historical Monument, where the ruins of the Indian villages have been preserved.

Sunset Crater today is much like it was centuries ago; the fumaroles and spatter cones look like they have barely had time to cool from the violence that formed them nine hundred years ago.

Sparse vegetation, like the gnarled ponderosa pines and aspens above, has taken hold on the foot of Sunset Crater's harsh lava cone. The volcanic eruption occurred in 1065.

ORGAN PIPE CACTUS NATIONAL MONUMENT

In 1853 under the terms of the Gadsden Purchase, the United States bought from Mexico a large tract of land at the southern extremity of Arizona Territory and so acquired a portion of desert unlike that of any in the country. The Sonoran Desert ranges from northern Baja California through the Mexican State of Sonora into the borders area of southern Arizona. Although most of this desert is in Mexico, Organ Pipe Cactus National Monument preserves a representative portion of 516 square miles of stark mountains, sweeping bajadas (outwash plains), rocky canyons, flats, dry washes and distinctive plants and animals.

The area is the merging point of three different kinds of desert vegetation—the drought-ridden California Microphyll (small-leaved) Desert, the upland Arizona Succulent Desert and the tall-cactus Gulf Coast Desert of the Gulf of California.

The most common plant is cactus. There are over thirty species here, and outstanding among these is the organ-pipe cactus *(Lemaireocereus thurberi),* found nowhere else in the United States. The second largest cactus in the country, it may produce over thirty unbranched stems up to twenty feet tall from one plant, bearing close resemblance to a church organ. This curious plant dominates the landscape on the lower slopes of mountains and along the ridges of the bajadas. In May and June each of the small greenish-white-to-pink blossoms bloom on the tips of the stems for only one night, opening after dark and dying shortly after sunrise. In midsummer fruits with a reddish, juicy sweet pulp mature and provide a plentiful source of nutrition for birds and small animals. Papago Indians call the fruit *pitahaya dulce* and they use it in many ways. Some is eaten fresh, some made into a native wine, and some is cooked, thus separating the pulp and seeds from the juice, which is then boiled down to a thick syrup. The pulp is dried and used to make jam, and the seeds are ground up for paste.

The rarest large cactus in the monument, the senita, meaning "old one," closely resembles the organ pipe except that it has very deep ridges between the vertical ribs. Clusters of long gray spines cover the tips of older stems, giving it the local name of whisker cactus. Found only along the southern boundary of the monument near the Mexican border, it sometimes spreads over many square yards along the bottoms and edges of washes and flats.

Other cacti found here are the large saguaro, several species of cholla and the barrel, hedgehog and prickly-pear cactus, all of which produce spectacular blooms of crimson, orange, pink, yellow, lavender, purple and pale green.

Cactus is not the only type of vegetation in the monument. If winter rains have been sufficient, spring may bring with it an array of desert colors— the bright red, showy flowers of the ocotillo; the greenish-yellow, nearly inconspicuous blossoms of the holacantha or crucifixion-thorn; and the pale yellow of the creosote bush. The brilliant red flowers of the desert honeysuckle attract many hummingbirds, and insects swarm over the drooping, pale yellow flower clusters of the mesquite. The leafless smokethorn or smoke tree from the California Microphyll Desert is covered in late spring with small, violet-to-indigo flowers, and in early summer the

large white, fragrant flowers of the night-blooming cereus open at dusk. The paloverde, with its dense mantle of yellow blossoms, forms a ribbon of gold over the land for many spring months.

The large variety of vegetation supports an equal variety of wildlife, and one of the most unusual is the javelina (collared peccary), which is a wild hairy pig that thrives in the monument. Other mammals roaming the monument include coyotes, ring-tailed cats, bobcats, cottontails, jackrabbits, foxes, mule deer and an occasional mountain lion. The raccoonlike ringtail is often confused with the coatimundi, though the former is much smaller and is distinguished by

The sun backlights a stand of jumping cholla cactus, accentuating the sharp needles of the branches and at the same time throwing a bluish shadow on craggy peaks.

Mount Ajo forms a scenic backdrop for the organ-pipe cactus to spread its tall stems above other desert plants.

its fluffy, ringed tail. Swift pronghorn antelope may sometimes be seen in valleys, and several bands of bighorn sheep live near the mountaintops. Adjoining the monument on the western edge is the huge Cabeza Prieta Game Range, which is managed by the U. S. Fish and Wildlife Service and protects the habitat of a herd of bighorns.

The rare, inch-long, shiny desert pupfish can be seen swimming in Quitobaquito Springs in the southern portion of the monument. As living proof that this area was once connected to the Gulf of California by the Sonoyta River, they also exist in some waters of Death Valley National Monument. A great variety of lizards and insects inhabit the area, and birds are surprisingly plentiful for a desert. Thrashers are one of the most common, and others include white-winged doves, black-throated sparrows, gilded flickers and warblers, as well as predators like the

red-tailed hawk and the golden eagle. The gila woodpecker drills nesting holes in saguaros and then abandons them, leaving them for elf owls who sleep in them during the day. Both turkey and black vultures are a common sight as they soar over the land or congregate at a dead animal's carcass. A great number of waterfowl use the springs at Quitobaquito, and larger birds include Gambel's quail and the roadrunner.

Looking like a skinny, long-tailed chicken, the roadrunner, a member of the cuckoo family, is best known for its comical appearance and striking behavior. Some Indians so admired its prowess as a rattlesnake killer that warriors would carry its feathers into battle. The bird dances, dodges and stabs at the snake's head until it finally grabs the head in its long beak, thrashes it on a rock and then gulps it down. Roadrunners use almost anything that moves

in the desert for food—lizards, grasshoppers, mice, sparrows. It is estimated that these birds can sprint up to fifteen miles an hour for a brief stretch.

The first European to visit the upper Sonoran Desert area was Melchior Dias, a Spanish officer sent by Coronado in 1540 to make contact with Alarcon who was exploring the waters of the Gulf of California. In 1699 Father Eusebio Kino established a cattle ranch in the area, and later a small Jesuit mission at Sonoyta, Mexico, just outside the monument. He pioneered the route paralleling the U. S.-Mexican border from the interior of Mexico to lower California; it was later called *El Camino del Diablo* ("The Devil's Highway") because of the brutal desert country that it traversed. During the California gold rush as many as five hundred men may have died of thirst along this roadway. The area is so sparsely settled that even today, aside from Government personnel at the monument and the game range, there

are only a few human beings inhabiting some three thousand square miles of land along the border west of the Papago Indian Reservation.

Established in 1937, Organ Pipe Cactus National Monument has a visitor center and campground beside the main road through the monument. The National Park Service has constructed two loop roads of twenty and fifty miles to take visitors along the base of Mount Ajo, at 4,800 feet the highest point in the monument, and through the washes and plains to Quitobaquito Springs. No visa is needed to cross the border to Sonoyta or to drive the now-paved *El Camino del Diablo;* however a visa is necessary to go farther south into the interior.

This monument and the Cabeza Prieta Game Range to the west have been proposed to be merged into a Sonoran Desert National Park. Conservationists should hope this plan comes to fulfillment soon.

A rising full moon in the late minutes of dusk (above) brings out the delicate cool tones which are in sharp contrast with the blistering, dry colors of daylight. A black-throated sparrow (below) ignores bristling cactus needles. Some birds even make their nests in cactus.

The Great Desert II

Echo Amphitheater, Carson National Forest, New Mexico

With the edge of the desert on one side and the Great Plains on the other, mesas, hills and flatlands in the warm Southwest exhibit features that sharply contrast with the arid stretches and grassy plateaus. The geographically young Capulin Mountain conspicuously juts its red, rusty brown and black crater above a relatively level New Mexico plain. Acres upon acres of dazzling white dunes catch the eye at White Sands. In the Chihuahuan Desert stand the Guadalupe Mountains that contain one of the largest exposed fossil reefs in the world, and Big Bend, a proud solitary stretch of country.

In the monument one can view the recumbent profile of Cochise Head, named for an Apache who roamed the range.

CHIRICAHUA NATIONAL MONUMENT

Grotesquely eroded spires, pinnacles, towers and massive battlements guard the canyons and shaded glens of the Chiricahua Mountains in the southeast corner of Arizona. In this fascinating wonderland of rocks, Cochise and Geronimo, famous Chiricahua Apache warrior leaders, fought against overwhelming odds to hold their Indian ancestral lands against settlement by outsiders. But the battle in the forces of nature forming these magnificent bulwarks against the arid grasslands below began millions of years ago — and continues changing the many faces of this ancient upheaval.

Rising steeply from the dry sparseness of southwestern New Mexico and northern Mexico into the corner of Arizona, this mountain range presents a verdant, forest island in a sea of grass. In 1924, after a bloody earlier period of American settlement, some seventeen square miles of the most spectacular section was set aside as Chiricahua National Monument. The fierce beauty of the monument fires the remembrance of the past of these mountains — a phantasmagoria of terrestrial upheaval and lean Indians hunting still abundant wildlife, their women picking herbs and flowers.

Mighty geological forces created the basic structures of these peculiar pinnacles and delicately balanced rocks during intermittent volcanic eruptions at least twenty-five million years ago. The explosive force of the eruptions shows now where various beds of lava and white-hot ash later cooled and were pressured into stone in Rhyolite Canyon. Remissions and recurring eruptions caused varying thicknesses in the lava layers, and during some longer periods of inactivity, allowed sediment layers to be formed in prehistoric lakebeds. These layers now show in the rocky ramparts which range in height from 5,160 feet to 7,365 feet. One explosive eruption must have caused a volcanic hailstorm. Marble-sized volcanic pellets cemented into a peculiar formation called "peanut brittle" rock have been eroded and are open for modern inspection.

An uplift and tilting of the earth's crust caused the mountainous terrain. Fissures and faults became wider and eventually became valleys and canyons. Changing climate, resulting in heavy summer downpours, eroded the cliff faces, while the winds, rain and storm continued the constant struggle between weathering elements and stone.

Massai Point, named for another famous Apache, "Big Foot" Massai, who resisted reservation life for a long time, looks out over a canyon populated by lava blocks.

In the changeless pace of ages, these breaches in the lava crust eroded, and rainwater channels carved the stone masses into a myriad of sizes and shapes. Other eroded shapes resemble a huge Duck on a Rock, the Old Maid, Punch and Judy and a variety of amazing likenesses of giant beasts and men in a ridge and canyon area of volcanic rock. Spires crumble, balanced rocks crash down—and while a generation sees little change, in geologic time, erosion extends its weird reformation of the rocky terrain. Softer rock parts were cut away and what remained balanced huge monoliths, wrinkled and etched.

As the rock weathered, soil formed and collected. Plants gained a foothold, then spread and began accumulating more soil. This activity caused the development of ecological niches and communities of varying altitudinal requirements that are a fascinating part of the monument today. Furthermore, because of their isolation in an arid grassland, the Chiricahua Mountains afford a haven for many plants and animals which are rare in the entire surrounding area.

Climatic conditions vary considerably—shaded slopes have much vegetation and varieties of both plant and animal life not found on the more arid slopes exposed to direct sunlight. Rainfall averages about eighteen inches annually, mostly in July and August. Temperatures have a mean of forty degrees in January and seventy-four in July. Each winter there are two or three snowfalls.

The biological consequences of the variety of elevations and exposures to sunlight have caused some botanists to estimate there is a greater range of plant life in Chiricahua National Monument than in any area of like size in the United States. For example, more than five hundred plant species are found here. Biologists learned, too, that the isolation meant that some forms of both plants and animals are distinctly different here than anywhere else.

Sunny slopes are characterized by desert type plants including the creamy-blossomed yucca, Palmer agave (century plant) and catclaw acacia, among others. These sun-exposed slopes meet the shaded declines which have scrub chapparal, a covering of oak, red-stemmed manzanita and bark-shedding madrones mingling with the chalky white limbs of sycamore and the feathery gray foliage of the Arizona cypress. Douglas fir and quaking aspens at higher elevations in the Chiricahua Mountains reflect the relatively moist conditions of the range. Wildflowers are found abundantly according to their natural elevation, moisture need and other environmental conditions.

The wildlife of the monument is almost as complex as the plant life. Two distinct species are the Apache fox squirrel and the green rock rattlesnake. "Visiting" species from Mexican highlands also come to the Chiricahuas. Among them are the coppery-tailed trogon and, rarely, the Mexican jaguar. The coatimundi—a long-tailed animal resembling a raccoon—also comes across the border to this attractive habitat. Larger animals include the javelina (collared peccary), wild turkeys and the Coues white-tailed deer. An occasional black bear is also seen in the monument.

A multitude of birds provide bright flashes of color and sound among the trees and canyons of the monument. In wooded glens are vermilion flycatchers, orioles, red-faced warblers and painted redstarts. A variety of lizards and other denizens of the Southwest United States and mountain country are plentiful.

There are campsites and picnic areas as well as the National Park Service headquarters and a visitor center. Motels are thirty-six miles away.

At Massai Point, in Echo Canyon or Heart of Rocks with its fairyland of imaginative likenesses, this land is vibrant and alive in a way that is little different from those earlier times of Indian stewardship when the sounds of night birds and coyotes closed the day.

CAPULIN MOUNTAIN NATIONAL PARK

A mantle of green trees and grass softens the violence which built this cone-shaped mountain of cinders and ashes. The reds, rusty-browns and blacks of the thousand-foot-high crater come from material thrown from inside the earth in volcanic eruptions many centuries ago. Although vegetation has partially stabilized the slopes, continuing rock slides in some places show this crater to be young in the stream of geologic time. It is one of the largest, most symmetrical cinder cones in the United States.

This is Capulin Mountain National Monument, 775 acres of recent geological history, established in 1916. Rising from a relatively level plain in northeastern New Mexico, it had become a conspicuous landmark as early as the nineteenth century during the days of the Cimarron Cut-off to the Santa Fe Trail. The main cut-off trail was about thirty miles to the east.

The cone's steep sides of ash and cinder, little modified by time, indicate that the volcanic eruptions which formed it occurred relatively recently, perhaps about seven thousand years ago. Successive eruptions at that time spewed out cinders and ash but little lava. Only two lava flows can be observed, one north and one south of the mountain. The heavier parts of the volcanic material fell back alongside the eruption vent, thus forming the cone, while the rest were blown away by the wind. Lava "bombs," tear-shaped or rounded stones, some nearly a foot in diameter, show how pressure hurled drops of molten lava high enough into the air so that it cooled into stone before falling. The mountain is quiet now, and although there is some question about future volcanic activity, many scientists believe it is unlikely.

An abundance of stabilizing vegetation enhances Capulin's quiet beauty with patches of ponderosa and pinyon pine, Rocky Mountain juniper and mountain mahogany. On the higher slopes are chokecherry, Gambel (scrub) oak and squawbush. The mountain actually was named after the Spanish word for chokecherry—*capulin*. From May through July many wildflowers bloom on the slopes including Indian paintbrush, bluebonnets (lupines), bluebells and daisies.

During late summer, ladybugs are hatched on the mountain by the millions. They are predators of mealybugs, scale insects and aphids and many are raised commercially outside the monument for use in fields and orchards.

Occasionally a great golden eagle can be seen soaring overhead, and many other species of birds and animals may be observed in the area also. In winter months, the relatively large porcupine popu-

Lone Capulin Mountain rises as a landmark above the surrounding plateau in northeastern New Mexico. The crater's name is Spanish for chokecherry.

lation is evident by the teeth-slashed trunks of trees and bushes.

Blustery, southwest winds prevail in the area, yet inside the crater trees seem to lean defiantly into that wind and away from the crater bottom, which ranges from 100 to 415 feet in depth. This strange phenomenon is caused by winds entering the crater at its lower edge on the southwest, circling inside the crater and then blowing the trees in the opposite direction as it spills over the rim. Although some of these wind-twisted trees are as much as 375 years old, a major part of the vegetation has grown in the past half century.

Many of the rocks have gray-green and orange lichens growing on them. These communities of fungi and algae aid each other in breaking down the stone into soil with each feeding the other in a cooperative existence.

A visitor center is located alongside a road which leads to the top of Capulin Mountain, where a rim trail circles the crater. The monument has a picnic area but no campground. Privately operated campgrounds and other lodging are available in nearby towns.

Here in the midst of mostly dun-colored northeastern New Mexico, the bright hues of flowers and trees on a dark cinder mountain make the eras of the relatively recent geologic past easy to read.

WHITE SANDS NATIONAL MONUMENT

White Sands National Monument preserves the most spectacular part of the world's largest gypsum dune field—great rolling hills of dazzling white sand that provide a severe environment for the animals and plants which have managed to survive in it. The monument is set in the Tularosa Basin of southern New Mexico that extends for over a hundred miles between mountains and highlands, the remnants of a plateau.

These mountains, including the forested Sacramentos to the east and rugged San Andres to the west, contain massive layers of gypsum rock that seasonal rains and melting snows have been eroding for centuries. Dissolved gypsum is eventually carried to Lake Lucero, the lowest part of the basin at the southern end, where the warm sun and dry winds evaporate the lake, leaving it a gypsum-crystal encrusted marsh much of the year. Gypsum also lies beneath the basin floor, evidence that it was once part of the high plateau around it. Capillary action draws the gypsum-laden underground water to the surface which, after evaporation, leaves extensive alkali flats north of the lake. Persistent, scouring winds from the southwest disintegrate the crystals in the lake bed and the alkali flats into brilliant white grains of sand, pile them into dunes and push the dunes across the landscape as new ones are constantly formed.

The winds blow the particles of gypsum, sometimes in a visible cloud, up the gentle windward slopes of the dunes as they continue to inch forward sporadically in a northeasterly direction. When the grains reach the dune crest they fall on the steep leeward side. Ripples on the flatter dunes are miniature examples of the same process. The dune area is now about thirty miles long and twelve miles wide. Dune peaks are as high as fifty feet.

Yet life survives, including over a hundred species of hardy plants. Even on the barren alkali flats some vegetation holds on with amazing tenacity—such as clumps of pickleweed or iodine bush. Sparse ground cover between the marginal dunes is made up primarily of delicate purple sand verbena, pink centauriums and rice grass. But their existence is temporary, for they are certain to be buried eventually by the advancing dunes.

The groundwater only three or four feet below the surface gives White Sands an advantage over most other dune areas, but it is only a slight one, for few plants can use the gypsum-laden water. Among those that can absorb it are the skunkbush sumac (squawbush), soaptree yucca, shrubby pennyroyal, rubber rabbit brush and cottonwood tree. As the sand begins to accumulate around its base such a plant will put on a burst of growth, thus stretching its "neck" to keep above the sand. As a result of this

The endless ranks of sand dunes (above) seem still, although these glistening gypsum mounds are always growing and moving. The marginal areas of White Sands monument (right) support a few vigorous plants like the hybrid varieties of woody-stemmed yucca.

222

Nocturnal animals leave tracks on this desert basin that is covered with gypsum sand which the wind constantly repatterns.

struggle for survival plants with stems as long as forty feet have been found. As the dunes continue to move, they gradually recede from these plants, leaving them elevated on pedestals of compacted gypsum bound by their tangled roots. The fourwing saltbush grows only among the stable dunes and its salty tasting leaves are palatable to wildlife.

Few animals live in the sands. Coyotes, occasional foxes, and the skunks, porcupines and gophers sometimes seen in the dunes come from the surrounding area. To avoid these predators, two species unique to White Sands have evolved white coloration to help protect them. A small pocket mouse *(Perognathus apache gypsi)* is seldom seen because he is nocturnal. In contrast with this white pocket mouse, the red hills nearby contain a pocket mouse that is a rusty color, and in the black lava beds north of the sands is a black race. The small white lizard *(Holbrookie maculata ruthveni)* can frequently be seen scampering over the sand during the day. It has no external ear openings and has overlapping scales on its upper lip to keep sand out of its mouth.

Prehistoric Indians apparently avoided the White Sands desert, although the remains of their fires, pottery and arrowheads have been found along its rim. Seventeenth-century Spanish explorers left behind a two-wheeled wooden cart, called a *carreta,* now on display in the small interpretive museum at the headquarters visitor center. The site of man's first atomic explosion is outside the monument, about fifty-five miles north of the visitor center.

Established in 1933, the monument has an eight-mile scenic drive into the heart of the dunes. Near the end of the drive is an immense picnic area with fireplaces and shaded tables, but there is no campground. Vehicles are restricted to roads because they can easily bog down if they are driven on the dunes. However, a brief walk to the top of one of the great dunes can bring you an exhilarating experience in a sea of glistening sand and sky, silent except for the relentless wind.

CARLSBAD CAVERNS NATIONAL PARK

If one person can be credited with initially exploring the yawning depths of Carlsbad Caverns, in the contemporary record of man, it is a determined, brave and dedicated cowboy named James Larkin White, who descended into these incredible hollows in 1901.

Prior to his descent, this now world-famous national park of southeastern New Mexico had been known to a handful of ranchers, when the austere desert lands of the Guadalupe Mountains were settled just after the Civil War. But like most of our great natural wonders, the existence of the caverns was known to the Indians of the region and their forebears for many centuries prior to the incursions of the white man.

Cooking pits, colored clay paintings or pictographs attest to historic and prehistoric habitation in the sheltering vaulted arch of the cavern's entrance.

For many years the awesome depths were known simply as the Bat Cave, from which hordes of the insect-eating mammals came wheeling and fluttering each summer day at sunset.

White so graphically described the bizarre features of this underground wonderland that the official interest of the General Land Office was aroused in 1923, and Robert A. Holley was assigned to investigate the authenticity of this vast natural wonder as an area possibly worthy of national preservation.

After thirty days of exploration, Holley was moved to state: "I am wholly conscious of the feebleness of my efforts to convey in words the deep, conflicting emotions, the feelings of fear and awe, and the desire for an inspired understanding of the Divine Creator's work which presents to the human eye such a complex aggregate of natural wonders in such a limited space."

On the basis of Robert Holley's enthusiastic official report, bolstered by the indefatigable efforts of James Larkin White, Carlsbad Cave was established as a national monument in 1923 and reestablished as a national park in 1930. Since then, about thirteen million visitors have experienced the profound awe of both White and Holley. The breathtaking height of ceiling, the vastness of many-acred floor areas, the variety of exquisite forms to be seen on cavern roofs, walls and floors present proof that this is one of our nation's most interesting and popular preservations.

On the surface of the park, especially in spring, there is a variety of colorful and bustling desert life. Birds, reptiles, raccoons, lizards and vultures thrive in the mountain-desert aridity which is emblazoned

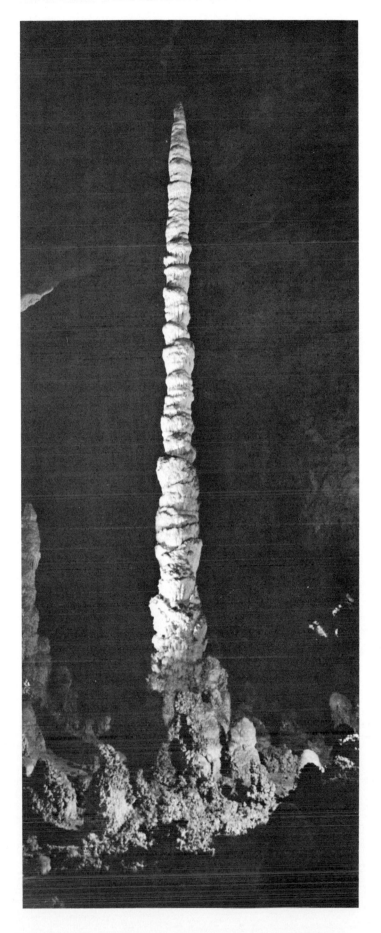

The Totem Pole is a huge stalagmite in the cavern known formerly as Bat Cave. Thousands of the insect-eating mammals spiral from the entrance at sunset.

with the bright yellows of the bladderpod and prickly-pear blossoms and blended with purple verbena and whitish pepperweed. Daytime temperatures in summer can be high, but evenings are cool. As summer wanes, the hillsides lose their color and reptiles go into hibernation beneath rocks. In winter the temperatures are mild, snow and ice are rare. Juncos, towhees and pyrrhuloxias become the most conspicuous of the birds.

And the bats still arrive en masse in spring, their return heralding the nightly tumbling black clouds of foraging flight emerging from the maw of the caverns. There is a proliferation of young bats each summer, but the chill frosts of November kill the insect provender, and mass migration southward again throws up a weird and sinuous cloud against exotic desert horizons.

Plunging to a known depth of 1,100 feet are the Carlsbad Caverns, hollowed by seeping groundwater in limestone beds laid down by an ancient sea. Appropriately named, the Big Room (above) has many acres of floor space: at one point the ceiling arches 285 feet above the mile-long perimeter trail. Formations (left) include stalactites on the ceiling, stalagmites on the floor, columns and twisting helictites to fascinate spelunkers in the New Mexico park.

227

BIG BEND NATIONAL PARK

The Great River, the Rio Grande, running a fairly straight southeast course, edging the United States and Mexico across the Chihuahua desert, suddenly bends around to its left and cuts to the north past the Chisos Mountains for a total of 107 miles. And before it turns south again it puts a heart-shaped lower boundary on Big Bend National Park.

Here is the wilderness. Here is the unexplored. Here is the West (with a capital letter) in all of its desert and mountain and storybook wildness.

In this day of overcrowding, bustle and hustle and nudging neighbors, parts of Big Bend National Park, which is within three hundred miles of El Paso, Texas, and four hundred miles of San Antonio, are still not fully explored. Parts of it are so untouched by this world of the twentieth century that a vacationer can ride his horse out from the comforts of a modern resort area and within an hour feel that he is alone in a world, uninhabited, untouched, and perhaps, before he himself looked upon it, unseen.

This is a proud solitary stretch of country, harsh without bitterness, austere without anger and silent with a proud and brooding unfathomable mystery.

Even the suddenly green pockets of lush cottonwood-lined oases along the river's edge seem like gentle guests (rather than settlers) of the sweeping mesa and rolling mountain land that tolerate their being there with the preoccupied hospitality of a host who has great matters on his mind.

This area has never been an easy one to know. It grudgingly permitted some acquaintanceship, but never sought or welcomed friendship; and it never offered itself or its resources to explorers, ranchers, miners or farmers. It wasn't until 1899 that anyone made a trip of record around the "big bend" of the Rio Grande. Others may have gone there before Robert T. Hill and five companions explored it for the Geological Survey in 1850, but the others went to raid, to smuggle or to hide.

Men who went there before the days of the park's development went there usually driven by motives which seemed better concealed than advertised. Train robbers, bank robbers, American fugitives and Mexican bandits slipped in and out of the area as they slipped in and out of the history of the outlaw-gunman West. Here, as late as 1916, Mexican bandits, possibly some of Pancho Villa's men, invaded the United States.

But today the men of violence are gone. Today if the visitor hears rustling in the underbrush, it is probably not a cattle rustler but a javelina or a mule deer, a cougar or a white-tailed deer.

In the middle of the park, the Chisos Mountains rise up like a string of fortified castles set to hold back the advance of the hordes of sage and cactus on the desert floor. The mountains throw their forest troops into battle lines against the invaders. In the front rank are the stunted oak and drooping juniper, and on the higher ground, the pinyon pine, Douglas fir and ponderosa pine.

The name of these mountains, "Chisos," is hard to translate. Part Indian, part Spanish, it carries the idea of ghostly wonder or enchantment in and out of both languages. And these mountains speak the mystery that surrounds Big Bend National Park.

Looking south from their south rim, a visitor knows in his mind that he is looking towards Mexico, but in the clear bright air and the isolated silence of a seemingly never-ending distance his heart begins to feel that he is looking over the edge of the world itself. He feels for just a moment on the edge of time itself so that, as a local saying has it, standing here on the side of the mountains of mystery, "on a clear day, you can see clear into the day after tomorrow."

Flowers begin to bloom in the lowlands in late February but do not reach the mountain heights until May. Spring also brings occasional "northers," sudden storms that bring chill winds and often dust. The mountains are particularly attractive in the summer when temperatures in the desert and valley hover around one hundred degrees. With the end of autumn—warm, gentle and delicately colored—comes the sparkling clean air of winter. Once or twice a year snow comes to the mountains, but usually in winter the heights are merely brisk while the canyons remain comfortably warm during the day.

The river and mountains have given the park three large canyons. Boquillas (*Little Mouth*) is where the river cuts the Sierra del Carmen in two. In some places it cuts with the stroke of a butcher's cleaver that slices the rock straight down to the water's edge, and in other places it hacks with hatchet chops that send chips of sand and tangles of willow a few feet up the bank.

But up river in the Santa Elena Canyon the Rio cuts the walls of the Grand Puerta (*Great Door*) with a 1,500-foot slash of its knife edge.

The third canyon, Mariscal (*Marshall*), is most remote, most difficult to reach, and most rewarding. Mariscal allows only boatmen to explore its limestone walls and view the fossilized remains of animals who lived in those distant ages of the deep past of our earth—times that still seem close beside the traveler within the remote and mystic silence, the emptiness and untouched grandeur that is Big Bend National Park.

The century plant, which, contrary to its name, blooms in a decade, stands before the Chisos Mountains in Green Gulch.

GUADALUPE MOUNTAINS NATIONAL PARK

In the middle of the Chihuahuan desert of southwestern Texas is an "island in the sky." One-quarter of the Guadalupe Mountain Range dips across the New Mexico border here, only a few miles southwest of Carlsbad Caverns National Park. These uplands contain a startling diversity of flora and fauna in an unusual mountain-desert setting, and it is fitting that, in 1966, Congress designated them as the nation's thirty-third national park.

The most notable feature of the Guadalupes is Y-shaped McKittrick Canyon—a deep cut in the northeastern mountains which embraces a unique, balanced ecosystem. Here the vegetation ranges from desert scrub to forests of pine, fir and juniper.

A wide variety of birdlife coexists with coyotes, foxes and bobcats which prey on various rabbits and rodents. Elk, mule deer and pronghorns drink from the self-replenishing streams and springs, and wild turkeys and quail dodge through the brush. A few blue-throated hummingbirds—a rare and endangered species—and spotted owls exist here, but there are also many varieties of birds common in distant sections of North America which are geographically isolated in this national park, including water ouzels, bandtailed pigeons and brown creepers. This area also once supported desert bighorns and wolves, but they among other species have been driven out, and black bears, mountain lions and golden eagles are now few in number. But McKittrick Canyon is still unsullied, for its high, precipitous walls and narrow canyon have fortunately discouraged "development" by man.

The park has many other fascinating features. Forming a V-shaped wedge pointing south and taking up a large portion of the park is a Permian marine limestone reef. Laid down in shallow coastal waters 280 to 290 million years ago, it is identified as one of the largest exposed fossil reefs in the world. At the point of the "V" is El Capitan, a sheer, thousand-foot cliff visible for over fifty miles. Nearby is the highest point in Texas, 8,751-foot Guadalupe Peak. Just inside the V-shaped highlands, and a part of McKittrick Canyon, is The Bowl, a 670-acre relict forest containing dense stands of ponderosa pine, limber pine and Douglas fir with a thick undergrowth. This small forest is very sensitive to environmental changes.

Archeological and historical remains document man's past activities in the region. Ancient cooking pits attest to the habitation of prehistoric peoples, and in the eastern part of the park are the ruins of Butterfield Stage station, which was a part of the famous Pony Express that preceded the railroads.

Climatic differences at Guadalupe are remarkable. Summer temperatures may be exceedingly hot at lower elevations while the mountain fastnesses are deliciously cool. Fierce summer thunderstorms often cause destructive flash floods, and in autumn, McKittrick Canyon is beautifully colored with the varied tints of its hardwood foliage.

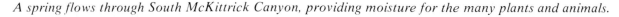

A spring flows through South McKittrick Canyon, providing moisture for the many plants and animals.

CASCADE CATHEDRALS
The Pacific Northwest

Sahale Ridge, North Cascades National Park, Washington

Crowning the Northwest, the Cascades form a gigantic precious gem in the diadem of our country's natural beauty. The Cascades majestically intercept the clouds fleeing east on the forceful Pacific breezes and drop their contents on ancient slopes, infinities of green forests, and jagged seashore cliffs. Some overwhelmingly huge facets of the gem seem particularly unpolished yet all the more intriguing, like Mounts Olympic and Rainier, with spectacles of ice lacing their surfaces.

OLYMPIC NATIONAL PARK

At Olympic National Park, in Washington, the civilization of man defers almost totally to the civilization of the tree. Amid these thousands of acres of mountain and coastal wilderness, 50 miles wide and 200 miles in circumference, the tropical-like luxuriance of rain forests vies in beauty and splendor with the majestic eminence of an immense conifer empire on primeval coasts and on the flanks of soaring peaks.

Such is man's deferment to this almost preternatural infinitude of green—the hushed, eternal realm of the Sitka spruce, Western hemlock, Douglas fir and red cedar, among others—that park trail crews often cut narrow, wandering foot trails through the wilderness. In the forest depths abound the natural civilization of wildlife and wildflowers—the animals, birds, and both familiar and exotic blooms, which flourish in a protective privacy redolent of the legendary preserves of Adam and Eve.

Fifty-six species of wild mammals inhabit Olympic park, with some of their more migratory marine members ranging from season to season along the coastline from Alaska, through British Columbia and Washington State, to Lower California, over a distance of four thousand miles. Around six thousand "Roosevelt" elk (also called American elk or wapiti) live in the park and can be glimpsed moving toward

the high country in the summer. More prominent residents also include the black-tailed deer and Olympic marmot, with mountain goat, bear, raccoon, mink, otter and mountain beaver quick and alive to the alert glance of the amateur naturalist. About 140 kinds of birds await the reverence and keen eye of the "watchers" with eagles, ravens and hawks more discernible along the wild seacoast and among the craggy heights of the park.

Riots of wildflowers carpet the alpine meadows around Mount Olympus, 7,965 feet high, and the other peaks, several of which rise above seven thousand feet. Of Olympic park's wildflower life E. B. Webster said in his book, *The Friendly Mountain:* "Flowers of every shape and hue. Flowers standing shoulder to shoulder, as thick as daisies in a pasture, or clover in the field. Red columbine, yellow and blue asters, scarlet paintbrushes, blue lupine, white valerian . . . all thrown together in one gorgeous blanket of thoroughly mixed color."

The Strait of Juan de Fuca separates the park area from Canada. In 1774 the Spanish sea captain Juan Perez sailed through these waters of splendor, discovering the Olympic Mountains and originally calling them El Cerro de la Santa Rosalia. It remained for Capt. John Meares of Great Britain to explore

Olympic (left) presents two distinct topographical faces to the visitor— glacier formed mountains and rugged sea coast. Maritime fog climbs to the steep sides of snow-crowned Bailey Range (above) near the Strait of Juan de Fuca.

233

*In Olympic, the highest amount of annual rainfall in the United States creates
yellow-green rain forests, a unique combination of towering conifers,
smaller moss-covered vine maples, swordlike ferns and soft ground cover.*

the area in 1778 during which he named the highest peak "Mount Olympus," a designation later charted by Capt. George Vancouver.

Pacific Ocean tides break, ebb and flow against the park's western shoreline. Eastward, Puget Sound and Hood Canal form the added gift of isolation, separating, with saltwater barriers, the peninsula and mainland of Washington State.

Along the fascinating shores, isolated conifers, twisted and misshapen, dot the shorelines. Then the fragmented shore, the home of the seal and wildfowl life of the sea, yields to sheer cliffs, fog-shrouded or sparkling in the sun, depending upon the day's weather. This massive moisture-channeling, aided by 142 inches of annual rainfall, nourishes, on the western side, the finest remains of the Pacific Northwest rain forests.

The overwhelming impression of the rain forest is in Andrew Marvell's phrase: "a green lamp in a green shade." Or as one park service man said: "When one is inside the forest and the sun comes out, it is like being inside a giant emerald." Here, giant cone-bearing trees rise to nearly three hundred feet above the forest floor. Red alders and black cottonwoods edge the stream banks where cutthroat, rainbow and brook trout thrive and steelhead seek the secluded streams in winter.

The lordly conifers dominate the realm, but here in the rain forest, the lesser fiefdoms of the tree kingdom are big-leaved and slender vine maples, burdened into arches by heavy veils of clubmoss. Most of this subsidiary civilization of the tree flourishes in openings under the dense conifer canopy. In the valleys of the Hoh, Quinault and Queets rivers, the wondrous renewal process of future growth continues interminably as spongy, rotting undergrowth returns the nutrients to the soil where new tree life is nourished.

The disappearance of the great rain forests, which once covered a coastal area from northern California to southern Alaska, highlights the preciousness of this magnificent "remnant" in Olympic National Park. It is almost as if a splendid tropical jungle lies at the foot of the more typically Northwestern snow-covered peaks which pierce the clouds at elevations of 3,000 to 8,000 feet. Majestic Mount Olympus dominates the uplands where more than sixty glaciers grow and recede, and these twenty-five square miles of ice hone down the mountains in the slow, eternal movement of time.

This mountainous interior lay unexplored until the winter of 1889-1890 when James H. Christie led the *Seattle Press* Expedition on the first crossing from Port Angeles to the Pacific Ocean. That summer Lt.

A common American wildflower, the tiger lily, finds an alpine home for its orange blossoms in a meadow at Hurricane Ridge.

Deep crevices ridge Blue Glacier, creating a spectacular setting for cross-ice pack hikes by seasoned climbers.

Joseph P. O'Neil led another expedition, crossing the mountains from Hood Canal to the Pacific.

Lt. O'Neil was the first to propose that the mountains would "serve admirably for a national park." A first step occurred in 1897 when President Cleveland created the Olympic Forest Reserve. A portion of the reserve was set aside as Mount Olympus National Monument by that champion of outdoor life, President Theodore Roosevelt, in 1909. The long struggle for the permanent preservation of this vast retreat of nature ended on June 29, 1938, when Olympic National Park was established under another Roosevelt, F.D.R. Further land additions were made in 1940, 1943 and 1953, expanding the park to its authorized expanse of nearly 1,400 square miles.

The park enjoys its most favorable weather in the summer and early autumn. Although impassable snows close the higher elevations from late fall to early spring, a road is kept open, Christmas through March, from Port Angeles to the weekend ski area at Hurricane Ridge. The high-country roads and trails are usually free of snow by July.

The park's many peaks challenge both the experienced and amateur mountain climber. During June, July and August, when all fourteen roads that enter the park are open, hikers and horsemen explore more than six hundred miles of trails except for portions of high country where barriers of immutable snow confront the venturesome.

This is Olympic Park, a gigantic, precious gem in the diadem of America's natural beauty, stretching from coast to coast. Here, still, the conifer is supreme, symbolized by the royal Sitka spruce, with needles hard and sharp as steel, sentinel of mountain and sea, spilling the wind in a sustained whisper, or twanging its branches in the brunt of the sea blast.

A young mule deer stands at attention in the evergreen forests of the Cascades, sometimes called the American Alps.

NORTH CASCADES NATIONAL PARK

Warm breath freezes in the wet coldness of the dark morning, as the mountains await the sun's heat. From the east, the first rays of the coming day edge over the vast land forms, and one by one the dawn's fingers touch the great peaks, illuminating their snow with a pink, then orange, and finally white light. The mists on the upper peaks begin to break and slowly dissipate, and the full majesty of these mountains comes into view.

To hike these valleys and climb the peaks is one of the most rewarding mountaineering adventures in North America. Montana's Glacier National Park and the Grand Tetons of Wyoming have their glories, but the vast rock cathedrals of Washington's northern Cascades have a scope and grandeur all their own.

Sometimes called the American Alps, these peaks, valleys and lakes sculpted by huge glaciers are con-sidered by many outdoorsmen to be the most scenic mountain wilderness in the conterminous U. S.

The Cascade Range stretches from British Colum-bia to northern California, but the North Cascades in Washington contain more spectacular scenery than any other section. Geologically, this mountain range has an unusual history. The first, or "dawn" Cas-cades, rose from the sea and were completely eroded away within a time span of eons. Then the ocean reflooded the area until about fifteen million years ago when earth convulsions raised the land once again. Erosion stripped these new mountains of their ocean sediment and about one million years ago, more earth movements broke the Cascades along fault lines and lifted the mountains even higher. Then vast ice fields reshaped the land again as three, possibly four, large glacial systems formed in the

Mount Shuksan (above) thrusts its 9,038-foot height above the autumn foliage at Picture Lake. The craggy peaks of the Chilliwack and Pickets ranges (opposite, top) reach above the misty clouds. Mount Redoubt, near the Canadian border, is in the foreground.

mountains and moved down the valleys, creating the jagged peaks, U-shaped valleys and sheer cliffs that can be seen today.

The high mountains intercept some of the wettest prevailing Pacific Ocean winds. Their heavy precipitation has produced a region of hanging glaciers, icefalls, ice caps, hanging valleys, waterfalls and alpine lakes nestled in glacial cirques. There are about 318 glaciers, most of which are stable or slightly retreating, and numerous snowfields within the North Cascades complex, which includes the north and south units of the park and Ross Lake and Lake Chelan national recreation areas—over a thousand square miles of mountain wilderness.

Over 130 alpine lakes dot the landscape and innumerable streams and creeks rush down the mountainsides, forming graceful waterfalls. Lake Chelan near Stehekin occupies a glacial trough exceeding 8,500 feet in depth, one of the deepest gorges on the continent. Fifty-five miles long and one to two miles wide, it has all the features of a Norwegian fjord.

Rain and an average of 516 inches of snow fall on the west side of the Cascades annually for a total of 110 inches of precipitation. On the drier, eastern slopes, however, the precipitation averages only thirty-four inches. The Cascade Range is thus responsible for the semiarid plains of eastern Washington.

Naturally there is extreme variation in plant communities between the moisture-laden west side and the dry east slopes. From western rain forests, the vegetation changes to subalpine conifers, verdant meadows and alpine tundra, and then to eastern pine forests and sunny, dry shrublands. The valleys and mountains below the timberline are covered with dense strands of huge Douglas firs, tall hemlocks and Western red cedars, Engelmann and Sitka spruce, ponderosa and lodgepole pines and silver firs. Mixed

A boat moves across the waters of Diablo Lake, whose setting resembles a Norwegian fjord.

with the conifers are many deciduous trees—alders, maples, willows and cottonwoods, among others. In the wet valleys on the western slopes, moss grows so profusely that it hangs from the trees.

The most colorful time of year in the high country is July when fields of red, white and yellow heather tint the slopes, mixing with the showy beargrass, and the yellow blossoms of skunk cabbage adorn the marshes around glacial lakes. Glacier lilies poke through the melting snow, phlox bursts into color in the meadows, and dogwood and chokecherry trees give the lower forests some added spring color. In summer whole fields of ripe blueberries await the wilderness gourmet on the high slopes. Tiny, fragile alpine wildflowers grow from every small bit of soil in the rocky uplands and tundras.

Bounding among these tiny flowers and jumping from rock to rock are numerous mountain goats. Black-tailed and mule deer are also present, along with foxes, black bears and coyotes. Though not plentiful, cougars, or mountain lions, have found parts of this wilderness isolated enough from civilization to live peacefully. Among the smaller animals are snowshoe hares, cottontails, aplodontia (mountain beavers), pikas, marmots, porcupines, weasels, beavers and a number of varieties of mice.

Waterfowl is plentiful with mallards, teals, widgeons, geese and goldeneyes sharing the lakes and ponds. Ptarmigan and grouse scurry through the underbrush, and various kinds of hawks and owls prey on the small animal population. In winter large numbers of bald eagles can be seen along the Skagit River feeding on salmon. The sounds of the Cascades' birdlife are varied with common loons and great blue herons adding their shrill calls to the singing of swallows, chickadees, nuthatches, wrens, robins, thrushes, warblers and sparrows.

Over 340 miles of hiking trails provide access to this scenic wilderness. Trails lead to many of the main vistas, such as Mounts Shuksan, Logan and Challenger, the Stehekin and Cascade rivers, Eldorado Peak, Cascade Pass and others. For hikers, numerous back-country campsites are available, and for boaters, several boat-in campgrounds are maintained on lakes Chelan, Ross and Diablo. There are also some developed, roadside campgrounds in Ross Lake National Recreation Area, and several other camps in surrounding Okanogan and Mount Baker national forests.

State Highway 20 follows the Skagit River into Ross Lake recreation area, which separates the north and south units of the park, and regularly scheduled boat runs are taken between Chelan and Stehekin on Lake Chelan at the southern edge of the complex. The most dramatic views, looking over thousands of square miles of snow, glaciated wilderness peaks and deep green valleys, are available only to hardy hikers from selected ridge vantage points. Reaching such overlooks is a challenging test for mountain climbers and high trail hikers.

The park presently covers only an area originally recommended by a Government study team in 1963, and some conservationists are still arguing that the park should be enlarged further.

Supreme Court Justice William O. Douglas, who has hiked this region for a long lifetime, has written, "The wilderness of the North Cascades is a national resource of the future, not merely a local commodity, and we need it all, as a nation." This park of towering, craggy ice mountains, flashing streams and waterfalls, blue alpine lakes, forested valleys, colorful flowers and abundant wildlife is, by any test, one of the crowning gems of the National Park System.

Moisture-laden clouds sweep in changing patterns over Mount Rainier which stands in the pale colors of dusk.

MOUNT RAINIER NATIONAL PARK

Rainier stands like a silent sentinel over the Cascade Range, a color covering of blue and green and tones of gray, clad in the white cap of cold and age, a garment which belies its fiery parentage.

The mountain soars above the Cascade Mountains of west-central Washington, rising 14,410 feet above sea level, her size so ponderous she covers a quarter of the national park's almost 380 square miles.

Deep, green stands of trees, alpine lakes, the diamond-tipped rush of icy water crashing over smooth boulders, delicate flowers hidden in shady glens, sprawling wildflower meadows — all are subdued by the spectacle of ice, laced like a child's finger painting across the faces of Mount Rainier. It has the greatest expanse of glaciers — about forty in number — found in the United States outside of Alaska.

Rainier, part of that once-spectacular circle of volcanic activity which rings the Pacific from the Americas to Asia, was not always so placid, so gently touched or so green. Volcanic eruptions flowed lava upon lava, cinders upon ash, until the mountain grew with a fury nuclear energy cannot match. The Cascades to the east were created in the

same manner, but Rainier retains more than a casual birthmark. At the summit are three peaks: Columbia Crest to the east, then two smaller but obvious volcanic craters. The summit crater on Columbia Crest retains small vents which whisper steam into the thin air, melting the snow which lies about.

Now Rainier is quiet. Time, water and glaciers have worn great canyons and raised ridges along its once-smooth sides, and glaciers now spread across its body, square mile after square mile of slowly flowing ice, an active reminder of the natural forces which helped shape much of our landscape today.

The water is the beginning of the various forms of natural life, irrigating lowland forests and alpine meadows. Douglas firs, Western hemlocks and red cedars tower above the brown-needled floor where beams of sunlight break through and give life to Oregon grape, western sword fern, bunchberry, dogwood and soft, green mosses.

Beyond the forests lie patches of green meadows, threaded by foot trails and sprinkled with a rolling panorama of wildflowers: the avalanche fawnlily, yellow lambstongue fawnlily, Western pasque-flower,

marsh marigold and mountain buttercup bursting into bloom with the last snow melting. The Indian paintbrush, spikes of lupine, speedwell, valerian and American bistort fill the voids in August when the seeds of the spring flowers have been sown by the four winds to bloom again another year.

Apparently oblivious to Mount Rainier are the birds, 130 species of them, and half a hundred mammals—mule deer, black bears, elk and mountain goats, raccoons, squirrels and chipmunks—feeding in this horn of quiet plenty.

High above are plants stunted by the cold and elevation, grasping rocks, with their roots seeking paper-thin fissures that nourishment might be found. The visitor here has taken a botanical "trip" far into Canada, for Hudson Bay is where this flora is generally displayed.

The snow which feeds Mount Rainier's glaciers originates as clouds over the Pacific Ocean. As the moisture-laden, westerly winds move inland, the first barrier they meet is the Cascade Range. Rising to pass over the mountains, they are cooled, and the condensing moisture falls as rain and snow. The heaviest precipitation falls on the windward slope, especially between five and ten thousand feet. Paradise Park receives about one hundred inches in a year.

For all its beauty, Rainier must have been a forbidding scene to the Indians, since none of the dozen nations that visited the region is believed to have established permanent settlements. The mountain, an object of worship to some, was a hunting ground for others.

Clouds and fog often obscure the mountain. There is, however, usually warm, clear weather from about July 1 to mid-September. In many years, Indian summer weather continues well into October, when autumn colors bring out still another kind of quality possessed by this magnificent mountain and the land that surrounds it.

A rocky hiking trail winding up Pinnacle Peak offers a view of 14,410-foot Mount Rainier.

Overleaf: *From Sunrise, the mountain looms skyward.*

243

Wizard Island, situated in Crater Lake, is actually a volcano within a volcano. The caldera holding Crater Lake was formed when the volcanic cone of Mount Mazama collapsed. Visitors can climb into the crater of Wizard Island.

CRATER LAKE
NATIONAL PARK

A quarrel between two mighty Indian gods created Oregon's Crater Lake—so goes the lore of the local prehistoric Indians who tell us that the earth collapsed to a depth of almost two thousand feet, forming the circular lake's basin, because of a raging struggle between "chief of the world above" and "chief of the world below."

The myth, not quite as old as the actual geological earth movement of seven thousand years ago, which carved out the second deepest lake in the Western Hemisphere, tells us that the underworld deity retreated below just as the chief of the upper regions let fall a mountain top on any possible exit to the surface.

Yet science more factually hypothesizes that predecessors of the Indian myth-makers may have seen the collapse of volcanic Mount Mazama, thousands of years ago, and built their myth, like most myths, on a residue of fact.

Crater Lake, astride the Cascade Range, thence gathered to itself the snows and rains of centuries, tinged gradually into the vast and stunning royal blue of its present setting.

It is said that the lake has only two seasons: an eight-month, snow-shrouded winter and an Edenlike two-month summer. But there is a brief snow-melting spring, and a haunting, chill-touched momentary fall. Yet, in all seasons, there endures the onslaught of arboreal beauty with hemlock, fir and pine clothing the pumiced slopes in varied shades of green, dappling the warm tones of summer and richly dotting winter's wide, white mantle.

Mount Scott, highest point in the park at 8,926 feet, commands the eastern side of the lake and overlooks blue waters twenty square miles in area. Multicolored canyon-like walls, 500 to 2,000 feet high, surround the crater depths of water, their heights majestic with conifers and bleak with sporadic barren surfaces.

The Pinnacles, near the eastern boundary, also contribute to the mute but striking evidence of earth forces that here wrought violence in the Olympian shaping of the now serene landscape.

John Wesley Hillman recalled, many years later, his initial encounter with Crater Lake on June 12, 1853. Only twenty-one, he was perhaps the first white man to look upon Deep Blue Lake, as his party of exploration chose to call it. His recollection: "It is really an impossibility to describe this lake as I first viewed it. The vast loneliness of the place, the sparkling water so many feet below, the beautiful

The Phantom Ship, with 175-foot spires, "floats" in the second deepest lake in this hemisphere, Crater Lake.

view of the whole thing are all too great to be described; one must see them to appreciate them."

Others followed Hillman, but not until 1869 did visitors from Jacksonville give the vast volcanic repository of handsome waters its present name.

William Gladstone Steel is outstanding among the lake's subsequent admirers. He came, for the first of many visits, to the brink on August 15, 1885. A six-day sojourn lengthened into a lifetime rendezvous. On one trip, in 1888, Steel was inspired to comment: "Standing alone, like a sentinel on the mountains of the Far West, (Crater Lake) looks down on the sleeping grandeur about it and is unique in all the world. The day is coming when the people of all nations will

gather to view its grandeur, then return to their homes to wonder that such things can be."

This indeed was a prophecy, aided and abetted by his own dedication and labors. Leader of the seventeen year campaign to create a national park, he achieved this goal when, on May 22, 1902, President Theodore Roosevelt signed the bill conferring on the wondrous waters their present status. Will Steel, later superintendent and U.S. commissioner for the park, has since been informally and gratefully called: "Father of Crater Lake National Park."

Thus was the immortal blue of Crater Lake preserved for the beneficence of mortal man and his posterity.

OREGON CAVES
NATIONAL MONUMENT

Oregon Caves National Monument is on the slopes of Mount Elijah, a peak of almost 6,400 feet in the Siskiyou Mountains of southwestern Oregon. Although long called Oregon Caves, it is in fact a single marble cavern consisting of an intricate complex of corridors. The main entrance is the northernmost and lowest point in the cave at an elevation of four thousand feet. The chambers in the southern regions of the cave are at considerably higher levels.

Located between the Rogue and Klamath rivers, the area is a transitional one between the California mountains and the Northwest evergreen forest. The region usually receives several feet of snow each winter.

Elijah J. Davidson discovered Oregon Cave in 1874 while in pursuit of a bear, and explorers were soon attracted to the cavern. Frank M. Nickerson found four different levels and opened several galleries blocked by stalactites. He served as a part owner of the cave and guide for several years. Joaquin Miller, the "poet of the Sierras," visited the cave in 1907 with a party that included Chandler B. Watson, a geologist. Miller made the cave so well known through his writings that it was established as a national monument in 1909.

The formation of the cave covers a vast period of geologic time. A shallow arm of the ancient ocean that covered the area 180 million years ago deposited a thick bed of calcium carbonate which later hardened into limestone. The intense heat and pressure created during the periods of mountain building transformed the limestone into marble, and it was raised above the sea as part of a mountain range. The uplifting process that formed the mountains fractured the marble in many places, and even though the openings along these fractures may have been relatively small, they allowed the passage of water. Groundwater, charged with acids from decaying vegetation, dissolved the marble.

The later stage of cave development began as streams in the region cut their valleys deeper and the water table gradually fell below the level of the caverns. They were drained, allowing the entrance of air. The resulting process of natural deposition created the decorative beauty that fascinates today's visitor. Drops of water reached the caverns and evaporated into the air, leaving minute deposits of calcium carbonate. Where the drops dripped slowly from the ceiling, stalactites were formed; where water fell to the floor, stalagmites were built up. Imperceptibly, this deposition process continues today for Oregon Cave is literally a "live" cave.

The myriad of shapes found in the cavern have caused many of the galleries to bear highly descrip-

Milky white deposits of calcium carbonate have coalesced to form this structure known as The White House.

tive names. Passageway of the Whale is a fine example of an enlarged crevice. The Wigwam Room has a formation called Chief Rain-in-the-Face. In the Banana Grove and Potato Patch is flowstone drapery that resembles bunches of bananas. Niagara Falls provides an example of cascading flowstone.

Life in the cave is not abundant but rabbits are frequently seen, and a ringtail or foot-long Pacific giant salamander wanders in occasionally. But of course the only mammals truly at home here are the eight species of bats. One of them is the Western lump-nosed bat, also called the long-eared bat. During hibernation it curls its large ears in spirals and folds them down against its neck, perhaps to reduce water loss from the thin membrane of the ears.

Guide service in the cave is furnished by a concessioner. Children under six are not permitted in the cave but a nursery is available. There are no facilities for camping or picnicking.

Joaquin Miller's "marble halls of Oregon," in their setting high on the slopes of the Siskiyous, easily live up to their reputation as being one of the most unusual caves in the entire West.

White clouds complement the curve of a black cinder cone which rises above the lava beds.

LAVA BEDS NATIONAL MONUMENT

From a distance the land looks fairly level, dotted in places with symmetrical cinder cones and craters. But closer examination reveals that the "level" blackness is extremely rough, jagged and rocky, for this is where the earth vented its anger thousands of years ago. California's Lava Beds National Monument, near the Oregon border midway between Lassen Volcanic and Crater Lake national parks, is unique among volcanic areas because no large volcano existed here; all the formations were caused by many small holes in the earth's crust.

The eruptions that took place here were of two types—the more common gaseous type which created the cinder cones and the fissure type, where great masses of thick, *pahoehoe* lava flowed like molasses from deep cracks in the ground. Rivers of molten lava streamed across the region, the outer material cooling and hardening more quickly than the interior, forming a crusty shell or tube through which the hotter matter continued to flow. When the eruptions ceased, the lava shells were emptied, leaving large tunnels or caves. About three hundred of these lava tubes have been found in the monument, and many more are believed to exist. Many of the cave roofs have collapsed in places to form serpentlike natural trenches 20 to 100 feet deep and 50 to 250 feet wide, with narrow bridges occasionally arching over them.

As the lava flow in the crusty tubes diminished, the cooling lava splashed against the ceilings, creating lava stalactites ("lava-cicles") and some of them were also formed when hot gases remelted pieces of the shell. Rivulets of lava on the walls of the tubes hardened into ribs.

Many of the caves are quite large and contain unusual formations. Catacombs Cave on the paved Cave Loop Road in the southern part of the monument is so named because of the niches in the walls,

which resemble the Christian burial caves of ancient Rome. Nearby Sentinel Cave was named for the stone figures which guard its passageway.

Many of the caves are so deep that the cold winter air does not have a chance to warm during summer, and groundwater seeping into the caves freezes. Two of the most spectacular ice caves are Merrill Ice Cave, which contains a frozen waterfall, and Frozen River Cave (not open to the public) named for a sheet of ice five to six feet thick and several hundred feet long.

The smooth, black cinder cones, about seventeen in number, rise from one hundred to over five hundred feet above the lava beds. Many small spatter cones can be seen on the beds, and some of them form deep holes resembling chimneys from the earth's hot core. One such hole, Fleener Chimneys, near the main road, is only three feet in diameter but 130 feet deep.

Plant life among these black lava beds is unexpectedly colorful. During spring and summer about 250 species of wildflowers, including purple sage, scarlet Indian paintbrush and blue wild flax, grow wherever there is sufficient soil. Scattered large spots of green in the beds are juniper, ponderosa pine, wild current, antelope bitterbrush and mountain mahogany. Colorful lichens adorn the rocks in all seasons.

Rocky Mountain mule deer, coyotes, foxes, skunks, weasels and badgers live in the monument area, as do cougars, bobcats and pronghorn antelope, although they are rarely seen.

The National Park Service has developed a campground in the headquarters area and a picnic ground at Fleener Chimneys for the use of visitors at Lava Beds National Monument. This grim and rugged landscape should be visited; it conjures up thoughts of other planets.

GRANITE DOMES AND PACIFIC SHORES
The Sierras to The Sea

High Sierra Wilderness Area, Sequoia National Forest, California

A vast tilted block on the earth where snowcapped peaks lie untouched and protected, the Sierra Nevada Range has a romantic and timeless appeal. In the wilderness dotted with glacial lakes mirroring the sun and its surroundings, one can hear the awesome crash of water plummeting down to distant pools, as well as the pastoral silence of flower-flocked meadowlands and cool deep woods. Around the ancient granite domes stand some of the world's oldest and largest living things, the sequoias. West of the mountains, a great variety of shoreland meets the ocean — rough, craggy palisades and sandy beaches which receive the full brunt of Pacific currents.

REDWOOD NATIONAL PARK

Along the coast of northern California stand some of the oldest living things on earth. In this redwood country there are groves of giant trees which were growing during the Golden Age of ancient Greece.

In order to save as many of these groves as possible for posterity, conservationists in 1918 formed the Save-the-Redwoods League and began a campaign for a national park in northern California. Exactly fifty years later, in 1968—after a series of stormy battles—their goal was finally realized. Embracing fifty-seven thousand acres of redwoods, bluffs and beaches, Redwood National Park also includes thirty continuous miles of beautiful California coastline. Within the boundaries are three state parks—Jedediah Smith Redwoods, Del Norte Coast Redwoods and Prairie Creek Redwoods—created earlier through the efforts of the Save-The-Redwoods League. These areas have been transferred to the park service and become integral parts of the national park.

Once growing the entire length of the Pacific coast from Oregon to the Big Sur peninsula, coast redwoods are now confined to relatively small areas, and some of these last groves are being logged as these words are written. There are also private landholdings within the park itself which will be logged unless they are added to the park; one hopes these areas will also be preserved in the near future to protect the ecology of the fragile watersheds.

The redwood is a living relict of the past. Redwood fossils have been found in Texas, Pennsylvania, Wyoming and even along the Bering Sea in Alaska. Redwoods once grew in Europe until an ice sheet forced them into the Mediterranean. In central China there are hundreds of what are called Dawn Redwoods, deciduous redwoods that have survived millions of years of floods, fires, droughts and ice.

The coast redwood's scientific name is *Sequoia sempervirens*. Sequoia comes from the Cherokee Indian, Sequoyah, who invented an Indian alphabet and taught his people to read and write; *sempervirens* means evergreen. Its close relative, the Sierra redwood *(Sequoia gigantea),* found in Sequoia and Yosemite national parks, is larger in girth and much older, but *sempervirens* is taller. The foliage of the *gigantea* resembles that of juniper, while the *sempervirens's* foliage is more like hemlock. The bark of the Sierra tree is a bright sienna, while the coast version's bark is a dull chocolate. Curiously *semper-*

viren's cones are only one-third the size of its cousin's to the east.

The park's area can be roughly divided into four main ecosystems. The redwood forest ecosystem is a special plant community adapted to the drainage, soil, relatively moderate temperatures and the abundant rain and fog found here—an annual rainfall of a hundred inches is not uncommon. Dominated by the large coast redwood, this ecosystem has an understory thick with smaller trees and shrubs, including flowering rhododendron, huckleberry, salmonberry and azalea. The forest floor, deep with redwood needles and other natural litter, is often out of sight under a cover of ferns. Where the duff is drier and the forest crown more open, acres of the floor are taken over by wildflowers—oxalis, wild iris, purple and yellow violets, white trilliums, and redwood and Olympia lilies.

Numerous streams provide a variation in plant life. Inland forest borders are dry from May through October and consequently have different kinds of vegetation, especially oaks and alders. Along the coast, moisture is so abundant that the redwoods must share the ground with hemlock, spruce, fir and cedar.

Wildlife is plentiful. One of the last surviving California herds of Roosevelt elk can be seen in the open meadows or on the coast. Also present are black-tailed deer, squirrels, foxes, bobcats, chipmunks, raccoons, beavers and river otters. Birds include Steller's jays, grouse, pileated woodpeckers, Western robins and various kinds of thrushes. The streams support a large population of salmon and trout.

The north coastal scrub ecosystem takes over as the forest thins on approaches to the cliffs and scoops in the coastline. This narrow strip is influenced by almost constant salty winds, rocky soils and poor drainage. Low-growing trees, woody shrubs and herbaceous plants dominate here.

The marine and shore ecosystem is fairy typical of the Pacific Northwest Coast. Offshore rocks are havens for seabirds, seals and sea lions, and migrating whales are often observed near the coast. Tidepools and saltwater and freshwater marshes have abundant animal life, and the sandy beaches and dunes are constantly renewed by the ocean's currents.

The cutover forest is a severely damaged redwood forest ecosystem and represents a drastic and sudden change in the once thriving redwood forest. The

Walking among the towering redwood trees, living relics of the past, is a unique and memorable experience.

Del Norte Coast Redwoods State Park, a beautiful meeting of land and sea, is one of three areas preserved by the Save-the-Redwoods League before the group succeeded in having the national park established.

effects of heavy logging and subsequent erosion of the land have created new conditions for plant and animal life. In theory, such areas will go through a succession of changes and will result hundreds of years hence in a different redwood forest ecosystem.

Notable individual features of the national park include the Tall Trees area along Redwood Creek where the world's tallest tree, 368 feet high, grows. An easy eight-mile-long trail leads to the Tall Trees from nearby U.S. Highway 101.

In Prairie Creek Redwoods State Park, Home Creek has cut through the bluffs, forming Fern Canyon, named for the five-fingered ferns and mosses that cover the canyon's fifty-foot high walls.

Highway 101 is the main route in the national park. Each state park is developed with campgrounds, picnic areas, visitor centers and hiking trails, and campgrounds are also found in adjacent Six Rivers National Forest.

At the signing of the bill authorizing Redwood National Park in 1968, President Lyndon Johnson stated, "The Redwoods will stand because men of vision and courage made their stand, refusing to suffer . . . any greater damage to our environment. . . . I believe this act of establishing a Redwood National Park in California will stand for all time as a monument to the wisdom of our generation."

Bumpass Hell, where steam rises from boiling mudpots, indicates that Lassen may be dormant but not extinct.

LASSEN VOLCANIC NATIONAL PARK

In the order of nature, often where there is chaos, great beauty is nearby.

This seems to be particularly true of the lush, sylvan beauty that neighbors on volcanoes in Italy, the South Sea Islands, South America and, in our own country, Lassen Volcanic National Park of northeastern California. For where volcanoes are, active or inactive, the slopes and lowlands of the tumultuous mountains are usually rich with the resources that satisfy the physical and spiritual needs of man: food and drink for his body, shelter for his family.

Lassen Peak, once called San Jose by Spanish explorers, is now an inactive plug dome volcano. But it was once considered the only active volcano in the United States, having erupted as recently as 1914 and 1915, remaining fire-breathing and occasionally rumbling until 1921.

The 10,457-foot peak was the habitat and wonderment of four tribes of Indians long before Spaniard Luis Arguillo discovered it in 1821. This once fierce, lava spewing mountain in the Cascade Range, not far from the Sierra Nevada, served as a territorial monument, dividing the regions of the Atsugewi, Maidu, Yana and Yahi, who foraged in its vicinity and lived in harmony around its slopes. In the park, also, the true American natives must have known the fearsome majesty of other volcanic heights now called Cinder Cone, Bumpass Hell and Devils Kitchen.

Now, as then, coniferous forests, flower-blanketed mountain meadows, sun-glinting and tree-shadowy lakes and streams characterize the 165-square-mile area. Deer are abundant in the fields of summer; over 150 species of birds beautify the foliage; golden-mantled ground squirrels, chipmunks, red squirrels and bears are permanent tenants.

The view from Lassen Park Road, extending from the southwestern to northwestern corner of the park, and half encircling the base of Lassen Peak, is stunningly comprehensive. Yet the leisurely assimilation of the park's beauty and bizarre landmarks appeals more to the view from behind a walking stick than through an automobile windshield. It is a hiker's and camper's park, demanding the effort, and offering scenic rewards not accessible to the automobile. The 150 miles of trails are highlighted by the path which leads to Bumpass Hell, a sixteen acre tract of boiling, sulphurous springs, named after K. V. Bumpass who discovered it in 1864.

The peak, the park, the surrounding national forest and a county — all are named after Peter Lassen, a Danish immigrant blacksmith, who familiarized himself and others with the area in the 1830's. He early acquired a large parcel of land at Vina, California. During the Gold Rush he guided migrants across these mountains from the East, into the Sacramento Valley. He used the peak as a storied landmark and his rancho as a hostel. Thus, the bestowal of his name on specific points and general area, by the U.S. Geographic Board in 1915.

Lassen's trail, however, did not wind into the area now included in the park. W. H. Nobles crossed through the northern part of the present expanse from Butte Lake to Manzanita Lake in 1852. Nobles' route was considered a more direct approach to the Sacramento Valley.

Lassen Peak and Cinder Cone were designated as national monuments on May 6, 1907. The eruptions in 1914 and 1915 electrified public interest in the American volcano and expedited the park's establishment on August 9, 1916. Here is a park and peak which Supreme Court Justice William O. Douglas must have had in mind when he wrote that some people "must find a peak or a ridge that they can reach under their own power alone."

Lassen Peak, reflected in a nearby lake, stands at the southern end of the Cascade Range. The largest plug dome volcano in the world dominates the park.

Point Reyes seashore is partly protected from the Pacific but is often shrouded in fog and wind-swept spray.

POINT REYES NATIONAL SEASHORE

Wind, waves and fog are the three elements which dominate the coast of the Point Reyes peninsula. The gusts, picking up force across thousands of miles of the Pacific Ocean, constantly lash this point of land jutting from the California shore. The winds push the water into powerful waves which batter the coast with spectacular force, creating tall, craggy palisades and smooth, sandy beaches. The monstrous breakers, whose wind-swept spray sometimes reaches a height of one hundred feet, are usually covered with a heavy sheet of fog stretching up to fifty miles out to sea.

The fog, which sometimes blocks out the sun for three or four weeks at a time, gives Point Reyes what may be the lowest midsummer temperature in the United States. During winter and spring, the fog is less common, and from the cliffs ships may be seen steaming toward San Francisco Bay, thirty-five miles south.

Inland on the peninsula both the terrain and the climate are different from the shore's. Sand dunes and rolling grassy hills enclose quiet lagoons, esteros and saltwater marshes; sharp ridges covered with evergreen forests surround freshwater lakes. The strong winds on the coast have become gentle breezes here, and due to the lack of fog, the temperatures are much higher. While residents of the hot, sun-baked San Joaquin Valley in central California enjoy the cool coast, visitors from the foggy San Francisco peninsula welcome the sunshine of the inland areas.

Point Reyes' only contact with the mainland is directly over the San Andreas Fault between Bolinas Bay on the south and Tomales Bay on the north. The fault, running northwest to southeast, is responsible not only for the long, thin bays, but also for the striking Inverness Ridge which parallels the fault on the peninsula. For the last eighty million years the peninsula has been moving slowly north along this fault, with an average rate of movement of about two inches a year. During the last recorded movement, the devastating San Francisco earthquake of 1906, however, the peninsula was shoved twenty feet out of line at Tomales Bay.

Because of this gradual movement, the rocks on the peninsula west of the fault are totally different in age and variety from those opposite, east of the fault on the mainland. The peninsula's rock is similar to that found many miles south near Bakersfield, California. Point Reyes is thus an isolated geological unit.

The human history of this area is no less interesting. Coast Miwok Indians lived here in relatively large numbers for centuries, depending on the sea for food. Sir Francis Drake is thought to have repaired his ship, the *Golden Hinde,* at Drakes Bay in 1579 while on his voyage around the world. Drakes Bay is a partly protected harbor formed by the point's turning south. His men couldn't understand why this land at the thirty-eighth parallel, the same latitude as the Mediterranean, was cold in midsummer. Notes taken by Drake's chaplain, Francis Fletcher, mention ". . . thicke mists and most stynkinge fogges. Neither could we at any time, in whole fourteene days together, find the aire so cleare as to be able to take the height of sunne or starre."

Point Reyes is a merging point of northern and southern California plant life. Stands of Douglas fir, normally found much farther north, are prevalent on the east slope of Inverness Ridge, while forests of

Bishop pine, common in southern California, inhabit the northern part of the ridge. A stand of coast redwoods, fairly common in patches as far south as Monterey, adds variety to Point Reyes' landscape. On the brushy slopes near the bottom of Inverness Ridge are coast live oaks and California laurels. Much of the lowlands are covered with tall grass which is used for extensive cattle grazing. It is thought that these grasslands were originally covered with brush, which early cattle and dairy farmers cut down and planted over with grass.

Wildflowers bloom everywhere on the peninsula from February to July. Some of them, notably a species of lupine, a blue or yellow flower often tinged with lavender, are exclusive to the area. Two kinds of manzanita grow only here and on Mount Tamalpais, twenty miles southeast.

Because of the varied climate and flora, wildlife is also diversified, ranging from shorebirds to mammals found in the dense forests. Point Reyes has 338 species of birds and 72 species of mammals, including black-tailed deer, raccoons, foxes and rabbits. Herds of California sea lions thrive along the rocky coasts beneath the white palisades, sharing the area with large colonies of seabirds which congregate on the offshore rocks. A few colonies of aplodontia, or "mountain beaver," have managed to survive here in the thickets and brush of the lower ridges. This seldom seen animal is not a true beaver, but a rather cute rodent, thirteen to eighteen inches in length, which exists in small numbers along the north Pacific coast. The aplodontia has sharp claws, which it uses for burrowing, and a tail so small that it is not even visible. Preferring moist soil near marshes and forests, it is strictly nocturnal and is hunted by many predators.

President Kennedy signed the bill establishing Point Reyes National Seashore in 1962. It contains about 64,000 acres, including tidelands and offshore waters up to one-quarter mile. Much of the land within the boundaries, however, is still privately owned and private property rights must be observed. A road leads from the headquarters, near Olema, where evidence of the San Andreas Fault may be seen, to the lighthouse at the tip of the point, which is not open to visitors. Various side roads lead to many beaches and Tomales Bay State Park, but only Drakes Beach with its visitor center is open for water sports. The Pacific beaches are a beachcomber's paradise and surf fishing is also popular.

There are nearly sixty miles of trails in the Bear Valley area which climb up and down the forested ridges and hug the coast. There are three developed "hike-in" campgrounds in Bear Valley, and numerous pocket beaches along Drakes Bay can be reached by the trails. Privately operated campgrounds and other accommodations may be found on the mainland, as well as public campgrounds in nearby Samuel P. Taylor and Mount Tamalpais state parks.

Although the forests and open pastoral spaces convey a sense of tranquility to visitors, the main attractions at Point Reyes are the rough, craggy palisades and the sandy beaches which receive the full brunt of Pacific currents. The huge breakers continually batter this magnificent seascape, seemingly unmindful of the chilling fog which envelops them. Point Reyes, for all who visit her precincts, is, in truth, an island in time where men and women may recharge "spiritual batteries" weakened by the ardors of civilization.

Adapted for almost total life at sea, sleek California sea lions populate beaches along the peninsula.

MUIR WOODS NATIONAL MONUMENT

From the hillsides of San Francisco you can see it, touching the sky twenty miles to the north. This is Mount Tamalpais, the Fujiyama of the Golden Gate, and in a valley at its foot is Muir Woods, a virgin stand of California coast redwoods.

To walk through a virgin forest is an experience in itself. Great varieties of plants do not clutter up the ground here; this is a forest that knows where it is going and has weeded out those plants which do not fit in with its natural scheme. Tall, stately redwoods stretch over two hundred feet above the soft, spongy forest floor, covered with redwood needles and cones, green ferns and rainbow-colored mushrooms of all shapes and sizes. The growth is so thick that only single shafts of sunlight can reach through and brighten the forest floor. Fog often covers the tree-tops during fall and winter, and a soft, misty rain permeates every inch of this evergreen park.

Many years ago, this relatively small forest was threatened by commercial timber cutting and to save it, Congressman William Kent of Marin County and his wife, Elizabeth Thatcher Kent, purchased the woods outright and donated it to the Federal Government on condition that it be designated a national monument in honor of John Muir (1893-1914). Muir was the famed writer, naturalist and conservationist who roamed the Western wilderness for many years and whom Kent greatly admired. Theodore Roosevelt proclaimed the woods a national monument in 1908.

Muir wrote Kent in gratitude: "This is the best tree-lover's monument that could be found in all the forests of the world. . . . Saving these redwoods from the axe and saw . . . is in many ways the most notable service to God and man I have heard . . . ."

The redwood's reproduction is unique in that it is one of the few coniferous trees that reproduces by sprouting from its own root system. Although seeds germinate readily, they cannot establish a strong root system fast enough to carry it through the summer drought season. The stump sprout already has a developed root system, however, and will quickly mature when the parent dies.

This is a primary reason why the forest survives today, for there is evidence that, over many centuries, a large fire would sweep the woods at least once every hundred years or so, killing many great trees but not the roots which supplied the new sprouts with life. The redwoods also resist fire by having a large amount of water in their wood, a very thick, asbestoslike bark and almost no flammable pitch. The charred stumps and deep scars easily visible in the woods resulted from the last major fire which occurred about 1845. Now with man's care these present redwoods will continue to grow even taller.

Muir Woods is noted for its redwood peculiarities of burls and albino shoots. Burls are large, lumpy growths on the sides of the trees. They are not caused by disease but rather by some kind of genetic disorder. Rare albino shoots are caused by the lack of chlorophyll, the chemical responsible for a plant's green color.

Other trees mixing with the redwoods include Douglas fir, California laurel, tanbark oak (tan oak), red alder and California buckeye. Ferns cover the forest floors, the most common being Western sword fern, ladyfern, Western bracken and giant chain fern.

The only large mammal here is the black-tailed deer, a cousin of the mule deer. Birds are numerous and active during the morning hours. Redwood Creek is also a spawning bed of silver salmon and steelhead trout, which can be seen in winter fighting their way upstream from the Pacific Ocean.

Muir Woods has no picnic areas or campgrounds (campgrounds are in surrounding Mount Tamalpais State Park), and is only open during daylight hours. However, a peaceful walk along these six miles of trails is all that is needed to induce feelings of serenity and remind visitors that these great trees are one of the natural masterpieces of this planet.

Sunlight filters through tall, stately coast redwoods which protect lush growths of ferns on the forest floor. The redwood is one of the few coniferous trees that reproduces by sprouting from its own root system.

PINNACLES NATIONAL MONUMENT

The shaded path called the Moses Spring Trail that skirts the Bear Gulch is invitingly cool on a hot May afternoon. A soft breeze rustles the tree leaves slightly. Suddenly, as the trail goes under a broad, overhanging rock face, a loud screech echoes from across the small gulch. The bushes near the boulder move and you are soon gazing at the prince of the wilderness, the rare cougar. For a half hour he roams along the rim, paying no attention to his observer across the gulch.

In California's Pinnacles National Monument, as in many of the wilderness areas in the West, the cougar is present but rarely seen. People lucky enough to view this splendid cat in the wilds never forget their thrilling experience.

The monument is a prime example of the type of habitat the cougar loves. Arid, rocky and rough, the Pinnacles region is located in the Gabilan Range a short distance east of the Monterey and Big Sur peninsulas. It was named for the spectacular spires, columns and jagged peaks, over one thousand feet high, which are found throughout the monument.

Mantling these rugged slopes is a dense, brushy plant cover called chaparral. The stiff-branched, leathery-leaved shrubs have many of the characteristics of desert plants and often grow quite large, thus chaparral is sometimes called a pygmy forest. The chaparral at Pinnacles is considered the best of the entire National Park System and is comprised chiefly of greasewood chamise, mixed with smaller amounts of manzanita, buckbrush (*Ceanothus*) and hollyleaf cherry.

The chaparral furnishes cover and food for numerous species of wildlife. The mountain lion is the prince of the predatory animals of the Western Hemisphere. It is perhaps the most mysterious and misunderstood of all the world's large carnivores. Although cougars avoid human beings at all costs, they have been hunted as though they were mortal enemies of man. Strong and ultrasecretive, the males may weigh up to two hundred pounds with a length of eight feet.

The cougar is a solitary animal who subsists on rabbits, squirrels, mice, wood rats, coyotes, deer and elk. They rely on stealth to achieve their kills, and there are very few recorded instances of attack on human beings—despite much folklore to the contrary.

Black-tailed deer live in the Pinnacles area, as do gray foxes, bobcats, ground squirrels, chipmunks and several species of bats, mice and rabbits. The raccoon is a frequent visitor to the campgrounds in the monument.

Birds are extremely numerous. Out of the 130 species recorded within the monument, seven are owls; there are twelve each of hawks and warblers,

Sheer rock faces of jagged mountain peaks are a common sight in Pinnacles. Many of these rock columns are over a thousand feet high.

six hummingbirds, nine flycatchers and phoebes, and five wrens. Soaring vultures glide over steep canyons, ridges and mountaintops, sometimes not flapping their wings for several hours. The vulture need not be quick because his food is already dead or dying, but the peregrine falcon is another matter. This predacious bird, of which there are few in the monument, feeds nearly exclusively on other birds and is surprisingly fast.

Entrance to Pinnacles National Monument can be easily reached only on the eastern boundary where a road leads to a visitor center, a picnic area and a campground at Chalone Creek. Fifteen miles of trail take the hiker through the chaparral range.

If it is solitude that is needed, Pinnacles has plenty. Although easy to reach by paved road, the monument has few visitors on the weekdays. The High Peaks Trail leads directly to the best of the rocky pinnacles and spires where the visitor can be alone with the wilderness and perhaps catch a fleeting glimpse of its prince, the North American mountain lion.

Half Dome, 8,852 feet high, rises majestically over Tenaya Creek in Yosemite.

YOSEMITE NATIONAL PARK

The dawn sun lies poised over Yosemite National Park, then the murmuring thunder of Bridalveil Creek seems to bring forth the hushed melody of the early morning wind blowing through spires of the groves of sequoias and evergreens as life stirs in this idyllic retreat in the High Sierra of California.

Whatever the season, winter of great snow or the pinnacle of summer, Yosemite lives on, its shape infinitely changing under the slow but persistent hand of nature.

Yosemite was born a hundred million years ago, but she carries her age with grace, growing more desirable with the millenniums. The Sierra Nevada gave birth to her, quaking with the pains of labor as the granite mass rose higher to the east, creating streams which drained into the Merced River.

The Merced grew in strength, not unlike a giant artery, flowing toward the San Joaquin Valley to cut a canyon two thousand feet deep in the rolling upland surface. In Yosemite's puberty, the glaciers came, gouging the V-shaped canyon into a wider and deeper U-shaped trough.

Bridalveil was one of the creeks—Yosemite and Ribbon were others—which lost their lower extremities to the mighty glaciers, leaving the valleys hanging. These streams then plummeted into the valley. Then the glaciers melted, leaving hundreds of tons of water behind a moraine, or a natural dam of rock debris, forming a lake which in time became filled with silt, sand and rock to form the level valley floor we see today.

The wonders of Yosemite range from the awesome crash of water to canyons far below to the pastoral silence of flower-flocked meadowlands.

Congress saw its great beauty in 1864, and granted it to the State of California. In 1890 the national park was created around this Yosemite Grant. California ended its control of the grant in 1905, turning it back over to the Federal Government to form an enlarged national park. There are now nearly 1,200 square miles for all to enjoy, protected forever against the encroachment of man and his penchant for reshaping the face of nature.

But man has not just recently discovered Yosemite. The Ahwahneechee Indians lived here long before it was discovered by the white man. Their name for it, taken from the tribal description, was *Ahwahnee,* or "deep, grassy valley in the heart of the sky mountains."

Then, a little over a hundred years ago, the Mariposa Battalion, a band of miners, entered the valley, seeking retribution for Indian raids. Some of the miners, awed by the expansive beauty of the region, argued around a campfire, trying to name their surroundings. They finally agreed on "Yosemite," perhaps meaning "grizzly bear." It was a derivation of *U-zu-ma-ti,* the name of a sub-group of Chief Tenaya's tribe which then inhabited the valley.

Bridalveil Fall drops between the Cathedral Rocks 620 feet, often swaying from frequent gusts of wind. Long recognized for beauty and scenic resources, Yosemite, the epitome of a national park, has been protected for over one hundred years.

While the Mariposa Battalion's visit was the first recorded trip by white men, it is believed the Joseph Walker party touched on part of the park in their journey of 1833. Nonetheless, to the growing nation just beginning to discover itself in those few short years before the Civil War, Yosemite enthralled the young country.

Members of the battalion wrote enthusiastically of Yosemite, and four years later, in 1855, James M. Hutchings brought the first tourist party. This group would, a shade over a hundred years later, be only a millionth of Yosemite's annual visitors.

Hutchings, the publisher of *California Magazine,* wrote glowing articles extolling the natural virtues of Yosemite, then where words failed, illustrated his pieces with sketches by Thomas Ayres. Hutchings' eloquent prose was reprinted by other publications, and soon Americans came to see for themselves. Californians, spirited by the great wonder which had been left in their midst, became concerned over Yosemite's future. In 1864, President Abraham Lincoln signed the Yosemite Grant, ceding it to California, to be held "inalienable for all time."

Thus, Yosemite became the first public park to be administered by a state government, and dictated the concept which has since served as the basis for the current National Park System.

It was fitting that this splendid region be such a first. There are hundreds of miles of trails leading from the valley through the coolness and fragrance of deep woods; across the sun-splashed meadows to high mountain lakes teeming with fish growing fat and ferocious in their chill depths.

But let us start at the valley, seven square miles of cragginess that becomes beautiful at once to the beholder. Mountainsides and cliffs overhang the canyon where the Merced River threads. A few miles later, the roadway widens to a flower-flecked meadow, dominated by El Capitan, a flawless granite monolith rising more than 3,600 feet toward the sky. Nearly as imposing are the Cathedral Spires, Sentinel Rock and the Three Brothers, named for the sons of Chief Tenaya whose land this was.

Water shaped Yosemite, and still is slowly wearing away rock as it must, seeking the lower levels and carrying with it bits of stone and vegetable matter, endlessly creating. The Upper Yosemite Fall drops 1,430 feet, and the Lower a bit less than a fourth of that. Water cascades with a roar over the top of cliffs for a total drop of 2,425 feet from the crest of the Upper Fall to the base of the Lower.

Not all is the sound and fury of nature. There is solitude in Yosemite to be found in her stands of sequoias, one, the Grizzly Giant, believed to have

In the center of the park, the immense Upper and Lower Yosemite Falls have a total drop of 2,425 feet.

been born from seed more than three thousand years ago. This magnificent cousin of the redwood is 209 feet tall and is more than 34 feet in diameter across the base. Growing silently, contributing to its grandeur, are the park's incense-filled forests of pine, fir, cedar and oak, providing habitat for band-tailed pigeons, pygmy owls, chipmunks and squirrels.

Deer and bear pause to feed here, then move on to the high country, a land of lakes and meadows, capped by high peaks casting great dark shadows on the rainbow of wildflowers below. Tuolumne Meadows at 8,600 feet is the largest subalpine meadow in the High Sierra. Though it can be best enjoyed on foot, there are auto roads leading to jewel-like Tenaya Lake and Tioga Pass, between granite boulders polished to a shine by glaciers and past high domes of the same stone. Another road leads from the valley thirty miles to Glacier Point, giving a panoramic view of the High Sierra and the valley 3,300 feet below.

In spring, there is a flood of color—brilliant yellows and soft blues with the dark green of the conifers filling the eye with the splendor of an untouched land. In winter, the high country is forbidding when giant snows fill the land, only to melt into the trickle of mountain streams which become the raging torrent to start life anew in this land of ten thousand wonders.

John Muir, the great Scots-born naturalist, saw its contrasts: "the most songful streams in the world . . . the noblest forests . . . the loftiest granite domes . . . the deepest ice-sculptured canyons."

DEVILS POSTPILE NATIONAL MONUMENT

The tremendous gray-brown mass of columnar stones, rising vertically from among the lush forests and wildflower meadows of California's high Sierra Nevada, resembles a pipe organ from some legendary age of giants. On a talus slope at the foot of this perpendicular facing are fragmented sections of polygonal columns strewn in a jumbled mass as though the giant, tiring of his prodigious toy, had smashed parts of it in a fit of anger.

Here 7,600 feet above sea level, this convoluted mass is the remnant of a million-year-old volcanic eruption. Dominating the surrounding forests and meadows, the entire formation is approximately nine hundred feet long, and as much as two hundred feet high. The columns are from forty to sixty feet tall.

This geological oddity, one of the most remarkable of its kind in North America, is formed of dark, basaltic lava flows, and is included in a one-by-three-mile area set aside in 1911 as Devils Postpile National Monument. It lies between Yosemite and Sequoia national parks on the John Muir Trail. Included in the monument are part of the Middle Fork of the San Joaquin River valley and Rainbow Falls on this river. Soda Spring—carbonated by carbon dioxide gases escaping into the water source from volcanic activity deep in the earth—also is in the monument, upstream from the Devils Postpile formation.

Volcanic eruptions higher in the Sierra Nevada, to the east of the monument, caused the original flow more than 900,000 years ago. As the mass cooled, the lava cracked (something like drying mud) into forms with three to seven sides. These forms extend from the surface downward into the mass, and seen in cross section, they resemble columns.

Several times in the last million years, glaciers, some as much as a thousand feet thick, flowed down the river valley and quarried away much of the lava deposits, including one side of the postpile. Only the more resistant columns, the ones seen today, remained standing. Most of the columns are vertical, but some are slanted and others curved, probably due to slight differences in composition, thickness and cooling rates. The tops of the remaining columns were exposed at right angles to the glacial movement and were polished to a high sheen, giving the appearance of a mosaic. In most places, however, they have been roughed by weathering during the time since the last glacial period.

Near upper reaches of the monument is a pumice flat which originated in the post-glacial era. This rock will float on water, but as it powders, it creates a fine dust. In some areas of the monument, this pumice is crumbly, making the footing difficult as one walks about. Some evidence of recent volcanic activity such as bubbly, hot springs are found nearby.

Rainbow Falls on the Middle Fork of the San Joaquin River, about two miles downstream from the Devils Postpile, provides a thrilling view of this rushing river as it plunges over a precipice 140 feet into a deep green pool below. At the foot of the falls are clumps of willows, Western white pine, hemlocks, alders, and numerous wildflowers.

A campground, open from mid-June to October, is maintained at the National Park Service ranger station in the monument. Two miles away from the postpile, at Reds Meadow, supplies, cabins, meals and both saddle and pack horses are available.

The awesome natural forces that sculpted this geometrically shaped Devils Postpile and the volcanic rubble from lava flows torn by glaciation make this monument a mecca for scientists and those interested in natural wonders.

Devils Postpile is a sector of huge basalt pillars, with four to seven sides each, left standing in the Middle Fork of the San Joaquin valley after a glacier removed the greater part of an ancient lava deposit.

SEQUOIA AND KINGS CANYON NATIONAL PARKS

The tree is king here, peering down over a majestic domain of gray granite mountains, deep forests and valleys making a harsh but welcoming slash in the landscape. It stands, holding silent court over a seemingly untouched panorama, beginning beyond one horizon and going past the other.

This tree is the largest living thing in the world—rivaling the age of any tree or other plant known—the sequoia, gently elbowing aside white firs and sugar pines, its cinnamon-red bark and pointed needles quite unchanged from the time when frightening creatures rumbled the earth with their ponderous tread.

One can count nearly four thousand years since some of them were born, and science believes none has died simply because of old age. They usually find their life-giving roots exposed by slow erosion, perhaps nature's way to return organic material to the soil. Then they topple and die with a crash, to lie fallen beside other warriors fighting the long battle against time in Sequoia and Kings Canyon national parks in California.

There are more than 1,300 square miles in the two parks, starting at the foothills of the San Joaquin Valley and reaching toward the crest of the High Sierra. It is some six thousand feet above sea level here, and the altitude makes the giant sequoias seem all the more regal. Perhaps at first, the height leaves one breathless, then suddenly the vista generates a catch in the lungs, for nowhere else does such a view exist.

Save for the efforts of a few, these mighty trees might have disappeared to the logger. The basis of the two parks gained Federal protection in 1890 so that they could be preserved. The culmination of this protection came in 1940 with the establishment of Kings Canyon National Park.

Hale Tharp was the first recorded visitor, a brawny, tanned cattleman seeking grazing land. He went up the Kaweah Valley near what is now Moro Rock, and listened to an Indian friend tell of the great mountain meadows lying beyond. Heartened, for cattle were his livelihood, Tharp followed the patrol of Indians to the meadows carpeted with deep, nutritional grass. There, in 1858, he beheld the Giant Forest's sequoias, and set up a temporary home in a fallen tree hollowed by fire.

Then, in 1862, Joseph Thomas discovered the General Grant Grove (now located in Kings Canyon Park) where several of the parks' outstanding trees reign. It took little time for their descriptions, and those of others, to create a national stir to preserve this virgin land.

The biggest and among the oldest of living things is the sequoia tree, Sequoia gigantea.

Old in appearance, the Sierras in Sequoia are geologically young.
Autumn colors cottonwoods below Mount Langely, 14,042 feet high.

Today, it all has changed. The parks are not what they were a century ago, nor are the trees the same. Although most of the changes are too small to measure, the valleys *are* a bit deeper because of erosion, the mountains a shade lower because of the torture of the elements, and some trees taller because the protective ring of the Government has given them life. If anything, Sequoia and Kings Canyon have grown more graceful, bearing their years with dignity.

The nucleus of a visit here is the General Sherman Tree, largest of all living things on earth, towering more than 272 feet above the ground and measuring more than 35 feet across the base. Because it is hard to imagine such a tree, perhaps this helps: The trunk alone weighs approximately 1,450 tons and has 50,010 cubic feet of wood, enough to build about forty homes. The General Grant is only five feet shorter and contains only a bit less wood.

These giants of the forest live in harmony with their smaller and shorter-lived brethren. The gigantic sugar pines and firs wrest life from the soil, and even without the sequoias their existence would be a pleasing sight. They are youngsters, however, for the General Sherman is believed to be more than 3,500 years old, a fertile tree when Christ was born and existing when the great pyramids of ancient Egypt were being built. It is a living link with history; no, more than history, the evolution of our planet. Only one existing thing has been proved older, the bristlecone pine. And the young sequoias may be living after our civilization has become history.

Smaller than the sequoias, but with much value of their own, are the flora and fauna of the two parks. The floor of the forest is covered with dogwood, colorful lupine and the red-flowered snow plant. Meadows are filled with wildflowers, Sierra shooting stars in June, Queen Anne's lace and Senecio later. Bear and mule deer roam at will.

This is a rugged land, existing almost as a separate entity from the rest of the West. Beyond the Giant Forest, named by that great, Scots-born naturalist, John Muir, is the Sierra Nevada's high country, a vast, tilted block on the earth where snowcapped peaks—crowned by Mount Whitney, the highest mountain in the United States outside of Alaska—rise to more than fourteen thousand feet to cast giant shadows on glacial valleys and ice-formed lake basins. This landscape is relatively untouched, existing as it is by Federal decree.

Here the bighorn sheep forages and the wolverine hunts among the alpine solitude, nuzzling through the luxuriant growth of a short summer, growing fat before the chill winds blow away the fragrance of delicate flowers and turn their vivid shades to dull brown, their colors not to return until spring.

*Smaller than the mighty sequoias but with unique values all their own
are the fruits of the forest floor, such as dogwood and lupine. Nestled among
decaying litter of pine and fir needles is the snow plant, a bright saprophyte.*

Great canyons are incised upon the landscape, among the deepest to be found in the United States. Gorges along the middle and south forks of the Kings River are more than a mile deep, their steep sides forming a canyon between the great peaks and the roaring waters tumbling over time-polished stones below.

Here there are valleys, miles long and a half-mile wide, created when small streams grew larger and carried infinitesimal bits of stone with their downhill fury, then finally hewn to shape by vast fields of ice jamming their depths. The valleys bear silent testament to their past; glacial moraines tell of when nature's strength rubbed, scoured and finally gouged its way through granite, forming the canyon walls we see today.

Some of these valleys are covered with forests of ponderosa pine, incense-cedar and white fir, towering above blue lupine waving in the summer breeze. Deer, bear and bobcats graze and hunt among the trees. Birds flutter against wind gusts, then swoop earthward to grasp an insect in their beaks and retreat to the forest a few wing flaps beyond to enjoy their meal and perhaps sing of triumph.

High above—nearly two miles on top of the level of the sea—is a mountain wilderness dotted with glacial lakes mirroring the sun and its spectacular surroundings.

Magnificent, even in winter when snow festoons the giant sequoias and fills the dips and small valleys, there is no word that does justice to the parks and their environs.

The region so moved John Muir that he wrote, "No doubt these trees would make good lumber after passing through a saw mill, as George Washington after passing through the hands of a French chef would have made good food."

The sequoias, thankfully, are living, for their peculiar makeup gives them an odds-on chance against every natural enemy—except perhaps man.

INYO NATIONAL FOREST

The Swiss have a special word, *Krummholz*. It means, literally, "crooked wood," but it refers to the dwarfed trees of gnarled shapes found in the Alpine mountains.

Krummholz reveals to the Swiss a lot about a tree and the setting in which it grows.

It tells them that here is a hardy species clinging tenaciously to life. It is a conifer, for a deciduous tree could not survive in such a harsh environment. The tree has withstood long icy winters and the flailing of many high winds, and has bent before the sculpture of these forces into a contorted shape. It grows extremely slowly in rocky, infertile soil, yet it will endure through a long life.

The earth thus unfolds itself to the viewer through the trees and forests that it produces. It speaks of rocks and their history, of weather, of soils, of water, and of all kinds of life forms, because trees never grow alone but are part of a life community.

High in the White Mountains above Owens Valley in Inyo National Forest, the landscape is bleak and severe. This region is one of the remotest in California. Here, in the Ancient Bristlecone Pine Forest, are the oldest known living things on earth. Some of the trees found at this location have been growing more than four thousand years. Methuselah, the oldest, has been dated at 4,600 years, a thousand years older than the oldest redwood. They are not, however, stately giants like the redwoods, but gnarled and twisted into many shapes and forms, and only twenty-five to thirty feet in height. The bristlecone pines have survived the most adverse conditions on exposed ridges of shallow, rocky soil, with little rainfall, and high winds as an almost constant companion.

The Ancient Forest was set aside within Inyo National Forest in 1958 as a botanical area for scientific study and public enjoyment, after scientific research had discovered the amazing age of the trees. They grow at elevations above nine thousand feet, accessible by a road that starts at four thousand feet and rises almost to twelve thousand, with views of the immense eastern escarpment of the High Sierras, including Tioga Pass, the jagged Minarets and Palisade glacier, the southernmost in the United States. Bristlecone pine also grows in scattered stands in high mountain areas of the Southwest, but this seems the appropriate setting for the masters of the tribe.

Limber pines appear at the lower levels of the Ancient Forest; however, there is no mistaking them for bristlecones. The limber is readily seen to be a younger tree. It can be differentiated from the bristlecone by the short tufts of needles at the end of branchlets, while the needles of the bristlecone run back for a foot or more like foxtails. And the purple-tinged cones of the latter have sharp bristles at the end of each scale. The Schulman Grove, at ten thousand feet, named for the late Dr. Edward L. Schulman, a relentless investigator who determined the age of trees by microscopic study of core borings, is an almost pure stand of bristlecones, a concentration of the oldest known trees. One of two trails leads to Pine Alpha, a 4,300-year-old tree, nearly four feet across but clinging to life with only a ten-inch strip of bark and living cambium tissue. All of these trees appear at first to be dead wood, but they bear a similar strand of bark twisting around the once living side or branch. This is their way of adjusting to the limitations of moisture and soil nutrient—they retard growth to the narrow lifeline, and let erosion polish the dead branches. Another, longer trail leads to Methuselah Walk and the oldest known tree anywhere in the world. It was already well along on this spot when the Egyptians were building the pyramids, fifteen centuries before Christ.

At the breeze-swept slopes eleven thousand feet above sea level, the Patriarch Grove contains the largest, most contorted bristlecones, including the giant of all, the Patriarch, with a circumference of thirty-six feet eight inches around its multiple stems. This great tree and others fling their bony fingers into the wind toward the mountain ranges of Nevada.

Covering almost two million acres in eastern California and part of Nevada, Inyo National Forest stretches between Sequoia and Kings Canyon national parks on the west and Nevada's desert ranges on the east, and is cut down the center north to south by the Owens Valley. When John Muir visited here he called the mountains the Range of Light. The Paiute Indians gave the name Inyo to the area, the Dwelling Place of a Great Spirit.

Overleaf: *On wind-swept rock-strewn slopes, bristlecone pines in Patriarch Grove are among the world's oldest living things.*

Sheer cliffs dominate Anacapa and Santa Barbara islands and offer nesting areas for seabirds.

CHANNEL ISLANDS NATIONAL MONUMENT

A brilliant expanse of treelike sunflowers on the springtime meadows and hills of Santa Barbara Island, thirty-eight miles west of San Pedro, California, serves as a golden beacon to ships at sea. This gleam is from the largest known stands of giant coreopsis in the world. Forty miles northwest, three tiny islets comprise Anacapa Island, a chain tipped on the eastern point by Arch Rock, a forty-foot-high wave sculpture, and isolated as a preserve where thousands of seabirds, rare seals and other marine creatures nest and breed.

These two islands are part of the Channel Islands chain which stretches from due west of San Diego northward to Point Conception and carries the archeological threads of prehistory for early man, plants and wildlife. Santa Barbara and Anacapa, like the other six Channel Islands, are mountaintops which were surrounded by ocean after the western parts of the ancient Santa Monica Mountains were submerged about a half-million years ago. These two islands were set aside as the Channel Islands National Monument in 1938.

Santa Barbara and Anacapa, comprising almost eighteen thousand acres, are a pristine outpost in polluted southern California. The surrounding ocean temperatures range between fifty-five and sixty-five degrees, offering a moderate climate advantageous to the many marine mammals.

Huge flocks of a variety of seabirds nest on cliff tops and the interior highlands of both islands. Anacapa Island is one of the few surviving nesting grounds for the brown pelican and the double-crested cormorant. Below, on narrow beaches and in sea caves gouged from sheer cliffs by the surging seas, the almost extinct Guadalupe seal finds hauling-out beaches. Sleek, brown California sea lions are common, while clumsy-appearing elephant seals, each of the bulls sporting a foot-long proboscis, populate coves and quiet beaches.

The six-to-eight-foot giant coreopsis is perhaps the most distinctive plant on Channel Islands, with its thick bark, gray, rigid trunk and stubby branches that appear lifeless during the dry summers. But come the winter rains, the plants show signs of life, and beginning in early April, bright green leaves appear with a gorgeous canopy of intensely golden-yellow blossoms.

The monument areas offer outstanding undersea environments for marine biological research in the tidal pools, coves and in the deeper surrounding waters. The islands are a museum of geological structures where one can find examples of faulting, fossils, volcanic action and canyon development as well as erosion of many kinds.

The monument is accessible only by boat, has no piers and, quite rightly, contains few man-made "improvements." Public camping is allowed, but firewood, food, water, and other supplies must be brought in by rough-it campers. Scuba diving off of either island is most rewarding. National Park Service personnel staff the areas only in summer months, though they patrol both islands year around.

These islands should be combined with the two largest Channel Islands, Santa Rosa and Santa Cruz, and be made into a true national park. This is the last national park option in southern California; it will be a sad chapter of conservation history if these islands are not converted into a superb park that will keep these unique island sanctuaries inviolate for future generations.

THE OUTER LIMITS
Alaska, Hawaii,
and The Virgin Islands

Turnagain Pass, Chugach National Forest, Alaska

The Alaska Range rises in a series of brilliant ridges, cornices and peaks, attuning the eye to the three-mile high magnificence of Mount McKinley, the top of the continent. In the last wilderness, snow fields and glaciers dominate the landscape, so that the multitudes of wild-life and the arrays of flowers go almost unnoticed. Almost a hemisphere away are the splendors of Hawaii, islands set in placid seas and dominated by gray mountains that spout lava and red fire into the sky. Then, the soft luxuriant and provacative moods of the warm Caribbean, at Virgin Islands National Park, provide a final look at the wonders of America.

276

MOUNT McKINLEY
NATIONAL PARK

The Wilderness of Denali is not tamed. It is raw and primal, and a man feels very small in it. Almost anywhere off the one road he is truly alone—and sometimes a little afraid.

It is a vast land, which dwarfs normal scales. Sprawling river bars, peopled with the swarming specks that are the caribou, wind out of immensity at the foot of the hills. The wind across the tundra is clean, untainted by mankind.

The spirit of the wolf hangs over the land. Unseen, his presence is felt. He is the warden and unwitting benefactor of the caribou, the superb culmination of the biotic pyramid—and the personification of the wild.

Over all, the Alaska Range rises in a succession of brilliant ridges, and cornices—each magnificent in its own right, but nearly lost in the greater picture. Higher they rise, leading the eye to the massive upsurge that is *The Mountain.* A full three vertical miles above the living tundra soars its peak.

Nothing lives on the mountain, but the mountain lives. Avalanches leap from its walls. Seracs crash; glaciers rumble and grind. Clouds swirl about its flanks, and a snow plume is torn by the wind from its uppermost crests. In the evening, the glare of the eternal ice softens, glows with the color of fireweed, then pales to ivory against the darkened sky.

No one knows what white man saw the country first. Russian traders knew the mountain, called it *Bulshaia Gora,* or "Big Mountain." Early prospectors knew it as Densmore's Mountain. The Indians of the area had perhaps the most beautiful and fitting name of all: *Denali,* "The High One."

But it was a young prospector, W. A. Dickey, who realized the importance of the 20,320-foot peak in 1896, and named it after the champion of the gold standard, President William McKinley.

It is fortunate that one of the earliest explorers of the area was a naturalist and conservationist, Charles Sheldon, hunting specimens for the National Museum, roamed the country for three years and felt its impact. Recognizing the intrinsic value of the landscape and its wildlife, he conceived the idea of making the area a national park while camping there in the summer of 1906. His vigorous efforts to create a refuge for the swarming wildlife, aided by the Boone and Crockett Club, brought about the establishment of Mount McKinley National Park just eleven years later. Today it is the only park service area which harbors the white Dall sheep and the barren grounds caribou, and its 3,030 square miles embrace more untouched wilderness than any other national park.

Unique to Mount McKinley in the park system, caribou can be seen along the park road.

Mountaineers answered the challenge of Mount McKinley early. On April 6, 1910, a hardy group of sourdoughs climbed to the summit of the north peak of McKinley, carrying with them a fourteen-foot spruce pole. It was an astonishing feat, for the group was inexperienced and poorly equipped. Modern mountaineers find the climb as dangerous and demanding as a Himalayan expedition, but each year a few manage to stand atop the continent.

Relatively little has changed since Sheldon fought to make this area a park. A single graveled road winds its leisurely way eighty-six miles into the park, climbing from the deep green spruce of the taiga to the sweeping tapestry of the alpine tundra. You may

The Teklanika River flows down from the Alaska Range through a broad gravel bed near the park road. A subarctic wilderness (right), Wonder Lake and Mount McKinley, is captured at summer sunset.

see from the road the same wild peaks and teeming wildlife that thrilled the first visitors. Over the tundra range groups of caribou, the bulls in late summer bearing brilliant white capes and towering, blood-red antlers. Moose, looking shiny black at a little distance, feed knee-deep in ponds or browse in willow thickets.

The deceptively lethargic-looking grizzly keeps his head down, gobbling berries, roots and grasses. Red foxes trot across the road, seemingly indifferent to man. Ptarmigan erupt into the air with a humorous, guttural croaking, their white wings flashing in startling contrast to their barred brown bodies.

In the ponds everywhere beavers are busy cutting willow. Golden eagles soar above. Gyrfalcons are sometimes seen, and marsh hawks swoop low across the dry flats. On the lower peaks, a spray of white dots becomes a flock of Dall sheep.

If you are very lucky, you may see a wolf. When you have seen the eyes of the wolf, you have seen the quintessence of wildness.

The park is generally accessible from June through the middle of September. In June and July the area is confronted with one of its few disadvantages— mosquitoes, which come after the late spring that leaves patches of snow at lower elevations even into June. During these same months there are eighteen hours of sunlight daily and only semidarkness in the remaining hours. Although the winters are cold, snow depths seldom exceed three feet on the level at lower elevations.

Whatever the season, the mountain, once seen, even if its persistent shroud of clouds allows only a momentary view, becomes an indelible recollection. The wildness of the park, once experienced, even if at some distance, leaves its mark on a man.

The glaciers flowing into the bay today are reminders of the "little ice age" that began four thousand years ago and reached its maximum extent into the bay in 1750. The fascination in glaciers lies in the dynamics of movement, the visible and invisible, from which to read the earth's history.

In Tongass one can relish the spectacular view from Harbor Mountain of the calm waters of island-studded Sitka Sound.

TONGASS NATIONAL FOREST

Alaska is very likely the portion of North America longest inhabited by man. Its beginnings are traceable to the age of Beringia, the ancient land bridge which the Wandering Hunters crossed from Asia, thus introducing the higher form of life to this continent.

Alaska is also the newest portion of North America, second youngest of the fifty states, the least developed and the least spoiled. Its naturalness is one of the marvels of the modern world, and therefore a special prize of all the nation.

The national forests, the Tongass and the Chugach, in turn, are among the oldest and newest parts of Alaska. Their establishment dates from 1892. The huge Tongass, a domain over 500 miles long, up to 100 miles wide and covering 16 million acres, is by far the largest national forest anywhere in the country. Second in size is the Chugach, with five million acres.

The Tongass embraces the coastal woodlands of temperate southeast Alaska, which are really an extension of the Pacific Northwest rain forest. Much of the land is composed of islands, while the mainland portion is deeply cleft by bays, inlets and large rivers, creating thousands of miles of shoreline—highly scenic, misty and moody places.

Sitka, now surrounded by the Tongass (except on the Pacific side), formerly the capital of Russian America and headquarters of Alexander Baranof, "Lord of Alaska," until the Seward Purchase of 1867, is now reachable by ferry on a voyage from Juneau through island-dotted channels; and almost adjacent to the ferry terminal lies the forest service's Starrigavan Campground, from whence one can (and should) drive upward through alpine meadows to Harbor Mountain. For in the Tongass one's senses become heightened. Art forms are implicit in the natural landscape of Alaska — the mist-shrouded low-lying coasts, the birds outlined in flight against a mass of snow and the composition of sky, forest, sea and tundra.

KODIAK NATIONAL WILDLIFE REFUGE

Kodiak Island, the largest island in the Gulf of Alaska, contains the 2,780-square-mile area of Kodiak National Wildlife Refuge, established in 1941. Unlike many other refuges, Kodiak has remained essentially unchanged over the centuries.

The island is wild and mountainous, with snowy peaks reaching four thousand feet above sea level. It is lush with vegetation in some areas while barren in others. Sitka spruce forests dominate the mountains of the northern part of Kodiak, while grassy slopes and rolling Arctic tundra are characteristic of the southern portion.

Numerous clear streams carry the water from the high alpine lakes to the long, fjordlike bays of the Pacific Coast. Often misty and dismal with low clouds surrounding the peaks, the island averages 105 inches of precipitation annually, and winters, unlike most of Alaska, are mild with temperatures seldom below zero.

The variety of birdlife is extraordinary, and particularily impressive are the almost two hundred pairs of bald eagles, the national emblem, which nest here on rocky pinnacles, cliffs and in cottonwood trees. The willow and the rock ptarmigan, the State Bird of Alaska, are numerous, and the call of the common loon is heard on nearly every lake.

Animals native to Kodiak are the red fox, land otter, weasel, tundra vole and little brown bat. Transplanted to the island after 1920 and gaining in numbers are black-tailed Sitka deer, snowshoe hare, beaver, muskrat, reindeer, mountain goat, red squirrel and Dall sheep. Sea lions, some weighing a ton, lie on the rocks of several offshore islands as thickly as bathers at Coney Island on a hot day.

But Kodiak Island is best known as the habitat of the Kodiak brown bear, sometimes called the Alaskan brown bear, the largest carnivore on earth. Weighing up to 1,200 pounds and growing to a height of four or more feet at the shoulders, the bear is formidable even without standing erect on its hind legs. When it does it towers ten to thirteen feet high.

The bears den from December to April, and during spring, early summer and fall they are mostly vegetarians. In July and August they are easily seen as they congregate in streams to catch the spawning salmon.

Cubs, weighing less than a pound at birth—the size of a small squirrel—are born in the dens during winter. They remain with their mothers for two years before the family ties are broken.

In spite of their size and clumsy appearance, the bears are quick-moving and agile when necessary, yet silent and cautious in the brush. Tremendously strong animals, they are able to kill a thousand-pound steer with one blow and break a tree four inches in diameter with a sweep of a forearm. They are, however, wary of man and will seldom charge unless cornered or injured.

When discovered by a Russian in 1763, the island was inhabited by people calling themselves Koniags. Numbering over six thousand, they were stronger and hardier than the Aleuts of the mainland, frequently swimming and boating naked in the cold. But imported diseases and ill treatment by the intruding traders gradually reduced their population; today there are only about eight hundred residents of Koniag ancestry left.

All of the Kodiak refuge is open to the public, but there are no roads. A scheduled airline makes two flights a day from Anchorage to the town of Kodiak, and several bush pilots and a local airline furnish air transportation to almost any part of the refuge. Commercial fishing boats can be chartered for trips around the island and to the beaches.

The world's largest carnivore, the Alaskan brown bear, may grow to 1,500 pounds.

KATMAI NATIONAL MONUMENT

Welcome to The Last Wilderness. Although other states may have patches of wilderness, only Alaska's is so primeval and untamed that you could wander for weeks without seeing another human being. It is the kind of wilderness that even people who know they will never see it are deeply satisfied that it still exists. Katmai National Monument, one of the largest units of the National Park System, protects over 4,200 square miles of this wilderness.

Located on the east coast of the peninsula leading to the Aleutian chain, this is one of the least visited of U.S. parks. The annual visitor rate can be counted in the hundreds; in Yosemite National Park that many people may visit every hour. And it is this very lack of human intrusion that keeps Katmai wild and beautiful. With no road or rail access, the monument is out of reach for the casual tourist. Private or chartered planes are needed to see the most scenic spots, for scheduled flights from the King Salmon airport on the Bering Sea side of the peninsula go only to Brooks River lodge and campground. Such isolation guarantees protection of prime wilderness values.

Katmai contains three distinct geographic sections. To the east is the seacoast on Shelikof Strait, a coastline of unsurpassed beauty. The central part is a series of deep fjords nearly surrounded by cliffs rising abruptly one thousand or more feet above the blue waters. The northern and southern coasts are comprised of wide, shallow bays with many extensive sandy beaches bordering large marshes and, in

Katmai Valley to the south, treacherous quicksand. Offshore are many small islets where Pacific hair seals and northern sea lions rest from the often turbulent waters of the strait. The great gray whale sometimes hunts in the bays and the northern sea otter plays in the shallows.

Inland from the coast is the Aleutian Mountain Range, forming the backbone of Katmai. These snow-capped peaks, as high as 7,600 feet, are continually being carved by glaciers and some of them are active volcanoes. There is little vegetation here because of the cold, the high winds and the short growing season; what does exist is of the subarctic tundra variety.

In the western portion of the monument is a huge mixture of grasslands, green forests and large, deep blue lakes. Two life zones meet here as on the seacoast: the Arctic zone above two thousand feet, comprised of short grasses and other low-lying vegetation; and the Hudsonian zone of forests of white spruce, balsam poplar, paper birch and dense stands of reed grass. Gradually the woodlands are replacing the grasslands in this part of the monument; the increased rainfall and milder climate of recent years has induced a rapid growth of trees.

Large mammals are numerous. The largest of them, the Alaskan brown bear, can be seen during summer in and along the streams as it fishes for salmon coming up the waters to spawn. In other seasons the bears eat grass on the open slopes, dig for roots or gorge themselves on the wild berries that are abundant in autumn. Moose are common and will always be found near the waters of the lakes or larger streams. Wolverines, the most far-ranging small mammals—found from sea level to three thousand feet—snarl at visitors if their prey is frightened away by man's approach. River otters are numerous on the lakes and along the shores of the bays.

The most abundant meat-eater at Katmai is the red fox, normally found in the lower elevations of the western portions of the monument. The lynx is the only member of the cat family living in this region and sometimes can be seen in the monument headquarters area at Brooks River. Beavers "log" the woods near the lakes and build large dams. Caribou and reindeer were once plentiful but have decreased to the point where none have been seen for many years.

Perhaps the most interesting mammal at Katmai is the wolf. This animal's howl is the trademark of the true wilderness. No other species has been so misunderstood by man. We now know that the vicious, man-eating wolf is a myth. Although in rare instances

The magnified sporophytes of mosses in the tundra zone at Katmai appear as forests of other worlds.

One in a chain of active volcanoes, Martin Volcano lies south of the Valley of Ten Thousand Smokes.

wolves have attacked man, they are wary of him and normally shun all areas where man intrudes.

Wolves basically look like large German shepherd dogs. Most of them in North America are dark gray, but they range in color from pure white in the Arctic to black in more southerly reaches. Their sizes vary with region and sex: Wolves of the north are larger than those to the south, and males are larger than females. Their average weight may be seventy-five to one hundred pounds, and from a distance they appear lean and rangy, much like a coyote but larger. These superb beasts are efficient hunters, and generally peaceful.

When running they have more endurance than speed and often have trouble overtaking hoofed animals. A typical family would consist of the parents, mated for life, one or two cubs, and another solitary adult that has been accepted as a part-time cub-sitter and hunting partner. They seldom quarrel among themselves and are quite friendly toward strangers of their kind, greeting them with play and dog-style tail wagging.

The wolf, like the cougar (mountain lion), usually attacks only the sickly animals for his food, thus weeding out those individuals whose continued existence is a burden on the rest of the herd.

Within Katmai's crater are the brilliantly colored Emerald Lake and a new glacier which is forming slowly.

An abundance of nesting sites, plant food, aquatic life and insects make Katmai ideal for birds. Waterfowl—ducks, loons and gulls—are plentiful on the lakes, and sea and shorebirds, including colonies of Arctic terns, populate the coasts. Bald eagles can be seen along the streams and lakes, and whistling swans inhabit the remote ponds during summer.

The monument's lakes and streams are dense with Dolly Varden, grayling, northern pike, whitefish, and rainbow and lake trout, giving both seasoned veterans and beginning fishermen a chance at prize catches. In late summer thousands of bright red salmon navigate up the streams from the Bering Sea to spawn.

In early 1912 no one would have thought that this magnificent, but still far away and unexplored, region would become a national monument six years later. But on June 6, 1912, one of the most violent seizures of volcanic action that modern man has recorded called attention to the area. The few natives were warned by pre-eruption earth tremors and they quickly fled, so there was no known loss of human life. Losses to wildlife, however, must have been enormous.

The activity began when Novarupta Volcano, halfway between the now abandoned villages of Katmai on the coast and Savonoski in the lakes region, blew up, spewing forth great masses of pumice and rock. Soon white ash began blowing out of the fissure, and within a few minutes two and a half *cubic* miles of ash had been tossed into the air. Over forty square miles of a nearby valley was buried in ash seven hundred feet deep, and even Kodiak Island across Shelikof Strait was covered with pumice. Trees on the mountain slopes above the valley were snapped off and carbonized by terrific blasts of scorching wind.

Steam and hot gases rose through innumerable small holes and cracks in this valley, pushing their way through the ash cover. Expeditions, sponsored by the National Geographic Society, were made into the valley later, and it was called the Valley of the Ten Thousand Smokes. The heat from some of these fumaroles reached nearly eight hundred degrees, high enough to melt zinc! The smokes have dwindled over the decades and very few are active today. The society's published reports on the volcanic occurrence as well as the stark wilderness of the region resulted in Katmai's being established as a national monument in 1918. It qualifies in every respect as a national park, and conservationists have urged Congress to give it this status.

After Novarupta had spent its own volcanic material, the base of Mount Katmai, six miles away, was sucked in by the volcano through an underground conduit. With its support gone, Mount Katmai collapsed with a roar that could be heard hundreds of miles away, creating a chasm three miles long, two miles wide and 3,200 feet deep. The hole has since partially filled with water, making a crater lake warmed by volcanic heat. Inside the crater above the water level a glacier has formed, perhaps the only glacier in the world whose precise age is known.

The last person to leave the doomed valley, the chief of the Savonoski villagers who called himself American Pete, said in 1918 of his experience, "The Katmai mountain blow up with lots of fire, and fire come down trail from Katmai with lots of smoke . . . Dark. No could see. Hot ash fall . . . Never can go back to Savonoski to live. Everything ash."

Katmai is one of our finest remaining wilderness parks. Its remoteness insures that it will always remain as a pristine outpost of nature.

HALEAKALA NATIONAL PARK

The land sleeps here now, resting under the warm Pacific sun after the long day geologists count in millions of years. To Haleakala (pronounced HA-lay-ah-kah-LA), it is night and a well-deserved rest, for this Hawaiian volcano helped form the lovely green fingers that probe the sea as part of our fiftieth state.

To Polynesians, it means "House of the Sun," and it was once that, belching forth angry torrents of fire and lava, making night as day, until it subsided in placid surrender to time, leaving as a heritage one of the showplaces of the National Park System so that all might understand the forces of geological evolution.

On a clear day — and there are many in the Pacific — the summit affords a spectacular view of the neighboring islands of Hawaii, Lanai, Molokai and occasionally Oahu. Turn the eyes a bit downward, and unfolding beyond the crater's rim is a vast hole in the earth, gouged by water erosion, leaving acres of symmetrical cinder cones painted with primeval colors huddled inside the great formations of cliffs whose tops are hidden in the moist clouds, lending even more vastness to the gigantic, dormant crater seven and a half miles long and two and a half miles wide.

Haleakala's history is shrouded in the still-growing science of geology, yet many scientists agree that this House of the Sun was once more than eleven thousand feet high, a summit about a thousand feet greater than the one we see now. She once slowed her volcanic eruptions, and water came to carve two deep valleys in opposite sides of the mountain which eventually met. Then, the fury of the subterranean eruptions began anew and lava flows cascaded into the valleys atop one another after their first outpourings reached the sea. The level of the valleys seen today is the height of the cooled, molten rock, save for a bit of topsoil created by time alone.

Cones of cinder were formed as high as six hundred feet, and volcanic bombs and spatter spurted from fissures in the earth, propelled by supercharged gases. Eventually, a water-carved depression, one partially filled, was created, resembling a true volcanic crater. Until 1961, it was hidden by distance from the rest of Hawaii Volcanoes National Park, when it was made a singular attraction of the system because of its size.

The House of the Sun is quiet now, for no eruptions have occurred here for centuries. But there is the appeal of something new, raw, a just-formed land, and in geological terms it is that. Lava is sterile stuff, for nothing can survive its heat. Generations of plant life have rained down upon the cooled rock until, in places, anyway, here and there a plant has been able to gain a foothold. That is fortunate, for they will flourish, then die, deepening the topsoil by a

When viewed from the rim above Kapalaoa Cabin, hikers on the Sliding Sands Trail can see the nineteen-square-mile crater floor many feet below the summit.

fraction of a millimeter so that other plants might follow eventually.

Life grows slowly at Haleakala National Park, for this is still a new land. But the silversword has fought grazing animals, man and the barren beds of lava to thrust its spheres of silvery, dagger-shaped leaves and three to seven-foot flowers, casting to the four winds thousands of seeds, then dying—the first handful of compost to fertilize the silent mountain.

Meaning "House of the Sun," Haleakala Crater (right) changes color almost hourly as the sun passes overhead, becoming most vivid at mid-afternoon. Within the crater are hundreds of cinder cones (below) formed by ash spurted through their vents.

HAWAII VOLCANOES NATIONAL PARK

Huge mountains, their gray, lifeless sides warmed by the Pacific sun, spout their anger at the placid blue seas around them, belching fountains of lava and red fire into the sky, pouring orange-red streams of molten rock down unresisting slopes.

This is a link with the past—geological history in the making as the Hawaiian Islands continue to emerge from the sea as they first did five to ten million years ago. Hawaii Island, largest of the chain, is the site of Mauna Loa, a 13,680-foot summit where Hawaii Volcanoes National Park begins, stretching southeast to the seacoast, a place of contrasts where umbrella-shaped palms and dense jungles of ferns lie near gaunt mountains and beside lava deserts.

The region has fascinated visitors for more than a century. The Rev. William Ellis, a British missionary, saw it in 1823 and said in his *A Tour Through Hawaii*: "... A spectacle, sublime and even appalling, presented itself before us. We stopped and trembled. Astonishment and awe for some moments rendered us mute .... The bottom was covered with lava, and the southwest and northern parts of it were one vast flood of burning matter, in a stage of terrific ebullition, rolling to and fro its 'fiery surge' and flaming billows."

The spectacle of the volcano, Kilauea, impressed Mr. Ellis and countless thousands since. Within the volcano at that time, at Halemaumau, was a great lake of rolling lava which spread across the floor, and at other times seeped into earth fissures to produce avalanches of fire. A later visitor stared at the sight, then told a guide, "I've seen hell. Now I want to go home." This "lava-lake" phase ceased with the steam explosion of 1924.

From the eleven mile Crater Rim Drive around the summit caldera of Kilauea volcano, Kilauea Crater, the visitor can see the destruction wrought by the forces of nature—cones of cinder, bluffs alive with steam and recent flows of lava. One of the most impressive sections is the "devastated area," which was denuded of vegetation during the 1959 eruptions of Kilauea Iki. The ancient Hawaiians made a deity of Pele, the goddess of volcanoes, whom they believed lived in Halemaumau, Kilauea's most active vent. It was her wrath, they said, which caused the eruptions, destroying villages and tilled lands.

From the summit caldera, the visitor passes along the Chain of Craters, part of the east rift of the volcano where the road winds past deep craters in which eruptions have recently taken place. In March 1965, a fissure on the side of Makaopuhi Crater poured forth a lake of lava almost three hundred feet deep. During the 1959 eruption of Kilauea Iki, lava spewed more than 1,900 feet high, filling a crater with molten lava to a depth of about four hundred feet. Until recently, the most spectacular of all volcanoes here was Mauna Loa, but it has not erupted since 1950.

From Makaopuhi Crater near the end of the chain, the island's newest scenic road passes along the southeast coast, past ancient villages and sites of religious temples. The mighty mountains of fire must have prompted these peoples to great religious fervor. At Wahaula Heiau near the eastern edge of the park is one of the island's best-known places of worship where it is reputed that one of the last human sacrifices was performed under the old religion.

Now the religion is appreciation of and humility before nature, which is protected within the boundaries of this park in a subtropical corner of paradise.

In 1959 a lava fountain roared at 1,900 feet, highest ever witnessed, filling Kilauea Iki (left) four hundred feet deep. Effervescing several hundred feet, the lava fountain (right) is considered to be relatively gentle.

Expert gliders, ring-billed gulls fly gracefully near the multihued sea and lush green woodlands. Dating from the mid-1700's, the Annaberg estate ruins (right) emerge from a green promontory.

VIRGIN ISLANDS NATIONAL PARK

The essence of the Caribbean's soft, luxuriant, provocative moods is nowhere better captured than at Trunk Bay of Virgin Islands National Park. The green waters are rich with multihued varieties of colorful coral, sponges and exotic tropical fish. The shimmering white beaches are fringed with palms. Off shore stands an occasional islet. Above, a royal blue sky. Inland, the dominant terrain is composed of rugged tropical forests and Bordeaux Mountain, 1,277 feet high.

The park constitutes two-thirds of the Island of St. John, which is nine miles in length. The islands form a geological unit with Puerto Rico and the Greater Antilles, being of volcanic origin. St. John Island is a typical offspring of subsurface volcanic eruptions, dating back millions of years. Steep mountains, deep valleys, gleaming white beaches and extensive coral reefs growing on an underwater shelf of rock are characteristic of this unique national preserve. These are the islands that were discovered by Christopher Columbus on his second voyage, in 1493. He named them in honor of St. Ursula and her eleven thousand virgins.

Strategically commanding approaches to the Caribbean and Atlantic as they do, the islands were of great interest to the security of the United States. Thus intensive negotiations, at first unsuccessful, took place between the American Government and Denmark, beginning in 1867. The islands were finally purchased in 1917 for $25 million, administered earlier by the U. S. Navy, and later by a resident Governor.

The relatively moist interior highlands of St. John, including steep-walled valleys, are dominated by a jungle forest of evergreen hardwoods. Drier slopes contain broad-leaved trees. Mangroves, turpentines, maho, cinnamon-bay kapok and soursop are the characteristic trees. Flowering shrubs and trees bloom in season, with a charm for the tourists increased by knowledge that hibiscus, bougainvillea and flamboyant are expensive commercial items in the floral hothouses of the States.

About one hundred species of birds abound in the islands with land birds more dominant. Herons, egrets, pelicans, gulls, frigate birds and terns can, however, be spotted along the shores. Pearly-eyed thrashers, smooth-billed anis, mockingbirds and hummingbirds are discernible in the forests and hills.

Six forms of bats are the only native mammals, although several species have been introduced, the best known being the mongoose. There are also toads, lizards, turtles, snakes and hermit crabs, which, oddly, live in discarded top shells. Insects are minimal with the exception of the mosquito and pesky sand fly which multiply after rainy spells.

Snorkeling is a major activity in the park. Visitors have a chance to snorkel along the underwater trail at Trunk Bay, participate in a naturalist-led snorkel trip at Turtle or Cinnamon bays or explore on their own in a number of other good snorkeling areas.

The northeast trade winds temper the intense heat of the tropical sun, yielding pleasantly warm days and cool nights. The average annual temperature is seventy-nine degrees with only about six degrees difference between the winter and summer seasons.

St. John Island's beauty, spiced with coral reef, tropical forest and history, is a matchless part of the national heritage.

101 WONDERS OF AMERICA

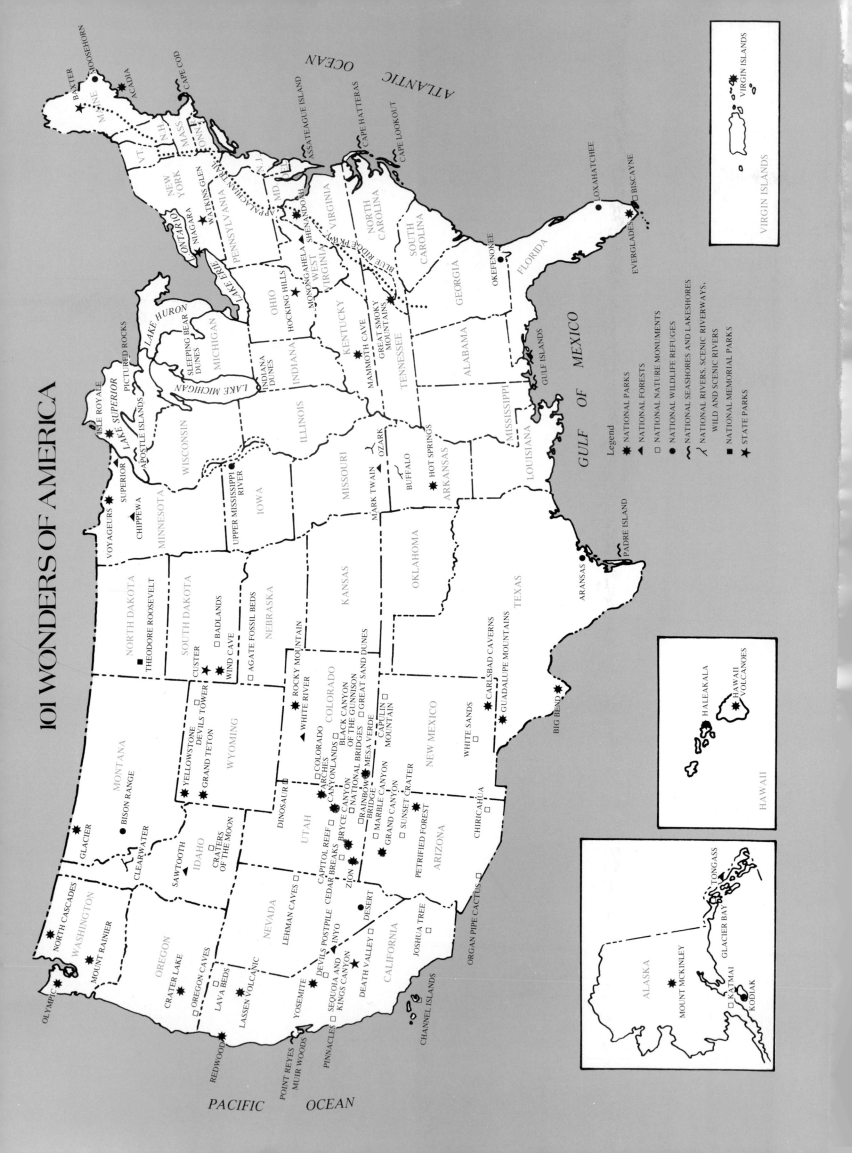